To Kevin Manning,

Thanks for joining in the "International business wars!"

Best regards,

Michael R. Tomczyk (signature)

4·25·91

THE
HOME
COMPUTER
WARS

THE HOME COMPUTER WARS

Michael S. Tomczyk

An Insider's Account
of Commodore and Jack Tramiel

COMPUTE! Publications,Inc.abc
One of the ABC Publishing Companies
Greensboro, North Carolina

Printed in the United States of America

ISBN 0-942386-75-2

First Edition, First Printing
10 9 8 7 6 5 4 3 2 1

COMPUTE! Publications, Inc., Post Office Box 5406, Greensboro, NC 27403, (919) 275-9809, is one of the ABC Publishing Companies and is not associated with any manufacturer of personal computers. Apple is a trademark of Apple Computer, Inc. Atari is a trademark of Atari, Inc. Commodore 64, VIC-20, and PET are trademarks of Commodore Electronics Limited. IBM PC and IBM PCjr are trademarks of International Business Machines, Inc. TRS-80 and TRS-80 Color Computer are trademarks of Tandy, Inc. TI-99/4 and TI-99/4A are trademarks of Texas Instruments.

Dedication

This book is dedicated to all the people who said I'd never make it, because they're the ones who made me try the hardest.

—MST

Contents

Acknowledgments

This book is based on my own recollections, impressions, and viewpoint. Those who helped fill in the facts and helped me recall some of the stories and conversations have my sincere thanks.

If I inadvertently left out anyone's contribution, my sincere apologies.

And the following people I'm pleased to be able to thank publicly here:

My wife Kim Tuyen, for making me feel like a genius when I felt like a shlub; my mother, Mrs. Dorothy Davis, for giving up her singing career so I could be a writer; my aunt, Mrs. E. A. Thomas, for helping me keep my perspective.

Kit and Lesley Spencer, who encouraged me to write this story; and to special Commodorians John Feagans, Lee Schreiber, Tony Tokai, Don Richard, Harald Speyer, Dick Sanford, Greg Pratt, Rich Wiggins, Tom Hyltin, Gail Wellington, Yashi Terakura, Chuck Peddle, Jim Bachmann, Eli Kenan, Jo Marinello, Pat Jones, and Sig Hartmann.

VIC commandos Neil Harris, Andy Finkel, Rick Cotton, David Street, Jeff Bruette, and Sue Mittnacht, for their constant *benutzefreundlichkeit*.

Mentors O. John Haering, Robert von Bergen, and the late Professor David Lippert, for introducing me to business and journalism.

Lisa Braden, Linda Thomas, and Steve Eisenberg, for contributing photos.

Robert Lock, for helping me get started in the computer

industry; and the entire staff at COMPUTE! Publications for their help and support, especially Richard Mansfield and Juanita Lewis who helped edit this book, and Gary Ingersoll, Stephen Levy, and Lance Elko.

Irving Gould, for his courtesy and generosity over the years.

And, of course, my continuing gratitude to Jack and Helen Tramiel, for inviting me along on the grand adventure and allowing me to chronicle those exciting years.

In 1980, when I joined Commodore, I made it clear to Jack Tramiel that, as a writer and journalist, I expected to eventually write a book on my experiences at Commodore. He and several executives I later worked for encouraged me to write "the Commodore story," and it was agreed that I would someday chronicle the experience when the time was right.

ONE

The next thing I knew, I was sitting in a foxhole with a bunch of smiling young geniuses. I poked my head out of the trench to see what was going on and a floppy diskette came whirring by. I ducked and it missed me by inches. Somebody handed me a chip and yelled, "Start computing!" That's the kind of war it was.

1979: Welcome to the War

The day I joined Commodore I had six dollars in my pocket. I was 32 years old and didn't know how I was going to make my next rent payment.

I sold my scuba equipment, my beloved Nikon cameras, and my coin collection, even the Mercury dimes from my paperboy days in Wisconsin. After all that, I still had only ten dollars in the bank. At one point I had to ask my friend Robert Lock, founder of COMPUTE! Publications, to wire me $50 overnight, just like in the movies.

It was ten-thirty at night and the world looked more black than white. I took the bus to the Western Union office, signed for the money, and away I went. I needed the money so I could drive to Santa Clara the next day to see Jack Tramiel about a job at Commodore.

I didn't realize that I was enlisting in a war: the Home Computer War. I was about to become an eyewitness, historian, high-ranking combat officer, and a member of a world-wide cast of characters including samurai warriors, political cutthroats, smiling young geniuses, nerds, hackers, wizards, robots, commandos, and millionaires. It was the opportunity of a lifetime.

Ironically my story at Commodore would begin, and end, at Atari. In the summer of 1979, the personal computer craze was just beginning, and the concept of home computers wasn't really accepted yet.

My background was already unusual, but easy to cover in one paragraph: I spent 21 years growing up in Oshkosh, Wisconsin, got an English and journalism degree at Oshkosh State University, spent three years in the Army (Airborne, Jungle School, Vietnam, and Korea), met a mentor in

3

Wisconsin who taught me how to be a business consultant, got an M.B.A. from UCLA, worked three years as a marketing consultant in Beverly Hills—and here's where we pick up our story.

One day the head of the company, Robert von Bergen, decided he wanted to retire and raise avocados in Escondido. It was a good time for a break anyway. I was tired of being a consultant. Consultants help other people make money. I wanted to be *inside* a company and keep a little bit of the money I helped make. After all, that's what graduate school was all about, learning how to manage a company. So I took a job managing a small computer graphics firm in San Francisco. I didn't know much about computer graphics, but the company was losing money and within three months I turned it around and we were making money.

Enter Atari. It was November and we were doing some graphics work for an Atari designer named Bill Hamlin. One day he gave us a new computer and a new game cartridge called *Star Raiders* and asked us to try them out. We didn't know it, but we had become an unofficial beta-test site. Remember, this was several months before the Atari 800 and *Star Raiders* were on sale to the public. Even dealers didn't have them yet.

The employees in the company went bonkers over the game, which was the first true-to-life, three-dimensional videogame. The TV screen became a window on space, and you had to find and destroy enemy spacecraft in different sectors of a giant grid, refuel at special space stations, and move through space by piloting your craft using a joystick or by jumping from sector to sector by warping. The visual effects were dazzling, especially when the stars whizzed by when you warped, or when the four kinds of enemy ships came zooming out of nowhere either behind or in front of you. A mini radar screen alerted you when enemy ships entered your sector. They shot at you, damaged your weapons, destroyed your shields, or surrounded and destroyed your fuel bases. The game was fantastic. But at first I didn't think so. I watched the guys play at the console and was

4

vaguely annoyed that they were playing on company time. Then the inevitable happened. I took the computer home for a night.

I couldn't hear the "Twilight Zone" music playing in the back of my life, but it was there. "Meet Michael Tomczyk," said Rod Serling. "He doesn't know it yet, but something has turned his television set into a video drug. He is about to enter a new realm, a realm of computer games and scan lines, a realm that could only exist in—you guessed it."

All at once, I looked up from the console and caught a thin band of light seeping through the living room curtains. It was dawn. I'd stayed up all night playing that stupid videogame. Ridiculous. Must be a lapse in my intelligence or something. I shrugged off the sleeplessness and went to work.

The second night, I told myself, "No way. I'll just play this thing for a couple of hours and go to bed." Six o'clock the next morning, I was still up. Come on, this is crazy. I've got responsibilities.

The third night I didn't even try to resist. I was hooked. Sweating profusely, palming the joystick to avoid the blister that had formed on my thumb, I maneuvered my way from Ship's Cook to Pilot to Captain, the elusive Commander rating still beyond my reach.

Okay. That's it. I'm a rational human being. I have a business to run. People rely on me. But wait a minute, if I, a rational, serious-minded businessperson—if I can get hooked on this crazy game, then *anyone* can get hooked on it, and if that's true, then I'm in the wrong business. Everyone's going to be playing this game in another few months, and who knows what craziness that will lead to?

Within a week I quit my job, turned down a participation in the company, and was living on my savings. Of course, I had to give up my Atari 800, so I started jogging over to an Apple computer store and hanging out to find out about computers. Next, I signed up for a five-night course in BASIC programming being taught by a high school teacher named Don Campbell who was moonlighting at the computer store.

Don *loved* Commodore, but as a marketing person I saw right away that Apple came packaged better. The case was more chic, the manuals were readable, and even the name Apple had a nice ring to it. The concept of opening up the case and plugging in different expansion boards was easy enough that anyone could do it, and techie enough to appeal to the new breed of hobbyists who were the vanguard of home computer owners.

"You're wrong," Don argued. "Commodore computers have a built-in screen and you don't have to mess around plugging cards and cables inside."

"But Apple's in color and Commodore's black and white," I countered.

"You don't need color," Don said.

Finally, I got stuck with a Commodore PET the first night and, grumbling, vowed to get there early the next night to get an Apple. But when I started using the Apple, I discovered that it didn't have any cursor keys. The Commodore computer had up-down and left-right cursor keys, but to move around on the Apple screen you had to press a control key and one of the alphabet keys (for example, ESC-D moved the cursor up). There were other things about the PET I preferred over Apple, and by the time the coffee break rolled around, I couldn't wait to get back to the PET.

But I still felt Apple would outsell Commodore, because Commodore had no pizazz or hype behind their product, and Apple was pure PR all the way. They had a free disk library for Apple owners to copy at the dealer's, and a whole assortment of reference manuals. Don suggested I visit Silicon Valley, which was about a 45-minute drive south of San Francisco, and get myself a good job.

"They're always looking for someone with your background," he said.

Bolstered by his matter-of-fact confidence, I launched a campaign to land myself a job. The first thing I did was buy every computer magazine I could get my hands on. Since I couldn't understand the articles, I studied all the ads. One day I spotted a new magazine on the racks which wasn't written in Greek or Aramaic. It was called *COMPUTE!*, and the articles were actually readable. The same day, I called Robert Lock, the editor/founder. Robert had just bought the rights to a popular Commodore newsletter called *PET Gazette* and melded the *Gazette* into his new magazine, which also covered Apple and Atari. All three computers used the 6502 microprocessor, which I later discovered was designed by MOS Technology, a subsidiary of Commodore.

I asked Robert if he knew of any marketing interviews I could read and he replied, "I have a policy. When someone complains because something isn't in my magazine, I tell them it's not there because nobody submitted an article on it yet; then I ask if they'd like to do the story themselves. So, since you're close to Silicon Valley, why not do some marketing interviews?"

He made sense. How could I turn down a challenge and opportunity like that? All I needed was some chutzpah, a tape recorder, and, easiest of all, a list of dumb questions. A little editing, a little typing, and, *voilà.* Instant articles.

A plan was beginning to emerge: my personal recipe for breaking into home computers. First, take a course in BASIC. I'd already done that. Second, get some articles published in computer magazines to use as credentials on my résumé. That was happening, too. Third, get an assignment to interview all the top home-computer marketing executives and find out their secrets. Fourth, put the touch on one of those executives for a job with their company. Fifth, get hired, learn everything I could about home computers, work my head off, and earn some money.

Right away I got a computer on loan from Atari. That was easy because they wanted to publicize the Atari 800 and my assignment from *COMPUTE!* made me legitimate enough to get one. I even got a *Star Raiders* cartridge. I set up the system in my small San Francisco apartment and plugged in the game, but I wasn't hooked anymore. I was too busy thinking of stories to write. Wait—the answer zoomed toward me on my TV screen. How about a story about the creator of the *Star Raiders* game? After all, *Star*

Raiders got me into this. Why not get some mileage out of those all-night game sessions?

It was easy to imagine the inventor of *Star Raiders:* cast in the mold of Steven Spielberg or George Lucas, a died-in-the-wool trekkie who attended Flash Gordon conventions and collected Captain Midnight kinescopes.

It turned out the world's master game designer wasn't even working at Atari. He was a chip designer named Doug Neubauer, and after spending six months designing *Star Raiders,* he got gamed out and migrated to Oregon to design computer chips for Hewlett-Packard. He received no royalties for his game because he was on salary at Atari while he wrote it. I did a brief phone interview with him but never found out if he was a trekkie. The interview appeared in the March/April 1980 issue of *COMPUTE!*. It was called *"Star Raiders:* The Wizard Behind The Game." The *Raiders* story was nice, but now I needed a technical article to strengthen my credentials.

I remembered an old journalism lesson: "Good journalists answer questions the readers would like to ask." So I looked around and found a good question to answer. Why don't microcomputers like Apple have 80-column display screens like minicomputers? After all, a typewriter page is 80 characters across, so how come Apples have only 40 columns?

The answer was that minicomputers used some high-resolution monitors as viewing screens, and microcomputers like Apple relied on TV sets. Monitors (which were still too expensive for home use) took their signals directly from the computer with little or no interference or fuzziness; but most television sets couldn't display 80-column-size letters because the coarse *scan lines* and signal interference on the TVs made it difficult to read the smaller letters.

A few years later in 1983, Commodore introduced a low-priced color monitor (under $300), and Jack Tramiel was surprised by the flood of orders. The demand for monitors was much higher than he'd expected, and Commodore was caught short by the unexpected surge in orders. It turned out that the world didn't really want 80-column adapters. It wanted an inexpensive color monitor for home use so computer owners could display 80 columns and see the screen without interference.

If the low-priced color monitor was available in quantity, computer makers could market low-priced 80-column computers for home use, but as long as home computerists used television sets, 80-column home computers were impractical. The solution ultimately came from the Japanese, who began building direct signal monitor lines into their component television sets, thus letting new television models double as monitors. At the same time, the cost of color monitors began to plummet, making possible low-priced home computer systems combining an 80-column computer with built-in disk drive and color monitor, for under $500. This revolutionary product, which I believe is the next step in home computing, was being worked on by several manufacturers in 1984 for possible introduction in 1985.

In 1979, most microcomputers used special tricks to get around the 40-column screen limitation. Radio Shack's word processor scrolled sideways to let you see chunks of the page. Others let you see 40 columns while you were typing, but printed 80 columns on paper when you used a computer printer.

Apple didn't make 80-column converters for the Apple II, but they were encouraging third-party companies to develop a cottage industry. The first 80-column board, called Sup'R'Term, was developed by two ingenious inventors named Marty Spergel and Bill Wobler, based in Sunnyvale, California. I drove down and met the inventors and wound up doing a detailed analysis of the three existing 80-column converters: Sup'R'Term, VIDEX, and Doublevision. The result was the first definitive article on 80-column boards for the Apple II. It appeared in the October issue of *Kilobaud Microcomputing* in early 1980. (I also did a Sup'R'Term review for *COMPUTE!*, but publishing in different magazines gave me stronger credentials.)

While working on the 80-column board article, I got to know some of the Apple people, including Steve Wozniak, Mike Markkula, and several programmers and product managers.

I started hanging out at Apple's sleek new headquarters in Cupertino, where I boldly wandered past the receptionist to go in search of whomever I wanted to talk to. Sometimes executives would encounter me in the hall and challenge me for not having an ID or escort, but I would tell them I was just there to see so-and-so and they would scowl and let me be. Apple people were already becoming a trifle paranoid about trade secrets and for good reason, considering all the trouble they had with imitators and copycats, but they were not Gestapo.

It's true that by early 1980 Apple was becoming a bureaucracy, but it wasn't the kind of bureaucracy that creeps up and strangles most large corporations. This bureaucracy was born partly from a desire to structure their explosive growth, and partly to insulate the company's young geniuses from vendors, journalists, and others who intruded on their creative domain.

I saw a lot of history being made without really realizing it. Andy Herzfeld, Apple's resident programming gnome, was experimenting with digitizing techniques that convert photographs and drawings into dot patterns which can be interpreted and altered or colored by the computer, then displayed on a TV screen. He had a disk filled with everything from Playboy bunnies to animated horses. Those stunning galloping horses later showed up on Apple's dealer demo disks and in public domain software, and undoubtedly helped sell lots of Apples.

Wozniak and Herzfeld, and probably others, were also experimenting with different types of character fonts which could be displayed on the screen and printed as well. The result of this early work clearly shows up in the Macintosh.

I have to admit I was attracted to Apple as a company. They were successful, growing fast, run by people about my age, generous, flexible, hard-driving, innovative, and unspoiled by success. There were many bright people in evidence, in almost every department, maybe too many.

One late afternoon I found myself sitting in the programming area with Steve Wozniak and Andy chatting about potential stories. Mike Markkula, Apple's president, happened by and asked some technical questions about page two of the computer's memory bank. Wozniak gave him an answer.

I was impressed that the head of the company was himself experimenting with the innards of the machine. Markkula had been hired by the two Steves (a nickname given to Apple founders Steve Wozniak and Steve Jobs). His mission was to provide professional management as the company skyrocketed toward the leadership position in personal computers. Markkula struck me as a quiet, suave, intelligent executive, with the emphasis on *executive*. He was without a doubt the right man for the job, in skill as well as temperament.

Wozniak was more of a hands-on tinkerer, at home with programmers and, later, rock fans when he staged several well-publicized concerts. He was amiable, bearlike, and tended more toward comfortable plaid workshirts and jeans than suits and ties or even California-style shirts and gold chains.

I didn't have much contact with Jobs, about whom much has been written already. He was known as the driving force behind the company, and his imprint on Apple's organization and product line was and is unmistakable.

Finally, someone at Apple said, "Michael, you've got the right personality for this company and you'd probably fit in very well." It was impressive that they were more interested in whether I'd "fit in" than in my credentials.

Mike Markkula said, "Why don't you do this—go in the cafeteria and look through the job requisitions. They're posted on the bulletin board. Find a job you're qualified for, go to Personnel, fill out an application, and when the application comes across my desk, we'll hire you against the requisition."

To someone attracted to the freewheeling, wildcat nature of a fledgling industry, Markkula's description of the hiring procedure sounded like the telephone company or civil service. I agree that those few simple procedures are necessary in most large companies, but to me and at that time, it hinted of bureaucracy, repulsive to a died-in-the-wool, card-carrying, antibureaucrat—Galactic Warrior first class.

Still, Apple had made me a solid job offer and I was thrilled to get it. I immediately stood up and rushed to the cafeteria, a small room with some vending machines and lunch tables. I found the list attached to the wall next to the doorway, but as I paged through the sheaf of fifty or sixty job requisitions, I was struck by their formality, and the way Markkula's offer had been made. Maybe I was spoiled, but I was used to being hired on the spot. My previous job offers had gone something like this: "Michael, you're exactly the person we need. You start work tomorrow, we'll talk about your salary in a day or two, and give you a job title next week."

I wasn't ready to work for a bureaucracy, even a fun bureaucracy like Apple. Next stop, Atari.

Early in 1980, Atari had just started shipping its two home computers, Atari 400 and Atari 800, and was getting ready to start marketing them full force. Conrad Jutson was hired in November 1979 as vice president of sales and marketing for personal computers, and I caught up with him in January 1980 after arranging an interview through Atari's PR person. At last I was going to have a formal chance to grill a computer marketing executive.

Jutson was an extremely thoughtful, erudite gentleman with twenty years in consumer electronics, most recently in the stereo field. His experience in that industry revealed a clear understanding of the computer as the central console in a *components-oriented system*. As it turned out, he and Atari were a little ahead of their time.

The day I did the interview, we sat with a tape recorder and I asked one or two dumb questions. Then Jutson started pouring out his marketing philosophy, which focused on the fact that a lot of the applications which made computers practical were still being developed. It was ironic that later on the Atari 400 and Atari 800 would gain reputations for not having much software, and many of Jutson's plans and dreams materialized at other companies instead of at Atari.

At the end of the interview, I slipped him a copy of my résumé and told him I was playing journalist so I could get a job in the home computer field. He looked over my résumé, and then, in a very calm, off-handed tone, he said, "Good. Well, come around when you're ready to go to work and maybe you can be director of application software, or something."

I thanked him and said I'd be in touch, but as I left the building I was mad. Now, I didn't really have a reason to be angry and it may seem foolish, but I was so naïve at the time that I resented the fact that he offered me a software job instead of a marketing job. I was so green that I honestly didn't realize that he'd just offered me one of the plum jobs in any home computer company, but I was too inexperienced to realize how important the software job could be. I wanted a marketing job, and to me that meant the job had to have the word *marketing* in the title.

When I look back on it, I feel a bit foolish, but in the end my foolishness paid off.

There were two other competitors in the home computer race—Texas Instruments, which had taken a game machine and upgraded it to a home computer, and Radio Shack, which marketed the TRS-80 fully assembled or as a kit, through their electronics chain. I never considered joining either company.

TI had an excellent reputation, but their computer had a goofy name (the TI-99/4) and was overpriced at $600. I figured if a giant semiconductor company that made its own computer chips charged that much money, they either didn't know how to control their manufacturing costs or were gouging profits at the consumer's expense. And since I was still technically a consumer, I resented anything that confused or befuddled the first-time computerist. Finally, and most important, TI was based in Texas and I wanted to stay in California.

Radio Shack was a subsidiary of Tandy, and their computers were sold to a captive audience through their 7000 Radio Shack outlets world-wide. I felt Radio Shack had an unrealistic view of the marketplace because at this early stage in the computer industry, almost anyone who was a Radio Shack electronics fan would consider picking up one of their inexpensive computers or computer kits. In essence, Radio Shack didn't have to compete with anyone because no other computers could be sold in their franchised store outlets. Later on, I would begin to feel jealous of Radio Shack's captive distribution system, but I had the last laugh when home computers exploded into popularity and Radio Shack got strangled by their own distribution system.

Apple had offered me a job, but they were too bureaucratic. Atari had offered me a job, but I was too stupid to appreciate the offer. There was only one personal computer company left in Silicon Valley, the puzzling company called Commodore.

"Okay," I told myself. "This is it. I'll try one more company."

My computer-store friends thought I was crazy. They teased me about Apple and Atari and urged me to give Commodore a try, arguing that Commodore made better computers for the money but nobody knew it because Commodore had lousy marketing, PR, and advertising. They said a mysterious man named Jack Tramiel—no one knew much about him—ran Commodore with an iron fist, and suggested I contact him.

The last week in March, I sent him a letter. It was terse, angry, and arrogant:

> *Dear Jack:*
>
> *Understand you need marketing help. I'm a marketing strategist. Call me if you need me. Résumé enclosed.*

To my surprise, his secretary Sue Anzel called me and told me, "Jack wants to see you." We set up an interview for Tuesday, April 1, at Commodore's Santa Clara offices, so I had a few days to ponder what I would tell him. Sue called him "Jack," not "Mr. Tramiel." That was a good sign. Ever since the Army, when people had to call me sir for three years just because I wore officer's bars, I had a mild aversion to being called sir, and I stopped calling people sir or mister.

As the day of the interview approached, I realized I knew practically nothing about Commodore. Everyone said the company was screwed up. I was going to find out what that meant.

The day arrived. I had to drive down to Santa Clara. Another 45-minute ride in my gas-guzzling Buick. It was getting down to the wire. I looked in my pocket and counted six dollars. All the cash I had in the world. Six dollars in my pocket and ten dollars in the bank. I had a little money coming from computer articles, but it hadn't arrived yet, and anyway it wasn't enough to cover my next rent payment.

Still, I was determined to hold out. I had offers from Apple and Atari to fall back on, but you don't get the special breaks in life if you don't make the sacrifice, take the risk, and pass on fourth down.

It was April 1, April Fool's Day. A bright, sunny morning. Commodore's headquarters at 3330 Scott Boulevard was just a few blocks off the San Diego Freeway. The buildings around Commodore were neatly manicured and unusually quiet. Palm trees lined the roads, and the neatly clipped grass looked like golf greens. There wasn't the usual ebb and flow of people you would expect to find at a large company. As crowded and important and busy as it was, this was a *quiet* place.

Unlike the roller-coaster streets of San Francisco, the streets of Santa Clara are perfectly flat and remarkably free of dirt, dust, or litter. The long periods of sun without rain seem to bleach all the color out of the roads, adding to the illusion of cleanliness, although in the air there is always the faint scent of bird droppings.

I paused on the sidewalk in front of the building. The outside of the Commodore building was more striking than

15

any building I'd seen in Silicon Valley. The architecture screamed high-tech. Made of a coarse, brownish gray concrete, with clumps of stones and rocks showing in the walls both inside and out, it was the first solar-powered building in the valley. The Santa Clara climate was so mild that the concrete served as both inside and outside walls, and the mandatory earthquake-proof construction made the walls sway back and forth whenever there was a minor tremor.

The front of the building was all glass, and was slanted in at a sharp angle. The inward slant seemed like a waste of floor space, but it was a stunning effect. Through the glass, you could see people holding meetings in the first tier of offices.

Jack's office took up the left front corner of the building. The ceiling-high windows were so huge that it was easy to see who was in or out, or in conference. Stringing out along the front of the building were a meeting room, two offices, the reception desk and front entrance, and a row of smaller offices to the right. The parking lot was located between the road and the main building. Most of the spaces were marked VISITOR.

I stalked into Commodore in my best pin-striped suit, wearing my arrogance on my sleeve. Sue Anzel, an attractive, California-style blonde who was into Jazzercise and decorative cakemaking, showed me into Jack's office.

Jack was seated comfortably behind a huge tabletop desk that faced the door. His office was comfortable but not ostentatious. There was a sofa against one wall for heart-to-heart talks, and a small, four-seater meeting table near the window for negotiations. He kept me at the desk.

We shook hands—he had a strong grip—and bade me sit down with a sweep of his hand while he finished reading some papers. He wasn't at all what I expected: short, balding, with a shopkeeper's tummy that gave him a totally round waistline. His heavy-lidded eyes seemed to stare straight into you, and he had an aura of—the only word I can think of is straightforwardness—that was immediately apparent.

He was 53, and the top of his head was completely bald, with a fringe of steel-colored wavy black hair slicked back on both sides. At the nape of his neck, small ringlets of hair curled up over his collar, giving him a slightly mod appearance and hinting that his outlook was more youth-oriented than bald.

His large dark brown eyes were set deep beneath thick wiry brows and tended to bulge slightly. He used this feature by making his eyes grow huge in their sockets to punctuate the conversation when he laughed, cursed, emphasized a point, or flashed a secret signal.

When he spoke, his lips curled, twisting and contorting into a thousand shapes and portraying a thousand emotions. He could jut out his lower lip in a pout and draw sympathy, open wide as if to yawn and laugh heartily, or tighten his lips into stony disapproval. Jack was a man whose lips shaped the words, but his eyes held the message.

His solid jaw and broad cleft chin gave him a massive appearance, and possibly provided the echoing power in his voice, which was deep and full with a resonance that carried in the air even when he spoke in hushed tones.

He had a stocky build, like a powerful machine that looked like it should be bolted somewhere. But he moved fast when he wanted, and everyone had trouble keeping up with him when he tore down the hallway in search of a fact, figure, or jugular vein. Sometimes he looked and moved like an Asian bear and was just as lovable—and dangerous.

His shopkeeper's tummy gave him a place to rest the palms of both hands, and made those who were fond of him worry about his cholesterol.

He had a slight Baltic accent that gave him a heavy European quality, an earthiness you might expect to find in a Russian general, and he had a peculiar kind of plasticity to his face that let him switch rapidly from a scowling roar to a beaming laugh in the blink of an eye. I guess you could say he had a schizophrenic face. It matched his moods, but then we were all rather schizoid at Commodore. You had to be. It was war.

I sat down and draped my arm over the back of the chair, my naïveté giving way to stronger feelings of arrogance and anger. I was the boxer, jutting out his chin. "Hit me," my posture said. "Come on, hit me with another meaningless job offer."

"Tomczyk—that's a Polish name. I'm Polish, too." He smiled and said, "You have an interesting background. How much do you know about Commodore?"

"All I know is what people tell me. A lot of people think you're a crook, but I figure if you're not in prison you're not a crook, you're just a shrewd businessman, and I'd like to learn to be shrewd like that." I hate to admit it, but I practiced those words in advance. I wanted to tell him exactly what I felt, in precisely the right words.

Jack smiled approvingly, then he found my résumé at the corner of his desk and without looking at it, proceeded to tell me more about myself in five minutes than most people learn in five years. It was uncanny.

He said he had the impression I was mainly a communicator and guessed I knew how to write well. He suggested I probably got along well in different cultures and languages, and declared that what I really brought to a company was an understanding of military organizations and—this was equally important to him—an understanding of Oriental business, especially Japanese. He was impressed that I'd spent two years in East Asia. He also knew I had a little computer experience, but not much. It didn't matter.

All this, just from reading my résumé? I know for a fact he didn't have any spies and hadn't investigated me. He just *absorbed* me like a mystic by looking in my eyes and sensing my vibes. I saw him do this often. He made a game of it. "What does this guy really want out of life, and out of his association with Commodore?" Whenever he hired someone, he always made sure he knew the person's "hot buttons," because the key to getting an employee to kill for you is satisfying his personal needs, whatever that meant—ego-gratification, fancy job title, big bonus, stock options, freedom to invent things—the list is endless and Jack knew all the pressure points.

He never studied Abraham Maslow, but he had a natural understanding of each individual's "hierarchy of needs." Jack knew we all have different personal values, and different ways of achieving self-esteem and balance. We measure ourselves by how important we are in the corporation, how much money we make, what kind of house we live in, the car we drive, the clothes we wear, the lovers we conquer, the power we wield, the things we create, the beauty of our children, etc.

Jack's first shot at meeting my needs was slightly off-target. I guess my chin was out too far, because he aimed too high.

He offered me the job of general manager in charge of sales in Europe.

"I don't really have a job for you," he admitted, adding, however, that something in marketing might open up in the future. "I do have one job in Europe. I need a general manager in charge of European sales. You could have that job if you want it."

"But I don't know any European languages except Spanish," I protested.

"You don't have to. All our people in Europe speak English."

"I—I really think you need someone multilingual," I stammered, "and someone heavier than me. I don't have much experience in sales, and frankly I think you can find someone more qualified for that job. To tell you the truth, what I really need is a six-month break-in period. I need some time to get to know your company, and to understand the industry. Then I'd feel more comfortable taking a heavier job." I didn't think much about it at the time—I was just being honest—but I guess sometimes you have to go backward to go forward.

At that instant, I became the only person I ever met in four years at Commodore who turned down a big job and asked for something lower.

Turning down that job was definitely the right thing to do. If I'd let myself be flattered and had taken the offer, I wouldn't have lasted thirty days. That was one reason a lot

19

of top executives got fired or had to quit. They jumped at Jack's first offer, whatever it was, and were so flattered to be a vice president or president that they took a job they couldn't handle. My honesty was my salvation.

"Let me think it over," Jack said, adding mysteriously, "A few months ago the company wasn't big enough and I couldn't afford the luxury of hiring someone like you, but maybe now." He leaned back in his chair and stared through me, trying to see where I belonged in the future, then he said, "Okay. I'm going to hire you, but I need some time to figure out what to do with you. Call me tomorrow and we'll discuss it."

Now, that's my kind of job offer. First you're hired. Then we'll figure out a job for you, and then we'll discuss compensation. It was exactly right. But wait, I still wasn't signed up yet. What I didn't know was that my first test as a Commodorian was lurking in the telephone lines. I was about to get a brief taste of corporate combat, Commodore-style.

The next day I dutifully called Jack's office. Sue Anzel told me Jack was in a meeting, but he'd get back as soon as he was done. An hour later I called again and Sue apologized that a long distance call had got in the way. Another half-hour. "You want me to poke my head in the door?" Pause. "Okay, Jack says he'll call you back in five minutes."

Five minutes stretched into five hours—six—seven—eight—nine—

Ten hours and ten phone calls later, it was seven o'clock at night. I had called all day long, each time reaching Sue, who told me in a sincere and pleasant voice that Jack really did intend to get back to me. *Really.*

I began to think Jack had had second thoughts. Maybe I was too green. Maybe he only wanted to hire a European sales manager and didn't have any other openings. I was getting angry again.

"Okay," I said out loud, "This is it. I'll call *one more time.* If I don't get you this time, then I'm not going to work for you, I don't care if you beg me on your hands and knees." I really meant it.

The phone rang twice, and then Jack himself answered. Just as I would see him do a hundred times, he was walking by the phone as it rang and couldn't resist picking it up. He often answered ringing phones, wherever he was in the building, just to touch and feel the different parts of the company.

When he answered, it was as if nothing had changed. He picked up our conversation exactly where we left off.

"Hello, yes, Michael, I've decided what to do with you. Come to my office tomorrow at nine o'clock and we'll talk about it."

Suddenly, I realized how busy the president of a large company is, and how unintentionally rude he sometimes has to be. I also began to sense the combat nature of the industry, for Jack operated on a war footing, even though the Home Computer Wars had not yet begun in earnest.

My six dollars was gone and I couldn't get my ten dollars out of the bank before my appointment. Frantically, I called Robert Lock.

"Help!" I pleaded, "You know that $50 for the *Star Raiders* article?"

"It'll be there in a couple of weeks."

"How about tomorrow?"

"Tomorrow?"

I filled him in on the morbid details and Robert agreed to wire the money that night. I took a trolley car to the Western Union office and picked up the money at tenthirty. Without it, I couldn't have afforded to buy the gas to get me down to Santa Clara.

The next morning I met with Jack and a young Englishman named Chris Fish. Chris was unofficially the number two executive in the company. Basically, he ran non-U.S. sales and was responsible for developing new foreign markets. He shuttled between the Bahamas, where Commodore was technically headquartered, and Switzerland, where most European operations were based.

Jack began by asking me what I thought I could do for the company. Overnight, I'd done a little more checking on Commodore and told him some of the things I knew were wrong with the company. "You have the best personal computer for the money," I explained, "but nobody knows it because your marketing is lousy. Your user manuals look like they're mimeographed. Apple has a two-color spiral-bound booklet. And you need some reference books like Apple, so programmers can write software for your computers.

"Your brochures are dull, I've never seen an ad for your products, and you ought to have a Commodore magazine like Atari and Apple. A lot of people I know tell me they have trouble finding good software for their Commodore computers. Apple gives their dealers 600 programs which their customers can copy free." I went on for several minutes, listing the deficiencies.

Jack began to get an idea of what I was all about. He began to see me as a user-advocate, sort of an in-house Ralph Nader. Chris and Jack exchanged meaningful glances that only they understood, then Chris left and Jack said, "I've decided what to do with you. You're going to be my assistant, but your job isn't going to be to assist me. You're job is to learn about the company. You'll be the only person in the company who's paid just to learn."

I didn't realize how radical that was until I found out later that one of the rules in Jack's business philosophy is, you don't pay people to learn or to teach, you pay them to do the job.

"To help you get to know the company—and let the company get to know you—you can write our annual report this year. You've had some experience in that area and we need someone who can do a good job." He added that I could fly around to the company's various offices and factories and meet the people as part of my annual report project.

"How soon do you want me to start?" I asked.

"You could start right away, or you can wait until I get back from Europe at the end of the month."

A month was like ten years. I winced. He rocked back in his chair and said, "Or—I'm just thinking—there's a corporate meeting in London. Maybe you should come and see how we work."

"I've never been to Europe, and you *did* say you wanted me to learn. What better place to start than in Europe?"

"Fine," he said. "Meet me in London April 14. Sue will make the arrangements."

London!

Visions of sugarplums danced in my head, but I didn't have time to get excited, because next came salary. Even that was a surprise.

"What's the lowest monthly income you can live on and be comfortable?" he asked. I told him $2,000 a month. Santa Clara is expensive. He rounded my figure up to $25,000 a year and said, "Okay, that's your salary. You'll also have an expense account, and I won't nitpick on it. If you want to fly someplace and have a good reason, go ahead. That's part of your compensation. I figure if I pay you a low salary I can invest a little in expenses, if it's gonna help you learn. So, work hard, learn the company, and I'll make it up to you in six months. I'll give you the kind of job you deserve, and which I think you can handle."

"Uh, can I have a computer system, too?" I blurted.

He scowled. "No!"

I shrugged disappointedly, but Jack broke into a broad grin and said, "Yes, sure." He liked to tease like that, swiftly switching his emotions between smiles, a pounded fist, insults, warnings, hearty laughs, and warm pleasure.

He paused, a little embarrassed to ask the next question: "A lot of people have been asking for employment contracts lately. If you need one—"

I already knew about Commodore's reputation as a revolving-door company, but before he finished I stuck out my hand and said, "Here's my contract. That's all we need."

Laughing, we shook hands, and in that moment we both knew I was destined to become a Commodorian, with all the rank and privileges and strangeness that would entail.

TWO

"I say," the old duke said stiffly, "what are all those people doing in our fox hunting lodge?"

"They're inventing computers and planning a war," his aide replied.

"Well, why don't they do it in their own country?" sniffed the duke.

"They say this IS their country!"

In the distance, the hounds began to bay.

Foreign Wars:
The Japanese Are Coming

London. Westminster Abbey—the British Museum—Shakespeare—the Thames—the Princess—fish and chips rolled up in a newspaper—beer as thick as mud.

I was still insolvent, so armed with a travel advance, I boarded a British Airways jumbo jetliner on April 13, bound for London. I was so hyper about the trip I couldn't stay in my seat. My veins kept popping and my nose was twitching like a rabbit. I could feel the excitement in the air, feel the future expanding wonderfully in front of me as the plane hurled us forward.

I made an unsuccessful pass at a stewardess. She had a stiff upper lip and didn't like men with twitching noses. I downed a complimentary beer, a glass of champagne, and wine with dinner. Relax, I kept telling myself. Relax! I wondered if it was okay to jog in the aisles. I paced up and down instead.

It was somewhere in the middle aisles that I saw Chuck Peddle, Commodore's engineering guru. He and his wife invited me to sit down and didn't seem to think it was strange that my nose was twitching.

Charles (Chuck) Peddle was without doubt one of the most interesting and intriguing characters in all of Commodore. His high, broad forehead, receding hairline, silver-beige swept-back hair, and sharp eagle nose gave him a marvelous alien quality that seemed suited to his status as computer inventor and guru.

He was suave, charming, intelligent, and spoke softly but with great assurance. His silky-smooth personality and boyish mannerisms made everyone like him, though along with his charm and brilliance came a streak of petulance that often placed him at odds with Jack Tramiel. It was said that Chuck was a first-rate engineer who thought he knew marketing. Chuck frequently tried to meddle in marketing. Jack and his other executives tried to keep him in engineering.

Chuck and his wife were extremely courteous and chatted for several hours until we all dozed off. The Peddles had a great formula for overseas flights: As soon as the jet took off, they laid claim to an empty middle row of seats and bracketed the row so no one else could sit there. When it was time to sleep, they put the arms up and one of them slept across the seats and one of them slept on the floor. That way, they both slept stretched out, very soundly. I slept sitting up, which for me is the same as not sleeping at all.

At the time I met Chuck, he was heading up a small group of talented engineers known as Systems Engineering. The systems group had their own building at Moore Park in Santa Clara, a mile or two from Commodore headquarters. The young engineers (most in their twenties) were fiercely loyal to Chuck, who had hired many of them during 1976–77 to work on Commodore's first computer (the PET).

The systems group reported directly to Jack, through Peddle, and worked in extreme secrecy. Even Commodore's own marketing people were cut off from the research/ engineering process. It was Jack's hard and fast rule: Marketing and engineering do not mix. Jack believed marketing executives only confused engineers and delayed new designs. He preferred to let the engineers invent the best and most sophisticated device they could possibly build, within cost/price guidelines suggested by Jack. If there was room for extra features or if mistakes or bugs were found, the marketers could suggest corrections *after* the product was invented.

"The job of marketing is to sell the products we give them," he said. "The job of engineering is to give marketing good products they can sell."

As a marketer and idea person, I was going to have to scheme, connive, sneak, and milk friendships to uncover new products and make early suggestions. While I resented having to wangle my way into the design process, I had to agree that marketing involvement tended to open up global debates which delayed new products months and sometimes years. At the same time, stupid bugs or engineering solutions were often allowed to get so far that the only way to correct them was to compromise by eliminating competitive features, or to leave the bugs in the first few thousand (or hundred thousand) products and make running changes later on.

The systems group's only outside contact, besides Jack, was with a small engineering group in Japan, and the chip designers at Commodore's MOS Technology subsidiary in Valley Forge, Pennsylvania. The Japanese engineers were needed to finish off and cost-reduce new products, and the chip designers provided new semiconductor devices which made the computers compute.

During our conversation, Chuck talked freely about his recent defection to Apple and his return to Commodore. Apparently, he'd had a dispute with Jack and gone to work at Apple for six weeks, but Chuck and Apple were even less comfortable with each other and he wound up coming back to Commodore.

Jack welcomed him back, but after Chuck's desertion it was obvious Jack had less patience with, or trust in, the engineer.

To the casual observer, Chuck still wore the official rank of guru with the rights and privileges of a Commodore general, but in reality he was being treated more like a colonel by Jack as well as by some top executives who had trouble forgiving his defection. The dispute between Chuck and Jack would flare up at the meeting we were about to attend, and their ongoing differences resulted in Chuck's leaving Commodore just a few months later in October, along with several of his best engineers.

Chuck had earned his guru stripes back in 1976 when he designed Commodore's first computer, the Commodore PET. He also designed the architecture for the 6502 microprocessor chip and the 6800 microprocessor.

He was working for MOS Technology, a small semiconductor company based in Pennsylvania, when Jack Tramiel popped up and bought it. The purchase of MOS was one of Jack's most brilliant moves, and one of the things that helped keep Commodore from going bankrupt after the Calculator Wars in the 1970s. MOS gave Commodore its own source of supply for semiconductor chips used in calculators and digital watches, and it also provided something else—the 6502 microprocessor.

When Chuck told him about the 6502 chip, Jack said, "You know what you've got here—you've got the makings of the first low-cost personal computer!"

Jack admits he didn't know what people would do with their own computer, but he sensed the opportunity and potential, and he guessed if he gave the public a low-priced computer they'd find something useful to do with it. He gave Chuck six months to produce the computer, and Chuck assembled a tiger team which included Bill Seiler, John Feagans, two Japanese engineers named Fujiyama and Aoji, and Jack's son Leonard.

Together, Chuck and his team developed the first self-contained personal computer: It had a keyboard, a built-in green phosphor screen, and a built-in tape cassette for storing and retrieving programs. The first unit came completely assembled, with a choice of either 4K or 8K of memory.

The product was officially announced in 1976, and Commodore's stock rose from $4.50 to $7.00 a share by December. It was the beginning of a historic rise in Commodore's stock that made the company one of the fastest rising stocks in the history of the American Stock Exchange.

The first actual machines were officially unveiled at the Consumer Electronics Show in June of 1977. By that time, the stock had reached $9.25 per share.

The prototypes shown at the Consumer Electronics Show were built by hand with housings made of wood and sprayed yellow to look like painted metal. Zenith television sets were built into the housings; the engineers used Zeniths because when they went to a nearby appliance store the Zeniths happened to be on sale for $89.95. The engineers took out the tube, stripped out the tuner, and rewired the electronics so they could use the black-and-white monitor as their computer screen. They also bought some Sanyo cassette tape recorders, added their own circuitry, and built the recorders into the housing. This allowed users to use ordinary cassette tapes to store any programs they wrote.

The keyboard was extremely compact, just a small rectangular patch of blue and red metallic keys. There was no space at all between keys and each key had graphic symbols on it, in addition to letters and numbers.

When I first heard the word *microprocessor*, I was about as technically literate as a fish and didn't understand it at all. In essence, a microprocessor is a tiny electronic circuit containing a set of instructions that control most of the functions of the computer. Physically, the chip is sandwiched between two rectangular pieces of plastic with metal pins which are plugged into the computer's main circuit-board. The microprocessor controls other chips on the board which, in turn, control such things as the video signal, keyboard, and external devices like disk drives and printers.

There are other kinds of chips too. For example, computers remember things the way we do: either short term or permanently in the two main types of memory chips, ROM and RAM. *ROM* (Read Only Memory) chips hold information which is written in at the factory and can never be changed. It's useful, for example, that a computer permanently remember the meaning of the word *stop,* so that's built into ROM. However, *RAM* (Random Access Memory) chips give the computer its temporary *memory,* which lets it learn new, but user-specific, information like your current salary.

The 6502 chip became the most widely used microprocessor in personal computing, thanks to a cross-licensing agreement between MOS and Synertek and Rockwell, which let those other companies make and sell the chip for use in other computers such as Apple, Atari, and Ohio Scientific.

Jack once told me that he gave Apple the 6502 chip when the two Steves were designing the computer in their garage, although Apple ended up buying most of their chips from Synertek or Rockwell, not MOS. Synertek and Rockwell were licensed to manufacture the 6502 chip under a cross-licensing agreement that gave all three companies licenses to each other's various chips. I was told that MOS, Synertek, and Rockwell cross-licensed different chips to each other in return for nominal royalties or at no cost, to settle infringement disputes.

The full name of the Commodore PET was Personal Electronic Transactor—pretty bad. But there was a method to this madness. The name PET was inspired by the Pet Rocks fad.

Apparently, when Chuck and Jack were trying to name the computer, Jack suggested they name it after something already famous like Pet Rocks. How about the Pet Computer? Or more simply, just PET?

Chuck agreed. (After all, PET's pretty close to Peddle.) But if they used the name PET, they had to come up with some sort of meaning for the initials. What could P.E.T. stand for? Those were tricky initials. Some people suggested Peddle's Ego Trip or Peddle's Electronic Toy.

After much careful thought, they gave the PET its official name: Personal Electronic Transactor.

In programming, that's called a *kludge*, something slapped together after the fact.

In France, they called it hilarious—it seems the word *pet* has something to do with farting. We would continue to have problems finding names for products that didn't mean something untoward in countries we expected to sell them. The name VIC, for example, startles Germans.

The first PET was previewed at the Consumer Electronics Show in January 1977. An original prototype still survives, thanks to John Feagans who discovered it in a warehouse and guarded it through the years.

The response was immediate and positive. Suddenly, everyone wanted a PET. People flocked to buy the new PET, but production delays created a swarm of angry customers and dealers. The public had tasted the future, and now they expected Jack Tramiel and his magic time machine to make it happen—*fast*.

So great was the demand that Commodore made the unprecedented move of asking customers to pay the full $795 purchase price in advance, then to wait up to six months for delivery.

And becoming a PET dealer was almost as hard as becoming a PET owner. New dealers had to have a service technician, a retail storefront, and a good credit rating, and had to send a large cash deposit to Commodore with no guarantees when items ordered would be delivered. The dealers, in turn, required—and got—prepayment from their customers. The money that flowed in gave Commodore the short-term capital they needed to rev up production.

This arrangement may seem a little like loan-sharking, but Commodore always knew how to make good use of other people's money. The company's accountants routinely crunched cash, cut costs to the bone, stretched out payables to vendors, and made dealers pay up fast.

A good example came in 1981 when the prime rate topped 18 percent. To take advantage of the high interest, Commodore practically stopped paying bills so it could deposit as much money as possible in interest-bearing accounts. That year, Commodore earned substantial interest income.

The PET continued to evolve. Commodore introduced a large typewriter-style keyboard, but because it was designed by and for programmers, they left off the period (you had to use the decimal point on the numeric keypad). As a result of this seemingly trivial design flaw, Apple and Radio Shack stole a large share of the fledgling word processing market.

The CBM 2020 dot-matrix printer was introduced in 1978 but had to be canceled for technical reasons. The 2022 and 2023 printers were successfully introduced later that year, along with a dual floppy disk drive called the CBM 2040.

The 2040 had two separate disk drives, which meant you could work with two disks at the same time. This made it easy to make duplicate disks or exchange files—and Commodore's engineers found a way to store up to 170 kilobytes of information, or about 50 typewritten pages, on each floppy diskette. This was considerably more than Apple (150K) and Atari (90K).

Meanwhile, Jack decided he'd made a mistake. The huge U.S. demand told him he'd priced the computer too low. His solution was to double the price and reintroduce the PET in Europe. It was an instant hit.

Some accused Commodore of greed in the extreme. In reality, it was simple economics. PETs were in short supply. Commodore could make only so many machines. If there are scarce resources—in this case, not enough PETs—you have to allocate what you have to where it'll do you the most good.

Choosing not to wage war on two fronts, Jack committed most of his resources to Europe. The strategy was simple. Starting in the U.S. meant competing head to head with Apple and Radio Shack. It made more sense to capture the world and then come back to the States, instead of starting in the U.S. and branching out to the world.

Jack decided to conquer Europe, where there was no real competition, and fight a modest holding action in the States. Later he could always use Europe as a bridgehead to come back and take the U.S. This, then, explained why Commodore seemed to be hiding its light under a bushel in the U.S., while in Europe the company shone like a beacon. The strategy worked.

In less than two years, Commodore captured nearly 80 percent of the microcomputer market in countries like Germany and the United Kingdom. In the U.S., with very little marketing push, Commodore became the third largest microcomputer company, behind Apple and Tandy (Radio Shack). By June 1979, Commodore's stock was $41.63 a share.

Still, Commodore's reputation in the U.S. was terrible. It had no customer support, a weak repair system, disgruntled dealers, and minimum advertising and promotion. Despite Wall Street's enthusiasm, a lot of people in the computer industry thought Commodore was down for the count.

But it was only a standing eight-count. Lazy marketers who relied on false research reports were about to receive a chess lesson: If you let a pawn cross the board, it's liable to checkmate your king.

By 1980, MOS Technology had expanded its chip-making capacity so much, it was starting to sell chips to outside customers and at one point became the largest supplier of ROMs used in Atari game cartridges. Jack was also setting up a manufacturing plant in Braunschweig, West Germany, to make computers for sale in Europe; this freed Hong Kong to support stronger sales in North America. It was time to bring the war home.

Until now, Commodore had all but ignored the U.S. market. Jack felt American consumers were too fickle—they had a "gimme" philosophy, expecting the same level of handholding and support with a $600 computer as they got with a $6,000 computer. Also, and more important, it was difficult and expensive to build customer and dealer loyalty in the U.S.

"European dealers know what loyalty means," Jack explained, pointing out that if you build a strong relationship with them, they're grateful and remain loyal over years, even decades.

"Americans always want more. They buy things they don't understand and get upset when they get it home. Europeans have to be careful how they spend their money. Before they buy a computer, they have to know what it does and what they're going to do with it. They buy on quality, not price, and when they buy something that doesn't cost much, they don't expect you should give them the moon."

This is why we had gone to London: to plan the strategy to bring Commodore back to the U.S. in full force. Would we succeed? Was Jack right? Was it time to confront the American market, or was it too late?

These questions buzzed through my mind as we landed at Heathrow International Airport in London. We made our way through the terminal complex, which was crowded with beautifully costumed people of every culture and nationality—Indians, Pakistanis, Chinese, Africans, Arabs—all British citizens, a consequence of Britain's empire days.

The first thing I learned was to stop calling this place England. It's Britain, or the United Kingdom. England shares equal billing with Scotland, Wales, and Northern Ireland. Most people call it the U.K. for short, as in Commodore U.K.

An hour by bus and taxi brought us to our destination: the Burnham Beeches, a delightful old mansion located in the countryside on the outskirts of London. The estate had been converted into an elegant and historic country club, without sacrificing the quaintness of its fox-and-hounds atmosphere.

The inn itself was architecturally bland on the outside, just a large white building, but the ambience was lovely. The inn was surrounded on all sides by a broad expanse of neatly trimmed meadows, broken here and there by a series of low white fences. I couldn't help imagining Jack on horseback, galloping across the meadows. I could see him dressed in a red and black riding outfit, blowing his horn and shouting "Tallyho!" But Jack wasn't the tallyho type. He was Teddy Roosevelt charging up San Juan Hill. Or maybe Napoleon.

Inside, the rooms were framed with deeply polished wood moldings, with tuxedoed waiters manning the small continental restaurant, and a tiny publike bar where I would soon get my first taste of a creamy liqueur called Bailey's Irish Cream.

After checking in, I went downstairs and found myself in the lobby with a group of charming European Commodore managers. It then dawned on me that you really can't understand a multinational company until you attend a meeting of international managers and find yourself outnumbered and surrounded (and in my case outclassed) by the Allies.

Among the two dozen managers in attendance were Harald Speyer from Commodore Germany; Christopher (Kit) Spencer from Commodore United Kingdom; Bob Gleadow, an Englishman Jack was grooming for a general managership; Jim Dionne, the 29-year-old manager from Commodore Canada; Dick Sanford, who ran Commodore U.S.; Ernst DeMuth from Commodore Switzerland; Chris Fish; Chuck Peddle; and a new U.S. sales executive named Dick Powers.

Despite the intimidating introductions ("Harald runs Germany," "Kit runs the U.K."), everyone accepted me right away—not because I was Jack's new assistant, but because anyone who showed up at these conferences automatically received equal rank. It was graphic evidence that, below Jack, rank blurred.

Still, it was clear that these were the company's generals and colonels. I was just a lowly general's aide, but I yearned to be a colonel. Put me in charge of the commandos, the red berets. I didn't want to be a general, I didn't need stars on my cap. I didn't even need rank. Just include me in this exciting international clique. Let me learn a little German, a little Italian, and some Japanese. Let me lead the paratroops when we go back and attack the U.S. market. I remembered our paratroop cry: "Airborne!"

We spent almost an hour milling around the lobby and loitering in front of the building, then a group of us went on a walking tour of the cobblestone streets around Windsor Castle, hosted by Kit Spencer's lovely wife Lesley and their daughter Marie. I seized the opportunity to corner each manager and sponged up as much information as I could, partly to wangle my way into the clique and partly to get material for the 1980 annual report.

I found that, as a group, the international managers were polite, friendly, smug, confident, extremely knowledgeable about their own countries and markets, but a trifle nearsighted and nationalistic when it came to understanding how they fit into the global scheme of things. It wasn't their fault. Jack encouraged this nearsightedness. He wanted each country to develop its markets according to the needs of its culture and people.

He knew computers would be used for different things in different countries, and he wanted each manager to find out what those uses were: educational, industrial, recreational, personal? Nobody knew. The only way to find out was to see what happened in each country. There was lots of time later to discover which applications were *universal*. For now, the world marketing plan was strictly *regional*.

In the United Kingdom, Commodore looked and acted and was seen as a British company. In Germany, Commodore spoke German. In Canada, Commodore was Canadian (French *and* English). Even in Japan, Commodore had a uniquely Japanese appeal.

Each country had different challenges to cope with, and different solutions. Harald Speyer recalled that in 1977 Germany had only the PET and no disk drives or printers to start with; so the enterprising Speyer marketed the PET as an industrial tool for use in laboratories and manufacturing plants. People started writing industrial software, and before long, there were PETs in factories and offices all over Germany.

In the United Kingdom, the PET was introduced as a hobbyist machine. Kit Spencer focused on getting machines into the hands of hobbyists or hackers, and encouraged them to write software for nonhobbyists. Within months, he had a whole catalog of software.

In theory, these successes should have been shared from one country to another, but in practice each country was treated as a fief reporting directly to Jack. The fiefs didn't communicate much with each other; they were too preoccupied with their own thrust forward.

Except for the quarterly management conferences, there was no real forum or committee which could circulate proposals or make decisions on international issues, such as moving excess inventory from one country to another, translating books and manuals, or negotiating world software contracts. As a result, it was possible for half a dozen countries to negotiate separate rights to the same software program, with each country paying a different royalty.

Most of the managers saw any attempt to consolidate activities as a threat to their autonomy. They liked the status quo and didn't mind duplicating efforts. Besides, everything was going well. Why tamper with success?

The night before the meeting, we had dinner together at a combination pub and continental restaurant. Crowded around a line of tiny square tables, we strained to talk above the restaurant noise. The main topic of conversation was the new 80-column version of the PET, called the CBM 8032. That computer was designed to put Commodore into the small-business and word-processing market. It came with a built-in green phosphor monitor, a business keyboard, and 32 kilobytes of memory which means it could hold 32,000 characters or symbols. Based on our discussions, it seemed clear that the future of Commodore rested on the PET and CBM systems. No one suspected that within 24 hours the future of Commodore and the entire computer industry would be turned in an entirely different direction.

The meeting got started around 8:30 the next morning, in a spacious, wood-paneled room with windows all around. We took our seats on the outside of a large rectangle of tables, facing each other like delegates in the U.N. Security Council. There were about two dozen executives there, mostly Europeans.

Everyone was smiling and the mood was calm and businesslike. There were no thunderclouds hanging over the room, no visible guillotines awaiting victims. No one fingered their collars nervously. The European managers were secure and good-natured and wonderfully unperturbed.

By rights, I should have felt like a dwarf in the land of the heavyweights, but by now I was beginning to feel like one of the gang. I took my place at the table next to Chuck Peddle. My nose had stopped twitching and I was outwardly calm.

Dick Sanford chaired the meeting, which was indicative of his position as de facto second-in-command. His star was definitely rising. The first few hours of discussion centered on the issue of international pricing and black-market computers. Several enterprising dealers made impressive profits buying computers from Commodore in the U.S. and exporting them to Europe where the retail prices were twice as high. It was decided that U.S. and European prices would be brought into line in the future.

By midmorning, the heat was stifling and we opened the windows to let in some fresh air. We also let in the noise of the gardener. For more than two hours the busy drone of his tractor faded in and out, in and out, as he rumbled back and forth scalping the meadows clean.

Jack arrived at midmorning and took a seat on my side of the table, a few seats down on the other side of Chuck Peddle. He winked at me as he sat down.

"I'm just an observer," he insisted, but no one believed him.

He leaned back in his chair, with one hand placed palm down on the table, and the other hand tucked inside the waistband of his slacks, a typical pose. He was wearing his usual attire—casual summer slacks, loafers, and a comfortable short-sleeved knit shirt. He wore suits and ties only at conventions, banking meetings, speeches, and investor presentations. Jack was a California person. Either that, or this was the way some millionaires dress after they become millionaires.

Jack's arrival caused some juggling of the agenda. There had been a quiet conspiracy to discuss certain topics when Jack wasn't there because the managers knew they could spark an explosion.

Chuck Peddle's briefing was hastily moved up, and he began his briefing with a rundown on his hottest research project, a new color computer which he called the ColorPET. Until now, the engineers had been calling the machine by its code name TOI (pronounced *toy*), which stood for Tool Of Intellects.

Chuck usually spoke with the smooth and earnest style that was his trademark, but today he spoke haltingly and his briefing seemed disjointed. I could tell from Jack's expression that there was something wrong. Either Chuck wasn't ready to give his briefing yet, or Jack was making him nervous.

Still, the features of the new computer were impressive: 80 columns, color, high-resolution graphics, programmable function keys, four-voice sound and music, an improved built-in BASIC (the programming language), expandable memory, and special connectors for outside accessories such as game joysticks.

It was during Chuck's briefing that I first heard the term VIC, a word that would soon have tremendous meaning in the home computer world. VIC stood for Video Interface Chip, a new semiconductor device which replaced the screen controller used in the PET and CBM. The VIC chip made it possible for new Commodore computers to use a color television set or monitor as a display screen like the Apple or Atari, instead of the green phosphor monitor built into the PET/CBM.

Two VIC chip configurations were planned—22 columns and 40 columns, although the 40-column version was not designed yet. The 22-column version had larger letters but displayed only 22 characters on each line, while the 40-column version would display 40 characters per line like most desktop computers. The 22-column chip was nonstandard, but the chip was essentially done and could be manufactured quickly. MOS Technology had in fact been trying to sell the chip to outside computer manufacturers since 1978, but no one wanted to buy the chip. So Jack was beginning to think about using the chip in a Commodore computer.

In his philosophy, we could either design the chips first and then design the computer, or we could start with the computer and then do the chips. Unfortunately, most engineers were either chicken people *or* egg people, not both. Quickly, a debate began between Chuck and Jack about what the next computer should look like.

Chuck argued that we needed to bring out a machine targeted head to head against Apple, Atari, and NEC (Nippon Electric Corporation, the leading personal computer company in Japan). He lamented the fact that we were two years behind those companies because we still didn't have a color computer.

Jack countered that the second or third company coming into a marketplace has an advantage because it can make improvements the first companies didn't think of, and find new ways to cut costs and reduce prices.

"There is no question that what I see, Chuck, is that if you come out a year or two later, you can still do better than somebody who came out brand-new. There is somebody called TI [Texas Instruments] who always comes in only second or third."

He went on to say that despite their head start and success with videogame machines, Atari was still small when it came to computers, and he made a strong point that being first wasn't always an advantage.

"If you're a leader in the marketplace, you don't have to be first with a product. *Only a newcomer has to be first.* I prefer to move in where the market is, than to start a new market."

Jack's message was clear. Since Commodore was already a leader in personal computers, we didn't have to worry if other companies were ahead of us in some segment, like color computers. As a leader, we already had the know-how and technology to leapfrog those companies that were in the market first, and thus beat them with better products. The debate continued. Jack wanted a low-priced computer and he wanted it immediately.

Chuck insisted we couldn't reduce the cost of the ColorPET any further. Jack disagreed and cited costs that were lower than Chuck's figures. He said the cost of color monitors was coming down, as an example.

He also complained that the engineers had been working on a color computer for nearly twelve months. He wanted a machine on the market at once. If a sophisticated computer wasn't ready now, maybe we should build a stripped-down version and improve it later. We could have several different models, each one better than the last. But we had to start with *something*.

There was some discussion as to whether a color computer needed a built-in monitor like the PET and CBM. Kit Spencer and Jim Dionne argued that built-in color monitors weren't needed for the education market, since most schools already had color TV sets. Someone raised the issue that sitting too close to a color TV could damage your eyes, or even make you sterile. No one really knew the answer at the time, although later studies suggested there was minimal health risk.

It was pointed out that Apple sold computers without monitors attached. And someone else suggested that if there really was a health risk we could use it against Apple in our advertising. Someone quipped: "Buy An Apple, Kill A Kid! What a great TV ad." Everyone thought it was a hilarious idea, but after the laughter died down we agreed to look into the health risk. Nobody wanted their eyeballs fried because they spent too much time using a color computer.

Finally, Jack leaned forward and said, "Gentlemen, as you know, I've been pushing for that machine for the past twelve months, only to try to have a low-priced color unit. And seeing where Apple was, it seemed like we had many discussions where people told us color is not the right thing. But it seems our engineering department still doesn't understand the consumer out there, and we have a problem in that particular area.

"I am trying to understand the market as much as I possibly can, and I'm learning, too. In the United States today, we're the underdog. We have to feed Dick Powers (the new sales vice president) with something which he will have that we can really bring forward. What is that product? Is it this color machine? At the same time I was thinking of having a machine exactly like this in black and white, for people who don't need anything fancy, just down and dirty. Those were my thoughts—because there are other people out there that will try to come in the same way."

He didn't know it yet, but he was predicting Sinclair's entry into the market with their low-priced, down and dirty ZX-80.

"I want to get started," Jack said firmly. "With the music and the features and everything else it's all beautiful, but if you come out with the machine the way it is now and tomorrow you want function keys and some other features, you can have model one, two, three, four, five, and six. Then you have something to talk about. You'll be constantly in the press.

"If we're convinced it's a good machine, we do it, because we can still change it if we want to, because to be in the marketplace I believe we need an encore all the time—constantly, constantly, constant encore. An encore which is proven already in the marketplace."

The discussion continued for a while and then the meeting moved on to other topics. Decisions on the ColorPET were tabled and Jack departed.

That evening, we all went with Chris Fish to a marvelous English pub where we all gained about ten pounds (American pounds). Meanwhile, Jack kept doing his homework *and worrying*. Encores were great, he thought, but you have to have a song before you have an encore, and as of then Commodore didn't have a song—or a color computer. He had to make a decision.

On the second day of the meeting, Jack surprised everyone by announcing his intention to develop and market a $300 personal computer. He reminded the group that Commodore was a pioneer in low-priced pocket calculators and had announced the first self-contained personal computer—the PET—in 1976. Now it was time to introduce a low-priced color computer.

As soon as he made the announcement, the entire room erupted in debate, with several groups talking simultaneously. Everyone wanted to debate the proposal with everyone else. Jack just smiled and leaned back as the meeting broke down into several smaller discussions on every side of the table. Refreshments were brought in. One or two people came up to Jack, but he waved them away and made them go join or begin a debate.

Most of the opinion was opposed to Jack's idea. Some felt it wasn't time for a computer priced that low. Others felt the new computer might undercut sales of the PET, and still others questioned whether it was economically and technologically feasible.

Finally, about twenty minutes later, Jack stood up and pounded his fist once on the table. The room fell silent. Then slowly, in his deep booming voice, he said: "Gentlemen, the Japanese are coming—so we will become the Japanese!"

The entire debate suddenly evaporated into the English countryside, like so many invisible spirits fleeing out the open windows.

The Japanese are coming—so we will become the Japanese. It was the simplest and most profound argument he could make, delivered in a single line, powerful and affirmative. Nobody dared speak.

Many of us knew he was right. We could debate the new computers and their features for years if we wanted to, but the threat was still upon us and all the talk and waffling in the world wouldn't stop the competition from coming in and crushing us if we didn't do the right thing, and do it fast.

Chuck had told us that every new feature in the machine meant another delay of a few days, a week, or a month. He argued for more time, but Jack was saying after a year's worth of development, time was up. Jack wasn't ringing the gong. The Japanese were ringing it for us, and there wasn't a single manager sitting around those tables who couldn't hear the hollow tones in the distance.

We all listened attentively as Jack explained that several Japanese computer companies (known collectively as Japan, Inc.) were already poised to enter the U.S. market. Japanese companies had already captured the television, radio, and small car markets, and personal computers were next on their list.

"We have to compete with ourselves," he warned. "Always. We have to be like the Japanese. We have to constantly come up with something new, something better. We have to believe that we are the competition. If we do this, no one can get ahead of us."

The entire room stayed quiet. We all knew a $300 color computer was a killer in a marketplace where the cheapest color computer sold for more than twice that price. Why was $300 a magic price point? There's no way of telling, except that Jack knew it. His nose told him it was the price barrier. Break down that wall, slice through that $300 price point, and the whole home-consumer market would open up like a flower. It was Jack's talent to sense such things—and be right.

I remember feeling a thrill after that session. History was really being made here.

Unfortunately, not everyone shared the enthusiasm. Chuck Peddle and his engineers still wanted the ColorPET. They didn't believe in the small computer. They didn't think they could get the costs down low enough. They didn't want a computer that was less powerful than Apple or Atari or NEC. They resisted, from the moment Jack made his announcement. And while Jack had his doubts too, he sensed he could get what he asked for, but he still didn't know quite how. If necessary, he'd go *around* the systems group. He had other engineers in Japan. And at MOS Technology.

Chuck continued to resist and lobbied against the small computer. Even Dick Sanford, the street-smart, scrappy hatchet man who ran U.S. operations, felt we should give away the small computer free to dealers who bought PETs and CBMs.

Jack turned to Jerone Guinn, president of MOS Technology. Jerone believed he could do it and volunteered his semiconductor design engineers, including a young chip designer named Bob Yannes, who was programming the VIC chip, and a brilliant engineering manager named Al Charpentier. Secretly, the small computer began to take shape in Valley Forge, Pennsylvania.

On the last day of the meeting, Kit Spencer invited us all on a tour of his U.K. operation in the London suburb of Slough. It was a lesson in successful marketing.

Christopher Spencer, called Kit for short, was a handsome, erudite Englishman in his midthirties, with a dashing air about him. He was slimly athletic and blonde with striking blue eyes, aristocratic features, and a cultured British accent. He *looked* like summer. If you saw him in California, you'd think he belonged at the beach. If you saw him in Antarctica, you'd still think he belonged at the beach.

For recreation he played pro-amateur tennis, held numerous trophies, and once competed in the Junior Wimbledon tournament. He loved sailing and occasionally ran in hash runs. His wife Lesley sometimes complained he carried the same competitive spirit into sports as he displayed at the office. Kit was like Jack, he competed to win.

During the meetings at Burnham Beeches, he wore a suit and tie like the rest of us, but his tie never once looked like it was strangling him, and he was totally unaffected by the heat. He always looked cool and never seemed to perspire.

He knew what it meant to rough it, too, and to scrape for a shilling. As a member of Voluntary Service Overseas, the British Peace Corps, he had spent a harsh year in the bush country of Uganda.

It is difficult to think of Kit Spencer without recalling Leo Tolstoy's description of Englishmen in *War and Peace:* "An Englishman is self-assured as being a citizen of the best-organized state in the world and therefore, as an Englishman, always knows what he should do and knows that all he does as an Englishman is undoubtedly correct."

As a manager, he was stylishly ferocious. He turned out newsletters, magazines, advertising campaigns, slogans, product recommendations, and presentations faster than anyone I've ever known. I've seen him sit down and hand-print an entire one-hour briefing on overhead transparencies on a few hours notice, and then speak from the viewgraphs as if he'd studied the whole thing for hours.

Surprisingly, his offices at Slough were modest, even slightly tawdry. The rooms were drab yellow and gloomy. And many of his programmers and writers had windows that looked out on assembly lines or warehouse aisles, although the people seemed cheerful enough.

Kit's management style was autocratic and tough, and I was impressed by his staffing formula: Surround yourself with young hobbyists who'll be doing what they'd be doing anyway, people who enjoy working by candlelight and on weekends. Don't pay them too much so it doesn't go to their heads. And do everything *fast*. The results were astounding. Through sheer force of effort and marketing skill, Kit and his staff captured nearly 80 percent of the

British personal computer market, and U.K. sales were higher than U.S. sales.

"And I have to sell my computers on an island!" Kit complained in mock agony. He loved to rub it in to the Americans, not for reasons of ego, but to spur the lagging U.S. team so they'd get their act together and go win the U.S. market. In fact, I think that he, more than anyone else, wanted Commodore U.S. to succeed.

Kit's marketing savvy was forged in the mid-1970s at the end of the Calculator Wars. When Jack recruited him to set up Commodore's British company, Kit was still working for Bowmar, the company that introduced the first handheld calculator.

Bowmar is often taught in business schools as the classic example of how a company which pioneers a new product can get bumped off by the competition. The lesson is that the second or third company entering a new market can leapfrog the pioneer company with new technologies or less expensive products. Some people have to go to graduate school to learn this lesson. Jack and Kit learned it firsthand because they were there.

In the case of Bowmar, it was Texas Instruments that drove them into bankruptcy, by introducing a $49 calculator while Bowmar kept selling calculators for as high as $500. Bowmar couldn't react quickly enough and went out of business.

Few people know it, but Commodore was primarily a calculator company in the mid-1970s, and when TI entered the market they almost went bankrupt like Bowmar. Both Kit and Jack learned valuable lessons at the hands of Texas Instruments. But they would have their revenge.

After the meetings ended, I got ready to go back to the States and Kit asked me in casual conversation if I was going on to Hanover.

"What's Hanover?" I asked.

"It's only the biggest industrial exposition in the world," he told me. "We're going over to launch the CBM system and see what the competition's got. I presume you're coming."

"I don't know. Jack didn't ask me so I guess I'm not going."

"Nonsense," he said. "We're all going. You want to learn about the company, don't you? You have to go to Hanover. I'll put you on the list."

The next thing I knew, I was scheduled for a seat on the PET Jet, Commodore's seven-seater corporate jet. It was ferrying people from London to Frankfurt. At this time, Commodore was the only microcomputer company with its own corporate jet. Apple got one later, but not until after they went public. The jet was shared by Jack and Irving Gould, Commodore's chairman of the board. Irving needed the jet because he split his time between the Bahamas, New York, and Toronto. Jack used the jet to hopscotch back and forth from Santa Clara on the West Coast to New York or Valley Forge or Toronto in the East.

The PET Jet was more cramped than a commercial airline, but it was elegant, besides being a major convenience and status symbol. It had a medium-sized luggage compartment and there was sometimes a struggle between suitcases and computers when prototypes were being taken to conventions.

Whoever sat closest to the small on-board kitchen had the duty of serving as steward, pouring drinks, breaking out crackers and cheese, and so on. Occasionally the passengers enjoyed such *haute cuisine* as lobster or steak.

It was said the air vent controls were gold-plated. They could have been brass, I guess, but they looked gold to me. It was a privilege to ride on the PET Jet, mostly because you usually traveled on it with Jack, and that meant you had time to catch his ear with a proposal. Above all, it was a good chance to go back to the well for Jack's wisdom, guidance, criticism, or encouragement, which he offered more freely and without posturing on the plane. In offices he slammed his fist on the table, but I never saw him slam his fist on a bulkhead or seat cushion.

We touched down at Hanover about 2:00 p.m. and were met by Harald Speyer, general manager of Commodore Germany. Harald was a tall, soft-spoken German with prematurely gray hair and a friendly disposition that made him popular throughout Commodore.

As a manager he was shrewd and resourceful, and ran his company like a well-ordered ship. If I was a guerilla and Kit was a field commander, Harald was more like an admiral. He loved to steer the ship, although Jack sometimes got on his case when he thought Harald might run the ship aground. Harald never sank, though. Whenever he ever got into trouble, he simply submerged like a submarine and stayed out of Jack's gunsites until he could resurface with a success.

He used to joke about how lucky he was because Jack wasn't around all the time to stir things up. Many of the Europeans expressed the same sentiment. They felt distance gave them more autonomy than their American counterparts, even though most of them spoke with Jack by phone nearly every day. For some reason, Jack felt the Americans needed more prodding, or maybe it's just part of his makeup to prod people wherever he is, and since he spent most of his time in America, that's where he prodded.

When we landed at Frankfurt, our baggage was brought into the terminal, but there was no customs inspection. Harald collected our passports, went away for a few minutes, and when he came back he said, "Okay, we can go now." I'm not even sure they stamped our passports to show we were there. It's possible Harald gave the government a personal guarantee we wouldn't be rowdy or make trouble and they let us come and go without the usual paperwork and hassles. Harald seemed to have good connections with the government.

For some reason I still don't understand, Jack, Harald, and Commodore in general had a lot of clout in West Germany. This is odd, considering there are Germans still living who had wanted to kill Jack and bury him in a ditch back in the 1940s. In fact, they almost did.

It was equally strange that Jack should choose to build a factory in Braunschweig, West Germany, in the country that threw him in a concentration camp for six years and made him work as a slave, building roads.

Perhaps from Jack's viewpoint, going back to do business in Germany was like getting back on a horse that threw you off. It was to prove to himself he could do it. I also suspected he harbored a secret feeling that he was collecting some debts.

On the German side, it didn't hurt to have a wealthy Jewish businessman coming back to start factories. Besides, Jack played by German rules, hired German management talent, and gave new jobs to Germans. He also worked closely with German bankers and there were even some government tie-ins engineered, I suspect, by Harald.

I've known other Jews who made it through the camps, but those Jews find it almost impossible to be around Germans.

I think the key to Jack's German connection lies in his view of time. "I live in the future," he told me. "Only the future. There's nothing else." That's how he handled his memories of Auschwitz. And that's one reason why he was able, more than anyone else, to *live* in the future of technology and work in that future just as skillfully and assuredly as most people work in the present.

We all crowded into two taxis and made our way to a wonderful inn called the Romerkrug, where Commodore executives always stayed during Hanover Fair.

The Romerkrug was a small German inn located on a quiet street corner in a residential area about five miles from the Hanover exposition site. There was a lively German restaurant on the ground floor. We stayed in rooms above the restaurant. The inn was run by an attractive German couple who treated us like house guests and made us feel extraordinarily welcome. Nobody spoke English, and that was the most fun of all.

That first night, I met Yashi Terakura and his wife Sumiyo. Yashi was senior engineer in the Japanese engineering group. Also joining us for dinner were Jim Dionne, the general sales manager of Commodore in Canada, and Dick Barton, who was newly in charge of manufacturing at Commodore.

Dick, who spoke fluent German, forced me to order from the menu and refused to translate one word. Everyone

51

went along with him and the next thing I knew, I was struggling to dredge up every German word or phrase I ever heard in a John Wayne war movie. It was a good thing I like Wiener schnitzel because that's the only word I recognized. We all drank great quantities of beer. The next day at the fair, I learned a new phrase: "Warum errotest du?" which means "Why are you blushing?" Harald had hired some attractive college girls to demonstrate software on the new CBM system, and I kept making passes at them. They practiced their English on me, and I practiced my line on them. If I got into trouble and got embarrassed, I would blush and ask them why *they* were blushing. "Warum errotest du?"

I told Harald I would learn German well enough to get by the next time I visited Germany. I never did. My German still comes from John Wayne movies.

Commodore's booth consisted of several eye-level displays showing software running on the CBM system, and complete systems set up on office desks along the aisles, with college students at each desk. If anyone wanted a demonstration, all they had to do was sit down with one of the students and get a free lesson.

At the back of the booth were some meeting rooms where business deals were negotiated. Jack used one of the rooms to talk with German bankers and officials who needed to talk with him about his pending purchase of the factory in Braunschweig. I discovered that I was allowed to drift in and out of meetings pretty much at will, a privilege which was worth its weight in gold because watching Jack Tramiel conduct such a discussion was a crash course in business. There was a trick. If you were there when the meeting started, you could usually stay. After the door was shut, admittance was denied.

The first afternoon, I wandered around and discovered why Hanover Fair had become the world's largest industrial exposition. There were twenty-one permanent buildings on a dozen square acres of land. Each building was as large as a factory or museum, large enough to suspend farm machinery from the ceilings and create giant waterfalls, or give factory-sized demonstrations of robotic car assembly. Virtually every major corporation in the world showed their new products and technologies here, and sellers and buyers came from the farthest corners of the globe to make deals. The pavilions were used during the first week of April. The rest of the year they sat vacant, waiting for the next fair.

In addition to the delicious German sausages and sauerkraut served by vendors at umbrella stands, there was a large Bier Haus pavilion with nonstop polka bands, sing-alongs, and dancing.

To get from one end of the grounds to the other, you had to hop on one of the small electric vehicles that came along every few minutes. International signs were every-where, and at every entrance and intersection you could hear small groups of businesspeople chattering in several different languages.

The office equipment and computer exhibition was the most intriguing of all because it gave me a chance to size up our real competition, which Jack had said was coming from Japan. NEC, Sharp, and several other companies had convention booths. Apple and Texas Instruments were there, too, but their booths were largely ignored. I went over and watched people looking at their computers, and the people, mostly Germans, seemed to yawn at their displays. The most crowded exhibit in the hall was Commodore.

Harald Speyer told me Commodore was the most popular and well-known computer company in Germany and throughout Europe. He said most people in Europe owned a Commodore pocket calculator at one time or an-other, or knew someone who owned one, because Com-modore was the first company to market low-priced calculators in Europe. This brand-recognition carried over into computers.

I checked this out myself by asking several people if they ever owned a Commodore calculator. They had. I was beginning to get a good feeling about the company I'd just joined.

For lunch, I stopped at an umbrella stand and had a long, dark brown sausage. I was surprised when the vendor handed me a greasy foot-long Polish sausage wrapped in a piece of thin paper, and a separate breadroll. The roll was too hard to split open and stuff the sausage in, so I ate like everyone else, by biting off a chunk of sausage, and gnawing like a rat on the hard roll. It was fun but a little messy, and I felt homesick for American hot dogs. Then I was hungering for one of those fantastic pork legs you can get only in Germany, the giant greasy kind where the meat falls off the bones, so I made Harald Speyer promise to go with me to a beer hall one day for lunch. It wasn't until the third day that Harald was able to get free.

The hall was tremendous. There were step-up balconies around the outside which gave everyone a terrific view of the hall, although most of us were more interested in the view of the buxom German waitresses scurrying to and fro in their scoop-necked national costumes. A loud polka band played constantly, led by a conductor who was more cheerleader than bandleader. He sang, told jokes, yelled at the band members, and kept exhorting the audience to stop eating and sing along.

It was impossible to hold a meaningful conversation above the noise of the music. Everyone around us was shouting and clattering plates and guzzling huge quantities of beer served in half-gallon glass mugs and pitchers. Harald ordered my pork leg and asked me if I'd like a beer.

"Sure," I said cheerfully, not knowing what I was getting into.

A few minutes later the waitress came back and gave us two 18-inch-high glass mugs, brimming with fresh German beer. "Drink up," Harald said, taking a huge swill. I grinned and followed suit.

Now, Harald Speyer is over six feet tall, and I'm just five-eight. Still, I *am* from Wisconsin, and we're beer-drinkers there, so when he started drinking, I figured I'd keep up with him, just out of courtesy. A few minutes later, he finished his glass and so I emptied my glass too.

When Harald ordered another round of beer, I still wasn't suspicious. We were just two guys having a beer over lunch. The pork legs arrived, along with two more pitchers of beer. Harald smiled, took the beer, and started drinking. Harald kept drinking and I kept up. After all, it was only two mugs of beer—the fact that these mugs were bigger than most pitchers in the States didn't occur to me.

Finally, we both drained our mugs, and by this time I was almost falling off my chair, but Harald was just sitting there, totally unaffected. I was ruined for the rest of the day. He was sober.

"Do you always drink this much?" I asked.

"Oh, this is nothing," he said politely. "When I was in the Beer Olympics—"

"Wait a minute. Hold on here. Did you say *Beer Olympics*?"

When he was in college, he was on a championship beer-drinking team, and one year they won a national beer-drinking competition called the Beer Olympics.

Needless to say, I crept off to a quiet corner to recuperate, but that night there was no rest for the dissipated. I wound up tagging along with Jim Dionne, the Canadian sales manager, who was driving Dick Barton to Braunschweig to look over the manufacturing plant Jack was negotiating to buy. We arrived about 10:00 p.m., took a quick look at the outside of the plant, dropped Barton at a hotel, then drove back.

A few weeks later in Santa Clara, I told Jack about our trip on the Autobahn and he told me, matter-of-factly, "I built that road."

Jack went on to explain that during World War II as a teenager he had been selected to work on the road gangs. He said that it was one way to survive, because they had to feed the people that did that kind of hard labor, or they couldn't work. "We built good roads," he said.

People who knew he was in Auschwitz were frequently shocked by the way that Jack talked about being in the camps. Sometimes he would get a faraway look in his eye and shake his head in disbelief.

"You know," he once told me, "it's hard to believe it really happened. But it can happen again. In America.

Americans like to make rules, and that scares me. If you have too many rules you get locked in a system. It's the *system* that says this one dies and that one doesn't, not the people. That's why I don't hate the German people. Individuals, yes. Rules, yes. But not all Germans." He shrugged. "They just obeyed the rules. But that's why we need more Commodores. We need more mavericks, just so the rules don't take over."

THREE

"Where am I?" I asked.

"Commodore," said the Dormouse.

"Commodore? What's that?"

"We're the third largest personal computer company in the world," he sniffed, "but nobody knows it."

Suddenly, from the recesses of Jack Tramiel's office, came a bloodcurdling cry: "OFF WITH THEIR HEADS!"

A dozen executives dressed like playing cards came tumbling out of his office and lay scattered on the floor.

"Gee, who's that?" I asked. "The Red Queen?"

"No, that's the Jack," someone said. Then they all tried to answer at once.

"Jack of Hearts. He's a teddy bear."

"Jack of Spades. He's a meanie."

"Jack of Clubs. He hits us with a club."

"Jack of Diamonds. He's so rich."

I shook my head and said, "I don't have to listen to you. You're just a pack of playing cards!"

"You're right," said the Dormouse, as they carried him off to be executed.

Captain Jack
and the Temple of Doom

Santa Clara, California, was oceans apart from Europe, in more ways than one. In Europe it was "Welcome to the club." In the U.S. it was "Welcome to the HMS *Bounty*." There was mutiny a-brewing.

Executives didn't exactly come flying down the hall like a deck of Alice in Wonderland playing cards, but there was definitely something wrong. "Off with their heads!" The threat lingered in the air.

Indeed, many of the managers in Santa Clara described Jack as Captain Bly, raining down floggings, threats, and wormy rations on the hapless crew, while he himself grew a tummy and became a smug multimillionaire. True, some of Jack's mannerisms smacked of Charles Laughton (with heavy Polish overtones), but he wasn't Captain Bly.

The closer I got to him, the more he became Fletcher Christian, damning the stiff-upper-lips and their abominable rules, sailing his ship on an uncharted course toward an island he knew must lie just ahead. And I got the impression that Jack would, if necessary, bash the whole ship aground on a reef if it meant saving the loyalists who stayed with him, and reaching that island and its sanctuary.

In his heart, he wanted safety and prosperity for everyone who fought beside him, and for their children's children and beyond. That safe future was more important than all the shiploads of breadfruit, and all the truckloads of PETs and CBMs.

Was Jack really Captain Bly, Fletcher Christian, or Captain Queeg? Maybe the crew could provide some clues. But

there were mutineers afoot. I got my first inkling of weird-
ness when a senior manager approached me in the hall and
said, "Michael, can you get me in to see Jack?"

I was shocked.

"What do you mean? Your office is only four or five
doors down the hall. Go poke your head in the door and tell
him you want to see him. That's what everyone else does."

The manager shrugged and turned red. He couldn't do
that because he was on the outs with Jack. He'd been
caught double-dipping. He was doing some computer business on the side and that was taboo. One of the things Captain Jack frowned on was moonlighting: buying a computer
store, going into the software business, making your wife a
Commodore distributor. He felt moonlighters and double-
dippers were motivated by greed, not need. If you were
really desperate for money, he expected you to tell him.

There were other signs of decadence, even some trea-
son. Keelhauling offenses, Mr. Christian. One married executive had transferred his mistress to his own group to keep
her from getting fired. Another executive had a part-interest
in a computer store and was using his influence to keep
other Commodore dealerships out of that location.

There was theft too. It cost the company as much as
$5,000 in sales every time a system walked out the back
door. Once or twice a whole truck trailer of computers was
stolen out of the parking lot. The few times I had been back
to the warehouse, the workers were rude, careless, and surly.

There was also a modest drug problem. One senior
executive was walking around with a squeeze-bottle of
Dristan, constantly squirting the stuff up his nose. "My si-
nuses are killing me," he complained. It turned out there
had never been any Dristan in the bottle. He was snorting
cocaine. We all had to admit it was an ingenious deception
and no one suspected, but he was only the most colorful of
the cocaine crowd at Commodore.

I moved into an empty office a few doors down from
Jack. I didn't know it then, but having a window is important in business. Managers tend to judge rank by where
you sit and whether or not you have a window.

The manager who was afraid to see Jack came in and started chatting about Jack's strange business philosophy. I was surprised that a senior manager could be so opposed to what was obviously a successful philosophy. Maybe being in the United States gave him a cockeyed view of things. Maybe he'd never been to Europe. Maybe he was burned out and poisoned by so much stateside neglect, and couldn't rise to the occasion now that Jack was finally bringing the war home.

He was full of complaints. Jack was chintzy on expenses, and insisted on signing checks and purchase orders himself. That was unheard of. Imagine, the president of a hundred million dollar company signing all the checks, one by one. Jack approved all new employees and sometimes got rid of superfluous people if their bosses couldn't justify them. He was constantly going back to vendors and making them reduce their prices. Sometimes he canceled deals that were already signed.

One illuminating incident concerned a former personnel director. It seems he wanted to show Jack that Commodore was seriously understaffed and needed more people. Secretly, he hired some personnel consultants to study the company, and one day he nervously took them into Jack's office. The consultants were expensive and Jack hadn't signed off on them. The consultants laid out all kinds of facts, figures, and statistics, and when it was over they concluded, "As you can see, Commodore is operating with half as many employees as any other company with your sales and number of locations."

Before they could show how they proposed to double Commodore's staff and bring them in line with all the other companies, Jack held up his hand and flashed a broad grin. He whirled on the personnel director and exclaimed, "Wonderful! I always knew my people worked twice as hard as anyone else! Now I know it! Gentlemen, I don't know what your study cost, but it was worth every penny. Thank you very much." Then he ushered them out of his office. It was a typical Tramiel reaction. A few months later, the personnel director was gone.

I began to see that the same people who criticized or laughed at Jack's blunt, earthy management style never seemed to mention that *it worked.* I had to get the real story from Jack, so I wandered into his office—a habit I picked up in Europe—and sat down. I started asking him about some of the stories I'd been hearing. He gave me a funny look, growled, shook his head, and exclaimed, "You're so green!"

"I never told you I wasn't," I countered. "That's why I'm here to learn."

It was an interesting moment. I think my real education began right then and there. He began to explain his philosophy.

Jack called his management philosophy The Religion. "You have to believe in it, otherwise it doesn't work," he said. A key element of this religion was people. He believed the minute you turn your back, people will go out and hire more people. Next to money, overstaffing is the single biggest problem associated with growth, so he kept his organization as lean as possible, with few middle managers and very short lines of command.

He believed managers had to be doers as well as managers. They had to be *involved,* a word he used frequently. "It's a disease," he said. "Nobody wants to get involved. Managers like to manage. They don't like to work. How can you know what's going on if you're not involved?" he asked.

Woe to the manager who presented a briefing, and when challenged with an easy question had to say, "Wait, I'll go get so-and-so. He knows the answer."

"I pay people to do the job," Jack declared, "I don't pay them to learn."

Consequently, he forced his staff, particularly vice presidents, to do the work ordinarily done in other companies by a second tier, the middle managers. At Commodore there was no second tier. The top managers had to sign off on all purchase requisitions, and Jack himself reviewed or signed off on all purchase orders above $5,000. Sometimes when finances were getting tight or receivables were piling up, Jack signed off on *all* checks written in the U.S., and checks above a certain level overseas.

It was a shopkeeper approach to doing business and sometimes it slowed things down, but that's what Jack wanted. Those who wanted to buy something had to be able to defend their purchases—or the prices they paid—directly to Jack, and that meant everyone had to be on their toes.

Once I asked Jack point-blank why so many managers got fired or resigned from Commodore. "Business is war," he said. "You have to be in it to win. Our generals are all in the trenches, so more of them get killed."

That was his off-the-cuff explanation. Closer observation revealed several reasons why top managers didn't survive at Commodore: (1) They couldn't or wouldn't practice The Religion. (2) They were offered—and accepted—high jobs they weren't qualified for, letting their ego say yes to jobs they should have turned down. (3) They didn't make friends with insiders and failed to realize that ignoring, or abusing, insiders, many who had no visible rank, was political suicide.

Jack's major ongoing problem was that the people who learned The Religion best and practiced it most vigorously were young people in their twenties and thirties. Many of this group were too young or too specialized to be general managers and handle money and administration as well as management and creativity. Therefore, until this group was seasoned enough to take larger jobs, Jack had to rely on conventional managers—presidents and vice presidents— hired from the outside.

Unfortunately, in the early 1980s there was simply no place to go to find top executives who understood the brand-new home computer marketplace. As a result, these executives had to undergo a sort of on-the-job training, and there was no way to tell until too late if they were up to the challenge or not. Many of them simply had trouble picking up a radical new business philosophy midway through their careers. The necessity of hiring seasoned managers with no computer experience collided head-on with Jack's philosophy of not hiring people who had to learn.

It became a joke at Commodore that if you asked a new manager how he was going to approach his job, you could tell from his answer whether he would survive or not.

Loser Line Number 1: "I'm getting my staff lined up. I've got headhunters out looking now, and as soon as I get my staff in-house, you'll see great things. I figure it'll take three months." Sorry. At Commodore, you did the work yourself. Staff? Who said you were going to have a staff? Three months was a decade in the home computer industry. Besides, this was war.

Loser Line Number 2: "I'm writing my business plan. As soon as I get my plan approved, you'll see great things. I figure it'll take two weeks." Wrong again. At Commodore, you hit the decks on the run. You were paid to do the job as soon as you got on board. You carried your business plan in your head and changed it as you went along. Nobody approved it. You just did it. If it worked you were in. If it failed you were out.

Loser Line Number 3: "I'm having trouble getting in to see Jack. He has to approve my (whatever). I'm really hung up. I can't get started till Jack signs off."

"What are you waiting for, Colonel? Get your artillery in place."

"I'm waiting for Jack. He's in Hong Kong."

Wrong again. You never waited for Jack. If something was important, you stood right smack-dab in Jack's doorway until he motioned you in, or if a meeting was going on, you lined up in the hallway and stood your ground until he was available. Even vice presidents. Waiting for a secretary to call you meant that all the stronger or younger insiders who ignored all the protocol and barged right in would eat up your time and keep you waiting in your office for—hard to believe, but true—sometimes *weeks.*

Of course, not succeeding at Commodore didn't mean a person was a poor executive. It just meant some executives, including some very good ones, simply couldn't or wouldn't adopt the Commodore business religion.

When executives moved on from Commodore, by choice or not, many moved on to success in companies to which their talents or personalities were more suited. I saw a lot of managers come and go. In fact, in the middle of

1980 I started collecting business cards of managers who left. When my stack got up to 100, the rubber band broke and I stopped collecting them.

There was another paradox which created upper management turmoil. The same success that put young managers in line to get higher jobs also made them rich enough to leave Commodore, which they did. Many young managers Jack had lined up for greater things got too rich too soon when Commodore's stock shot up into the stratosphere in the early 1980s. Quite a few heirs to the throne decided to take the money and run, and never stayed long enough to fill a presidency or any other key role.

I estimated it took an average of seven years for an individual who got stock options and bonuses to become a millionaire. Kit Spencer and I once sat down and counted 27 millionaires created by Commodore—and this in 1984 after the stock fell from $60 to $20. We didn't count those who slipped back below the millionaire mark because the stock skidded, and we didn't include those poor souls who became only half-millionaires. We also didn't count stockbrokers and shareholders who could have turned $565 into over $100,000 if they bought 100 shares of Commodore in 1970 and held them until 1982.

Fortunately, not everyone was a mutineer, and not all the generals got shot in the trenches or became suddenly wealthy. John Calton, whose office was a few doors down from Jack's, had been with Commodore for nearly 25 years, making him the longest-lasting employee. The two friends met in New York City in the early 1950s. Jack was selling mechanical adding machines and repairing typewriters. At night, he drove a taxi to bring in extra money.

As I heard the story, John arrived in New York as an Irish immigrant. Apparently, he started walking the streets the first day he stepped off the boat. When he got to Jack's store he went inside and said, "I like the looks of your store. Can I have a job?" Jack hired him on the spot.

A quarter of a century later, John had lost most of his Irish brogue and was Commodore's purchasing vice president. All components, subassemblies, and materials were purchased through John. You could hear him negotiating with vendors on the phone. "I need ten cents," he would say. He knew he could get it because he always knew the vendor's costs, to the penny. That was his secret of buying things.

Jack's purchasing philosophy was clear. Make sure you know the vendor's costs before you buy something. Decide if it's cheaper or more convenient to make it yourself. If you decide to buy it outside, take the vendor's cost, add a reasonable profit, and make the vendor sell it to you at that price. The same thinking applied to ROM and RAM chips, wires, cables, paper clips, staples, software disks, desks, file cabinets, or posters.

When it came to negotiations, there was more corporate wisdom: Don't negotiate a deal unless you're prepared to turn it down. Don't be afraid to walk away. Being ready to walk away from the deal if it wasn't what you wanted made Jack Tramiel one of the strongest business negotiators in industry. People would come to him with money-making propositions, but if it wasn't enough money or a low enough cost, or wasn't the right deal or the right timing, he'd leave it.

"But we can make you a lot of money," the deal-makers would argue.

"No, thank you," Jack would say.

The Santa Clara factory came alive for me when Jack himself took me on a tour of the giant earthquake-proof shell. It was still my first day on the job. "Come on," he said. "I'll show you the plant." Off he walked at a brisk pace, me hurrying along behind.

As far as I could tell, the building was divided into prestige areas: the hallway near Jack's office, at the left front corner of the building; the rest of the hallway on the other side of the reception area; a large area with administrative offices and cubicles; a matching area for programmers and technical staff; a factory behind the offices for assembling and testing computers; and finally, in the very back, the high-ceilinged warehouse.

The front offices included Jack's corner office, a long conference room, my temporary office, John Calton's office, and an office used mostly by semiconductor executives. The administrative offices looked like a tornado had just swept through a business forms plant. There were file cabinets, desks, and stacks of papers everywhere, seemingly at random. The arrangement of offices and desks changed almost from day to day as the accounting, purchasing, and sales staffs kept shifting around and crowding closer to make room for more files or an extra clerk.

The technical area was fun. This was where Chuck Peddle's group at Moore Park brought their goodies to be fine-tuned, tested, and debugged, and to have software written. There were half a dozen offices along the outside walls, and the center area was partitioned into tiny cubicles with low walls that you could see over when you stood up. The technicians, engineers, and programmers seemed to be constantly busy, often wrestling with a technical problem until late in the evening.

Two of Commodore's best software people were Bob Fairbairn and Penny Galant. Bob was a talented curmudgeon in the making, capable of debugging operating system software, authoring assembler development systems, and writing applications software such as chess programs. Penny was an excellent programmer with an appealing personality. She kept pet rats at home and talked about their antics like most people talk about their pet dogs and cats.

There were also two talented Japanese engineers, Fujiyama and Aoji, whom Jack greeted in Japanese: "O-genki desuka?" To which they replied, "Genki, desu." Jack always had a special fondness for his hard-working Japanese engineers who toiled incessantly, were incredibly loyal, and had a habit of accomplishing impossible tasks in no time.

As they explained what they were doing (too technical for me), Jack kept snapping, "Hai, hai,"—Japanese for "yes" or "okay." Jack used the word like a riding crop. Instead of snapping the crop against his leg, he barked out the words, "Hai! Hai!" so sharply they sounded like snapping wood.

When it was time to move on, he bowed to me and gestured for me to go first, saying, "Dozo" ("Please," or "With your permission"). It was Jack's way of thinking

Japanese and reminding himself that Japanese companies were his most serious competitors and that to defeat them in the coming Computer Wars he would have to understand and outfox them.

The factory was located in a separate area behind the offices, and the warehouse was behind that. The white tile floors of the factory were exceptionally clean. The assembly area was staffed mostly by Koreans and Mexicans, who were hard-working and conscientious. One whole area was reserved for testing, and PETs and CBMs were stacked up to the ceiling, their green screens flashing and blinking with test patterns. Every machine was tested like this for 24 hours or more.

If they make it through 24 hours, Jack quipped, they'll probably last 24 years, since computers have no moving parts except the keyboard. That's why we have to keep making new products, he stressed, so the customers have a reason to buy better computers before their old computers wear out.

The pieces of the computers came from many different places in the world. Most of the computer chips were made at MOS Technology in Pennsylvania. The tiny half-inch-square chips were sent to Hong Kong to be packaged in plastic sandwiches and inserted into electronic circuit-boards which formed the guts of the computer (peripherals like disk drives and printers were bought from outside companies, although the electronics were designed at Commodore). Metal housings for the PET/CBM were manufactured in Toronto, Canada, where Commodore had an office furniture division—the largest manufacturer of budget-priced, metal office furniture in Canada. Final assembly and testing were accomplished in various worldwide regional centers where the computers were going to be sold: Hong Kong, Santa Clara, Toronto, Slough, soon Braunschweig; and later Corby, England, and West Chester, Pennsylvania.

Jack wanted everything to be done as locally as possible, from manufacturing to marketing. It was a concept we referred to as the country concept. "Next year we'll need all this space for computers," he said prophetically, waving his hand across the plant. I didn't realize it, but he was already thinking of putting Commodore into the mass-market, low-priced computer business. He knew this meant higher volume, lower margins, and more factory capacity.

He spoke of another concept I would hear over and over again at Commodore, a phrase that would become the company's—and Jack's—special trademark. It was called *vertical integration,* and in layman's terms what it really meant was not counting on anyone to make your products for you. Do everything yourself.

Vertical integration means that a company is involved in two or more of the processes in getting a product from the idea stage to the selling stage. In the case of computers, being vertically integrated in the production of both computer chips *and* computer systems gave Commodore its winning edge.

Most computer companies have to buy their chips from outside companies like Intel or National Semiconductor, which raises the price of the computer or peripheral. By owning its own semiconductor company (MOS Technology), Commodore was able to design and manufacture its own computer chips, which not only lowered its costs, but made it easier to design special chips which the computer engineers asked for. No other company whose business was solely personal computers could do this.

Even so, MOS made ROM chips, not RAM (short-term memory) chips, and when a world-wide shortage of RAM chips occurred in 1982–83, Jack's immediate response was to buy the manufacturing rights to 64K RAM chips from a company called Micron in Idaho. The first RAM production line was set up at Commodore's semiconductor plant in Costa Mesa, California, toward the end of 1983. The idea was to make Commodore less vulnerable to future industry shortages of RAM chips. Of course, this might also cut the cost of RAM chips used in Commodore computers.

This was an excellent example of how Commodore reacted to an industry crisis—the shortage of RAM chips—by integrating its manufacturing operation. The rule: Any outside vendor is potentially unreliable.

New computer designs cannot be bought from other companies, at least not at a bargain. Commodore invented and manufactured its own computers, including subassemblies, plastic cases, metal housings, cables, circuit boards, cables, and more. If Commodore didn't do the work in its own plant, it leased an existing plant, negotiated a joint venture, or developed cast-iron business relationships with vendors in Hong Kong, Taiwan, and Japan. The costs of items that had to be bought outside were constantly being hammered to get them lower.

The only area in which Commodore was not vertically integrated was peripherals and accessories. In 1980, Commodore sold complete computer systems which included disk drives and dot-matrix printers as well as computers. The disk drives came from Tandon or from Japanese suppliers, and printers came mostly from Epson. Our engineers worked with these outside companies to develop the interface electronics which made their peripherals talk to our computers.

Nevertheless, sometimes Tandon couldn't supply enough drives because they supplied drives to many different companies and demand was outstripping their ability to keep up. Later, in 1983, Commodore integrated disk drives into its operation by forming a joint partnership with Mitsumi Electric Company in Japan to design and produce floppy disk drives, but printers were a different story.

In 1980, a Japanese company named Epson was supplying small, inexpensive printers to Commodore on an OEM basis. OEM means Original Equipment Manufacturer; the original manufacturer, in this case Epson, sold its products to another company to be packaged and sold under that company's brand name. For example, the Commodore Model 2023 Dot Matrix Printer was really an Epson printer masquerading in a Commodore housing.

When the printer business took off in mid-1981, Epson decided to switch its emphasis from OEMing and start selling printers direct, under its own name. Within a year, we found Epson selling its own printers in the U.S. under its own brand name, including an *improved* version of the one being sold by Commodore, and at *reduced prices*. Of course, Epson could do this: When it came to making printers, they were *vertically integrated*. You couldn't blame them. After all, why sell a printer to a company like Commodore when you can sell it directly to computer store dealers and get twice the price?

As a result, we had to scramble to find other, less expensive printers so we could continue to compete. The subsequent hodgepodge of printers from different manufacturers (it seemed that we bought a new kind of printer every six months) made it virtually impossible to have total compatibility among all Commodore printers. This became a major problem when we introduced two or three different dot-matrix printers in 1983 and phased out the previous model.

Most people buy printers to work with word processors and spreadsheets, but our existing Commodore software worked with the *old* printers, not the new ones. The answer was to take a step backward in technology and change the ROM chips in the new printers to make them work like the old printers. It was a mess.

Companies which do not, or cannot, vertically integrate their operations face many dangers. I'm convinced that any company in any business which does not vertically integrate will ultimately be knocked out of competition by companies that are integrated, if only because the competitors' costs are lower. Vertical integration was Jack's guiding principle in business. If Commodore had a company flag, that would be our motto.

When we reached the marketing area back near the front offices, Jack introduced me to the key executives there, then glared at me and commanded, "Learn!" He pointed me toward one of the offices and walked away.

I found myself standing at the other end of the front hallway, at the opposite end of the building from Jack's office. This was Marketing Land. No Commodore executives came flying down the hall, but there was something definitely wrong here.

The marketing department was being run by a personable executive named Dennis Barnhart. In an ironic and sobering tragedy, Dennis became famous three years later for the way he died—crashing his red Ferrari sports car on the very afternoon his company, Eagle Computer, went public and made him a millionaire.

Dennis was likable, creative, and egocentric. His black hair, thick mustache, and driving personality reminded me of the stereotyped casino owner in a B Western. Dennis was well-liked by his staff, and he struck me as what gamblers would call a high roller.

The day I met him, he was still bristling from the appointment of Dick Powers as head of U.S. sales and marketing, which meant Powers was his boss. Dennis had been given two options: resign or take a lesser job under Powers. It didn't crush him, though. He was very close to his staff and hinted that the clubby marketing group would band together to make sure Powers didn't succeed.

"I'll be running marketing again in three months," he told me.

To make matters worse, Jack was pressuring everyone in marketing to move East to Pennsylvania. Pennsylvania was Siberia to these Californians.

That was to be my next stop: Valley Forge, Pennsylvania.

FOUR

Before anyone could say another word, the Walrus and the Carpenter had eaten all the oysters.

Everyone, including Alice, seemed to have an opinion.

"I like the Walrus best," said Alice, "because he was a little sorry for the poor oysters."

"He ate more than the Carpenter, though," said Tweedledee. "You see, he held his handkerchief in front, so that the Carpenter couldn't count how many he took: contrariwise."

"That was mean!" Alice said indignantly. "Then I like the Carpenter best—if he didn't eat so many as the Walrus."

"But he ate as many as he could get," said Tweedledum.

This was a puzzler. After a pause, Alice began, "Well! They were both very unpleasant characters—"

Just then, the Dormouse crawled out from under a desk, rubbed his eyes with a great deal of weariness, and said, "No matter. The oysters deserved to be eaten. That's what they're there for."

The Walrus and the Carpenter

There was no time to worry about mutinies in Santa Clara. In a flash, I found myself dispatched to all the farthest reaches of Commodore's empire in North America—Toronto, Dallas, Valley Forge, and New York. I began a series of cross-country trips that made me feel like a shuttle diplomat, sleeping in a different city almost every night. My apartment in San Francisco began to accumulate dust. I developed a taste for roast duckling. My shoes began to disintegrate and the handle broke off my suitcase.

I made a nonstop series of visits back and forth across the country, mostly between Santa Clara and MOS Technology in Valley Forge, Pennsylvania, with side trips to Toronto, Canada, to see our factory; to Dallas, Texas; back to Santa Clara; then on to New York for a meeting with Steven Greenberg, Commodore's investor relations consultant.

"How do I get from the airport to the hotel in Dallas?"

"Take the hotel shuttle. Use the phones in the lobby."

"How do I get from the hotel to the Dallas office?"

"Rent a car."

"How do I do that?"

"Learn!"

Jack's command kept ringing in my ears.

The first thing I learned was that they don't teach you any of these things in business school. I began to think my M.B.A. degree stood for Mighty Bad Ability. I was renting cars, making hotel reservations, getting the cheapest plane fares, exchanging international currencies, hiding Cuban cigars (I don't even smoke), filling out expense reports, keeping taxi drivers honest, tipping porters the right amount, and moving gigantic boxes from one city to another.

"Michael, you don't mind taking some boxes to MOS for us, do you?" asked the engineer.

"Sure," I said helpfully. "No problem."

A Commodore business computer is big and bulky. Add some six-inch-thick Styrofoam and heavy-gauge cardboard, wrap it in a box, and you've got a package the size and weight of a Sears top-loading washing machine. Now give three of those boxes to someone who's having enough trouble finding his way to the right gate at the airport, and send him to Pennsylvania.

MOS Technology was located on an out-of-the-way country road (no sidewalks) about a mile from Valley Forge National Park, and less than a mile (as the crow flies) from the Audubon Wildlife Sanctuary. The MOS building was a boxy two-story building that looked like it had been built in the 1950s.

The semicircle driveway in front was marked NO PARKING on the curb, but everyone seemed to ignore it. That was a good sign. There were mavericks lurking hereabouts, my kind of people. The cars in the driveway were parked bumper to bumper in both directions, ignoring the two enormous parking lots at the side and back of the building. Lazy people, these Pennsylvanians. Either that or they liked the prestige of parking in front. It turned out that they weren't lazy. Their interest in prestige was another matter.

On the way in I spotted several small holes in the front windows. The thick glass had been punctured clean through, and there was a weblike circle of shatter lines around each little hole.

Inside, a pleasant gray-haired receptionist doubled as the switchboard operator, and I had to wait for her to finish answering calls before I could ask.

"Uh—excuse me—what are those little holes in the windows? They look like (gulp) bullet holes."

She laughed and shook her head.

"Golf balls."

"Huh?"

76

"Golf balls. There's a golf course across the street and once in a while a ball hits our windows. I've been meaning to get those fixed."

Just then, a young girl riding bareback on a giant brown horse rode by the front of the building. She had dark flowing hair and seemed to be going nowhere in particular.

"Horses?" I said out loud.

The receptionist laughed again.

"Didn't you know? This is horse territory. People ride by all the time."

I said to myself, "Not bad. Anyplace where you have to duck golf balls and clean up a little horse manure can't be all bad."

I made a quick walking tour of the building. The front hall had offices only on the window side of the building. At the end of that hall, a left turn led into another long hall with more offices. At the end of that hall you could turn right and go through the door to the parking lot, but then you'd need a special ID card to open the door again.

In the hall on the left was the semiconductor area, where the chips were made. There was a small maze of corridors with windows cut in the walls so you could see people working over microscopes. They worked in *clean rooms*, which meant they had to wear hair nets, beard nets, mustache guards, dust-resistant gloves, smocks, and pants, and booties over their shoes. Going into the clean room, you stepped on a sticky floor mat to take the last traces of dust off your booties, then you stepped into an airlock, closed the door, pressed the buzzer, and went inside.

The class-A clean room. It looks like the inside of a space shuttle. Everything's spotless. It has to be, because one speck of dirt, one hair or piece of lint can ruin a whole batch of chips. In the lab, there was a room with a red light where the microscopic circuits were photographically engraved on the chip material, then a yellow room where the chips were developed, an oven room for baking the silicon wafers, and several testing areas filled with microscope benches.

The clean room not only kept dirt out of the circuits. It also made it hard for industrial spies to wander in and get a full picture of how chips are made, which is possibly one reason why other countries fell so far behind in semiconductor technology—except, of course, for the Japanese.

Leaving the clean room, you dumped your special clothing into a special container for laundering. The exit of the clean room was all the way around, at the back of the building. You found yourself at the opposite end of the front corridor. Up the stairs was another corridor. That's where the semiconductor group had its offices. Window side for managers, other side for technicians and engineers. The atmosphere was relaxed, but there was no room for airheads, shirkers, incompetents, or meanies. Or so they said.

Behind the offices were the engineering labs where chips were invented and debugged. One room contained art tables where design artists drew large posters of chip circuits, which would later be photographically reduced and etched in metalized silicon.

One room was totally dark. The moles who worked here sat in front of special CAD (Computer Aided Design) computers. It was their job to design the different pieces and layers of circuits needed to make a chip work properly.

The research lab was a room inside a room, marked NO ADMITTANCE. Imagine a TV repair shop set up in a kitchen cafeteria. That's what MOS Engineering looked like. There was electronic gear of all sorts strewn about on long benches. The engineers sat on stools, peering over prototype circuit-boards or staring transfixed at a black-and-white or color monitor screen or a green oscilloscope. They were perpetually hunched over some magnificent tiny contraption, their noses inches from the tip of their smoking soldering guns as they wired jumper cables from one chip or circuit to another.

Few people know how tough it is to make everything balance between the computer chips and the computer— timing, video scanning, processing speed. You even have to find ways to reduce heat because too much heat hurts the sensitive chips and reduces the life of the computer.

You couldn't just plug some ROM and RAM chips into a board, wire them together, and turn it on. Often the chips wouldn't work and had to be debugged. Sometimes a computer wouldn't work because someone substituted a tiny component which was cheaper but slightly different from the engineers' specifications.

As I got more involved, I discovered that no computer was ever introduced that didn't have at least one bug in it. It's a good idea to wait six months after a computer is introduced before you buy one. And make sure you get the latest revision.

It was hard to realize how much important inventing was going on at MOS because everyone was so quiet and most of the work went on behind closed doors. In May 1980 they were still finishing the 22-column VIC chip. Bob Yannes, a light-featured, 23-year-old chip designer who did most of the work on the chip, looked about thirteen and was constantly being kidded about his youthful appearance. Al Charpentier, a likable shirtsleeves manager, was in charge of chip design, and Charlie Winterble, a humorless technical manager I always thought of as semitough, headed semiconductor engineering. Shiras Shivji, a brilliant senior engineer of Indian heritage born in Africa, was also a key player. All were in their twenties and thirties.

At the top of the semiconductor pyramid, key managers included Tom Rizol, Sr., Elton Southard, Tom O'Donnell, and Jerone Guinn. Tom Rizol, Sr., was a sober, wry-witted executive at the vice president level who had worked at MOS for more than a dozen years. He was a major survivor at Commodore, and the only manager I'd bet money would still be around to collect his pension—if Commodore had a pension plan—when he reached retirement age.

If anything needed to be done administratively, from his specialty, import-export, to renting a car or setting up the company picnic or Christmas party, you'd hear "Go see Tom Rizol." He must have had IOUs spread throughout Pennsylvania because whenever anyone needed something, all they had to do was go see him and he'd smile pleasantly and say, "Give me a little time. I'm sure I can arrange something." Tom's wheeling and dealing was effortless. Like a master magician, when he produced the coins in midair, you never knew where they came from.

Elton Southard consistently held the number one or number two slot in engineering, semiconductors, or both, despite the musical chairs in the Commodore organization. Elton was a stylish, silver-fox Texan in his early fifties, with a penchant for Corvettes and expensive cowboy boots. He had a reputation for being knowledgeable, reliable, and congenial, and Jack could always count on him to make insightful recommendations and decisions. He was the kind of general who'd do well in a real war—too mod to be crusty, too smooth to get flustered, too involved to make a mistake. He was constantly driving to make Commodore completely self-sufficient in semiconductor production. We shared something in common, in that when Jack hired him and asked about employment contracts, Elton stuck out his hand and told Jack that was good enough. He was the only other person besides myself who made a point of sealing his employment with a handshake.

One rank below Elton were Tom O'Donnell and Roy Thomas, the operations managers in the semiconductor group. On a par with Elton, though technically his boss, was Jerone Guinn. Jerone (everyone called him Jerome by mistake) was a tall, quiet Texan who, like Elton, was well-liked throughout the company. He was quiet, thoughtful, and reserved. I never saw him lose his temper which was remarkable, considering the constant pressures in the semiconductor group: bugs in the chips, delays in design, bad batches in production, and constant, straight-up expansion. Jerone later assumed overall responsibility for manufacturing, but left the company in 1982 after a dispute with Jack while organizing the ill-fated cash-register division in Dallas.

In 1980, Jerone was one of the handful of true believers in Jack's $300 home computer. He enjoyed debunking the myth that such an inexpensive computer just wasn't possible, and committed his semiconductor engineers to the task. It's not widely known, but Jerone's personal commitment and push helped make it happen. He and his chip engineers believed they could build Jack's computer before his deadline, which was the June Consumer Electronics Show, a little more than one month away. Meanwhile, Chuck Peddle was still pushing for a more up-scale computer and was quietly resisting the project.

In the background, you could hear the clock running down. And downstairs there was a powerful doubter. In the big front office sat Dick Sanford who was in charge of the entire operation. Dick was one of the many executives who didn't believe in the $300 computer. He felt Commodore would be better off giving away small computers with the larger CBM and PET systems ("It's a toy," he said flatly). To him, the small computer was best used as an incentive for dealers and customers, but then he was ultimately responsible for U.S. sales and tended to think in terms of the near-term bottom line.

I had first met Dick Sanford in Europe, where he was introduced to me as head of U.S. operations. Dick was in the process of becoming the number-two man in Commodore International, under Jack. Dick was short and athletic. He jogged every day and liked to enter marathons. His smoky black hair was getting a bit thin on top, and his tough, dark brown eyes burned with intelligence and energy. He was in his late thirties and had the look and mannerisms of a street fighter. When he was angry, or when he sensed a gauntlet thrown down, his eyes flashed his determination, his lips pulled back tight over his clenched teeth, and his fists tightened. His hands looked like they belonged to a boxer. His fingers were short, square, and his nails trimmed close. No one wanted to get hit. Not that Dick would ever hit anyone—but no one knew for sure.

When he spoke, he had a soft, authoritative manner, especially when he clenched his teeth. He communicated a kind of tough enthusiasm. His attitude was that of a street-smart general who'd come up through the ranks and hadn't forgotten any of the hand-to-hand combat he'd learned as a sergeant.

Dick first drew Jack's attention while working as an accountant with Arthur Andersen & Co., Commodore's accountants. A few weeks after Jack hired him as company controller, Dick called Jack and proudly announced, "I just earned my first year's salary, with bonus." And he had.

He'd maneuvered Arthur Andersen into reducing their accounting fees. It was more heavy-handed than masterful, but it worked. He had first asked Andersen to reduce their fees by a substantial amount. Of course, they refused. Next, he'd called Peat, Marwick, Mitchell and asked them to bid on the account. It seems that whenever a new accounting firm bids on an account, they have to notify the old accounting firm and the old firm has to open certain records to them. Apparently Arthur Andersen agreed to Sanford's request for a reduction in fees, shortly after Peat, Marwick notified them that they'd been invited to bid on the account.

Some people thought Dick was Commodore's hatchet man. I remember a professor at UCLA telling us that every large organization has a hatchet man, whose job it is to deal with various unpleasantnesses the president or chairman prefers to sidestep. Sometimes the hatchet man fires people. Sometimes he sets them up or gets them ready to be fired. Sometimes he invites them to resign. Sometimes he reorganizes the company and hires new bosses for people who don't think they need bosses, or opens and closes new offices—absorbing the structural shocks that such changes inevitably bring.

Dick told me once how, when he was still controller, he'd fired a general manager. He was making an inspection of the general manager's operation and was chagrined to find things in a total mess. Things were so bad that Dick had to take drastic action.

"You're fired," he told the manager.

"You—you can't fire me!" the manager exclaimed. "You're only the controller!"

"You're welcome to call Jack if you doubt my authority," Dick threatened, "or I'll throw you out myself." The manager was intimidated enough to pack up and leave. Then Dick called Jack and told him he'd just fired the general manager. Jack approved.

That was one of the peculiar things about Commodore. Authority was where you found it. It wasn't usually pinned on your chest. If you wanted responsibility, you could just look around the hallways. There was always a lot of authority lying around, waiting for someone to pick it up and run with it. That's one reason some people with no real rank wound up with more authority than many senior people who had fancy titles.

Dick's one weakness was that he was good at short- and medium-range tactical combat, but he wasn't a long-term strategist. It was often said that he lived from quarter to quarter, because there was always a huge flurry of activity in the last two weeks of every fiscal quarter as the U.S. sales executives flew around the country making last minute deals—arm-wrestling large dealers to help clear out inventories, and snapping the cat-o'-nine-tails over the shipping and warehouse crews so they could get all the orders out the door, therefore officially shipped, before the quarter closed.

Needless to say, there were always a lot of cranky people around Commodore the last two weeks in March, June, September, and December. It was a good time to take a vacation, if anyone ever took a vacation. I only took about two weeks in four years.

Dick and I got along well starting with our first meeting. I saw him as the best and toughest of the generals in the trenches. He was tough as nails but also loyal to the people who worked for him, and more sensitive to what his employees thought of him than he ever revealed. He was absolutely fearless in tense situations, outside the company in tough negotiations, and inside the company when the political wolves started howling.

But Dick Sanford wasn't just tough. He was also shrewd. One of the best examples of his shrewdness was his involvement in setting up Commodore as a Bahamian chartered company. By most accounts, Dick was a driving force in taking advantage of the tax benefits which resulted when Commodore moved to the Bahamas in 1976.

Moving the company offshore had tremendous tax advantages. To begin with, Commodore could manufacture computers in Hong Kong and sell them to its sales companies in each country. By selling products to its own companies, Commodore generated international profits which were technically earned in the Bahamas, where the corporate tax rate is as low as 1 percent. Of course, each sales company paid taxes in its home nation, but the profits and taxes paid in each country were much lower because of the international transfer cost. Excess cash could also go into the Bahamas and draw tax-free interest on the deposits, especially in years when interest paid on deposits was high.

Setting up the organization was a complex process, and the details were handled by an outside consulting organization. At the top, safely sheltered in the Bahamas, was the parent company: Commodore International Ltd., called CIL for short. Between CIL and the rest of the organization was a special manufacturing company called Commodore Electronics Ltd., or CEL, technically based in Hong Kong but later moved to Switzerland. CEL provided manufacturing between the Far East and the various Commodore sales companies scattered around the world, and was the umbrella organization that sold products to the sales companies. The only risk was whether the Internal Revenue Service would one day swoop down and disallow the system, so during the 1980s Commodore became more and more conservative in the way it treated its international manufacturing and transfer costs.

In 1980, the income tax gnomes hadn't yet started to bedevil the company, but during 1983–84 an Internal Revenue Service audit sent shivers through the organization. Dick Sanford was gone by then, and no one in finance could even remember how or why Commodore wound up in the Bahamas, anyway. Several people asked me if I knew the answer, and I kept imagining the IRS auditors saying, "Okay, guys, how come your headquarters are in the Bahamas?" To which the whole room would shrug their shoulders and someone would say, "Gee, we don't know. The people who did it aren't here anymore."

Before long May 1980 had come and I didn't have time to worry about taxes. I had to figure out how Commodore was organized so I could research the annual report.

Below CIL and CEL, there were sizable sales companies in seven major countries: Canada, Hong Kong, Japan,

Switzerland, the United Kingdom, the United States, and West Germany.

MOS Technology was technically a subsidiary of the U.S. sales company. Frontier Manufacturing, based in Costa Mesa, California, manufactured a special kind of semi-conductor called a CMOS chip. These low-power chips were used mostly in digital watches and calculators because they didn't need much power and could be run on min-iature batteries. Micro Display Systems Inc. (MDSI) was a watch-making company which Commodore acquired in 1979 from Tom Hyltin, its founder, and from his partner, Seiko (the watch company) in Japan. Jack once called it the worst business deal he ever made. The acquisition involved giving 100,000 shares of Commodore stock to Seiko, and MDSI wound up losing money for Commodore. Meanwhile, Commodore stock went up substantially and Seiko made money.

Jack spent several years trying to get the stock back from Seiko and finally succeeded in getting half of it back in 1981. It irked him that a large Japanese firm owned so much of his company, and the rising price of Commodore's stock made the MDSI deal look increasingly expensive. The Japanese were worthy vendors, partners, and competitors, but they were also a threat. Jack knew what could happen if he left even a small door ajar for the Japanese to come in.

Commodore had become quite a far-flung empire. In addition to the sales companies, there were seven major manufacturing facilities, including Santa Clara and Costa Mesa, California; Valley Forge, Pennsylvania; Dallas, Texas; Toronto, Canada; Hong Kong; and Braunschweig, West Germany.

Keeping track of the organization was Jack Tramiel's major challenge. But with everything so spread out, that meant Jack was constantly traveling, which in turn made it hard to keep track of Jack. So we all became Jack-watchers.

I often volunteered to ride with Jack from Valley Forge to New York. He always insisted on driving, and was very proud of having once been a New York City cabdriver. In New York, he'd usually hold some meetings with Irving

Gould, chairman of the board, or Steven Greenberg, investor relations consultant, then stay over in a hotel for a night or so before flying on to Toronto, Europe, or Santa Clara. I inherited the task of returning the company car to Valley Forge.

During these trips, we often discussed company plans and issues, and occasionally family affairs. As early as 1980, Jack told me about his dream of bringing his sons together in some way, as difficult as that seemed at the time. He had three sons, all of whom looked like younger, slimmer versions of Jack.

Sam, the oldest, was 32, my age. He was most like his father in personality and business sense and was the only son who was involved on a day-to-day basis in the company. Leonard was the intellectual of the family, living in New York and studying for his Ph.D. in astrophysics which he earned in 1984 from Columbia University, New York. Few people knew that he was involved in the design of the original PET, had often brainstormed with engineers, and as a graduate student was involved in at least two experiments sent into space on the first Columbia space shuttle.

Gary, the youngest, was still an undergraduate in 1980, but he was already demonstrating prowess in financial matters, as manager of the Tramiels' multimillion-dollar investment portfolio. After college he worked briefly as a stockbroker for Merrill Lynch and then went on to bigger things later.

In his desire to bring his sons together, Jack told me he even considered putting some kind of clause in his will which would make it more profitable for them to work together. He didn't really want to do that, though, and kept hoping they would somehow come together of their own accord, as brothers. The concept of family was extremely important to Jack. It was part of the Jewish tradition and central to Jack's belief about the collective strength of a talented, close-knit family—both at home and in business.

As I bobbed my way around the country, on red-eye specials to conserve daylight hours for business, I discovered that wherever I traveled, the constant, haunting presence of Jack was always there, regardless of where he really was. He was like a huge Cheshire cat, lingering in the air, likely to appear anywhere, anytime.

Whenever I arrived at an office he had just visited, I would see stunned people—active, but dazed. It was like showing up at the end of a rock concert. The people would be walking around with an incredulous expression on their faces, their brows tightly knit as they fought to understand the lessons Jack taught, or to solve the problems he brought to the surface by digging until he struck blood. People were constantly saying "Jack wants this" or "Jack wants that" or "If Jack were here, he'd tell us to—"

Jack was not just a president or company founder. He was a *presence*, like Mahatma Gandhi must have been a presence. Jack reinforced his philosophy wherever he went, and that philosophy was always the last thing to disappear when he left.

Obviously, it worked, because everyone was constantly looking over their shoulders, and Jack-watching was something everyone indulged in. "Where's Jack?" was a common question; for knowing Jack's whereabouts and destination not only gave you advance warning when he was coming, but it also provided some strong clues to what was going on in the company. Learning to read these clues was learning to be a top manager at Commodore.

If you overheard someone say where Jack was, you needed to understand the code. Here's a brief code breaker:

Jack's in New York at an analyst meeting. This meant Commodore's stock would probably jump up a few points because, after talking to Jack and Irving, stockbrokers and analysts often walked out of the meeting and bought stock right away or published buy-recommendations. I once saw a broker go over to a phone while the meeting was still in progress and buy 50,000 shares.

Jack's in the Far East. This meant he was probably solving some production problems or, more likely, negotiating or renegotiating stepped-up production of computers, peripherals, or components at a factory in Hong Kong, Japan, or Taiwan.

Jack's in Europe. When Jack gave his remote European managers an injection (or transfusion) of religion, he almost always brought back a flurry of new ideas he wanted us to try in the U.S. It was typical of him to open his briefcase, hand you a brochure like Kit Spencer's software catalog, and ask, "Why can't we have software like this in the U.S.?"

Jack's meeting with the bankers. This often meant some of us had to hustle to prepare bits and pieces of company profiles or financing packages, or answer long and detailed questionnaires. Sometimes the questionnaires forced us to get the answers to questions we should have had but didn't. Jack once told me he was in deep trouble one time and went to Germany to try to get help from a German bank. He was a little nervous going into the meeting because he thought banking was a rigid discipline and you couldn't break the rules. By the end of that meeting he'd learned that "banking's just like any other business." The rules are negotiable and deals can be made.

Jack's at MOS. This meant he was expanding our ability to make more chips, shortening production schedules, pumping up the engineers, or mediating between U.S. and Far East production. Jack wasn't an engineer himself, but he was a spark in search of some kindling material. He would push into the specifics of a problem or process until suddenly an engineer or technician looked up and said, "Hmmm, come to think of it, we might be able to cut a few weeks off the top if we—"

"*See?*" Jack would roar with delight, then send away the experts to work out the solution.

Jack's at the show. Commodore attended most of the major industry conventions during the year: Computer Dealer Exposition (COMDEX), Consumer Electronics Show (CES, Las Vegas and Chicago), Hanover Fair (Germany), National

Computer Convention (NCC), the PET Show (London), and West Coast Computer Faire (San Francisco). With the cost of attending each show somewhere between $100,000 and $1 million, Jack worked all aspects of the show to get every penny's worth, and was never really satisfied with the results or cost/benefit ratio. Still, he admitted, shows were something that had to be done.

Jack's at the ranch. The ranch (in California) was his personal retreat, a modestly furnished ranch-style home with horse stables, set on the very top of a hill overlooking cows grazing on the side of a neighboring hill, which rose steeply on the other side of a small stream. Across the highway from his home was a long string of lakes created by the topsy-turvy, earthquake-fault geology of the region, which kept pulling the coast out toward the sea and forming miles of deceptively picturesque inlets as the water seeped in to fill gaps in the shifting land masses.

If someone was there with him at the ranch, it meant he was plotting drastic strategy, or maybe offering his guest a bigger (or smaller) job. A stay at the ranch might include a trip to a nearby pier for some fresh seafood, or a fantastic ethnic meal served by Helen, his wife and constant companion of over 30 years. When home, they preferred to eat simple Polish-style meals, which Jack called peasant food, because they ate so much restaurant food while traveling. Helen was quiet, elegant, humble, and considerate, but also opinionated on important issues, and she occasionally enjoyed playing the stock market with their son Gary.

"I like lasers," she said to me once at a convention, without a word of warning, and went on to explain in her light European accent that she was considering investing in companies which were involved in laser technology because she was convinced that lasers were the wave of the future.

One day when I was at MOS, Dick Sanford said to me, "I get the feeling the marketing guys aren't supporting Dick Powers."

I told him I had to agree, but there wasn't much we could do.

"I know what to do," he said flatly.

He happened to be flying to Santa Clara and the next day he called me and said, "We don't have to worry about the marketing group. We just fired them."

"The whole department?"

"All except one, a software guy."

When I got back to Santa Clara the next day, I found the three marketing managers and most of their staff already gone. When Commodore fired people or asked them to resign, or if someone quit, it was company policy to ask them to leave immediately. Sometimes they were asked to leave now and come back later to clear out their office. It was the cancer theory: Cut it out before it spreads.

One of the managers was invited to stay if he would move to the East Coast, but he chose to resign instead because he wanted to stay in California. The software manager who hung on was a talented young man who had let things get slightly out of hand. Jack asked me to investigate and give him a report on the status of our U.S. software program. All morning long, I was like a gadfly (definition: "any fly that goads or stings domestic animals"), lunging into the software manager's office, then back to Jack, then back to software. Jack kept giving me more questions to ask, more facts to find out.

Things were dismal there. Problems ranged from royalties not being paid to software authors, to software being sold with no contracts at all. But what irked me most was finding two final notices—including a telegram (how can anyone ignore a telegram?)—complaining that we had defaulted on a royalty payment and as a result our contract to sell *WordPro* was being canceled. This famous and excellent word processor was essential to marketing our CBM business system. If we wanted to renegotiate the license, the price to us would be triple what it was before.

That was the last straw. I blew up in the manager's office and then I blew up in Jack's office. *WordPro* was my favorite word processor. How dare they let the contract lapse, and for something as inane as not paying royalties or not answering two telegrams.

About 11:00 a.m., I went on a side mission for Jack to collect some information, and an hour later when I went back to the software manager's office, he was gone.

"Where is he?" I asked a secretary.

"Gone," she said. "He was just fired."

Apparently, Jack walked down and gave him the boot. He was gone *immediately.*

One of the problems with a career in marketing is that business goals change so fast, if you set off down one road and start doing well, the company's liable to change directions without telling you and leave you sitting on a side street. Often, top management changes direction without telling you, then they sit in meetings and talk about how marketing seems to be going in the wrong direction. Frequently, marketers aren't going in the wrong direction, they're just going in the *old* direction—going there so fast that when the company changes course, they shoot out in a straight line and are flung into space.

At Commodore, Jack was *the Commodore.* He set the course and ran the ship, and if you didn't listen to him constantly, you fell behind. Jack ran fast, turned corners at breakneck speed, stopped on a dime, and gave you nine cents change.

Unfortunately, some executives were too egocentric, stubborn, set in their ways, or simply opposed to Jack's philosophy. Jack took 25 years to develop his philosophy. He had the scars to prove it. It was unique, it was his, and it worked. If you wanted to join, or stay in, the Commodore family, you had to learn it and practice it.

During the next four years, I saw it happen over and over: executives and managers, even presidents, who just couldn't bring themselves to learn and absorb and live the Commodore religion.

The departure of our marketing crew left only three people in the department: Dick Powers, a new employee he'd just hired to handle conventions and shows, and part-time, me.

Incidentally, there was a long series of top-notch women managers. Most prominent among them were Marge Jillett, Edith Silverglide, and Julie Bauer. These hard-driving women oversaw some of the most difficult areas of the company, where pleasing a dozen executives was almost as important as keeping costs low and turning projects around on impossible schedules. All of these women were doers more than managers. They designed and wrote magazine ads and brochures, planned and supervised special events including trade shows, and arranged flight reservations. They also had to juggle hotel rooms, which was no mean task, since it wasn't unusual for someone to ask for twenty or thirty extra hotel rooms just a week before a convention that had been sold out for three months.

They worked with huge budgets and managed a squadron of creative artists, printers, and typesetters whom they persuaded to work overtime and on weekends, and still produced quality creative results.

The upcoming NCC was one of those tricky marketing events. It was to be the launch of our CBM computer line. We rushed to gather the proper fact sheets, brochures, and dealer materials; and to bolster our small sales force, we imported a few friendly dealers and software vendors to help staff the booth.

"We don't need marketing people at the show," Jack advised. "We need salespeople."

What did Mickey Mouse, Donald Duck, and Goofy have to do with computers? Someone must have seen a connection, because in May of 1980 the National Computer Conference (NCC) was held in Anaheim, California, just a short distance from Disneyland. At that time, the National Computer Conference was the most important convention for personal computers, drawing dealers from throughout the U.S. and beyond, and we were going there a matter of days after firing most of our marketing staff.

Commodore was using the show to introduce the new CBM system which included an 80-column 32K computer (the CBM 8032) and a new high-density dual floppy disk drive (the CBM 8050). The system was shown with another manufacturer's letter-quality printer. For about $5,000 retail, including an NEC or Diablo printer, the system was a bargain, and beat just about anything on the market in terms of features. The green phosphor screen reduced eyestrain; the business keyboard had a separate numeric keypad for fast calculation; and the disk drive stored up to half a megabyte (half a million characters) on each 5-1/4-inch floppy diskette, and let you work with information on two disks at once.

It was a great system, and the computer dealers who came to the booth were enthusiastic despite our weak dealer-relations and marketing in the U.S. Dealers kept telling me, "I've got one of the original PETs—serial number two forty three—and it still works fine," or "I got mad and tried to close out the Commodore line, but I couldn't do it because too many school districts use your computers."

Our two-for-one and later three-for-two giveaway programs made Commodore PETs the most widely used educational computer in the world. Jack's idea was to give away one PET to every school that bought two. In theory, the giveaway reduced Commodore's revenues by 30 percent on computers sold to schools. In truth, the giveaway allowed Commodore to write off the third computer as a tax-deductible charitable donation, another one of Commodore's exotic tax loopholes.

One of the things I wanted to do at the NCC was make friends with computer magazine editors, most of whom were anti-Commodore. At first, Jack didn't think this was so important because these magazines catered mostly to hobbyists, but I argued that *any* new computer-buyer reads the hobbyist magazines first to find out which computers do what. If the magazines are against Commodore, it trickles down to all purchasers, not just hobbyists.

"The editors keep knocking us in their magazines because we keep ignoring them," I said. "Communication is the key to good relations with the press. All you have to do is talk to them. Even a polite *no comment* is better than no response at all."

Jack gave me the green light and was soon encouraging me to talk to my friends in the press, as he put it. I was also given the privilege of being one of the few people in the entire company authorized to talk on the record to the press. Jack left it to my discretion what I said and to whom. He knew I used to be a journalist and figured I knew what to say.

Most of the editors were pleased to see someone trying to make contact: Chris Morgan at *BYTE Magazine*, Wayne Green at *Kilobaud Microcomputing*, and of course Robert Lock at *COMPUTE!*. The founders and editors of computer magazines were still forging new ground in 1980. I remember Robert Lock being thrilled when his circulation reached 23,000 that spring. By 1984 his circulation was up to half a million in the U.S. alone, and he was publishing books (including this one) as well as magazines.

I reserved the back cover of *COMPUTE!* exclusively for Commodore ads, which was good for the magazine and good for Commodore, although later I had to fight off a succession of less than brilliant Commodore executives who kept trying to cancel our magazine ad-space. Every time a new marketing executive or ad agency appeared on the scene, it seemed they wanted to suspend our magazine ads "just for a month or two until we formulate our new strategy."

What they didn't realize was that locking up space on the back of any magazine is tough because everybody wants it. If you drop off the back cover once, you've lost it forever to the next savvy company waiting in line to make the permanent commitment. Besides, advertising on the back of a hot computer magazine gives some readers the impression that you own the magazine, or are somehow closely associated with it.

When *Personal Computing*, a very bland, pulpy magazine with no targeted audience, was bought by Hayden Publishing, I seized the opportunity to get the back cover of that magazine because my instincts told me the magazine would do very well, which it did. Jim Mulholland, president of Hayden, was extremely helpful and obliging.

In contrast, David Ahl, founder of *Creative Computing*, was downright rude. When I sought him out at his NCC booth, he told me he was canceling his Commodore column and wasn't interested in discussing a revival. He practically told me to get lost. Still, anyone who wears glitzy black T-shirts at conventions can't be all bad, so I kept working on him. Within a year we restored good press relations with *Creative Computing*, and Dave Ahl and Betsy Staples, the editor, became good personal friends and Commodore supporters.

Chris Morgan, who edited *BYTE*, was especially generous in welcoming me to the computer industry. He showed me some great magic tricks, too. At the risk of getting banned from the magic castle, I'll reveal one. He would drop a quarter on the floor, pretend to pick it up, but really flick it under his shoe. When he opened his hand the coin was gone. Chris always had a few coins under his shoe or in someone's ear or up his sleeve.

He told me a story once about his first corporate meeting after *BYTE* was acquired by McGraw-Hill. When it was his turn to report sales and earnings, he stood up, gave a one-sentence reading of the results, said "Our results will be even better next year," then used the rest of his time to play the banjo. Later, Chris became marketing vice president for Lotus Corporation, where he helped popularize *Lotus 1-2-3*.

Wayne Green, founder of *Kilobaud Microcomputing*, *RUN*, and a half-dozen other computer magazines, was known as an irascible pundit and curmudgeon in print. Few people today remember that Wayne founded *BYTE* and lost the magazine in a dispute with his wife. He didn't suffer much from the loss, though, because a few years later, in 1983, he sold his magazines and business interests for about $60 million.

The result of all these contacts was a marked improvement in Commodore's image, and some personal friendships which continue to this day.

In any case, we did end up going to Disneyland, compliments of Apple. Apple bought out the whole amusement park for one night of the NCC. You had to pick up the

95

tickets at Apple's booth, and a group of us went over and charmed the Apple hostesses into giving us two or three dozen tickets so we could get in. Someone mumbled something about how I was the enemy, but we got the tickets anyway and had a wonderful time.

That evening, I was accompanied by my girlfriend Kim (later my wife) and by John Feagans, one of the inventors of the original PET. John was a mild-mannered engineer with a boyish face, a friendly personality, and an essence that I can only describe as peace of soul. John was a born inventor and tinkerer. At age eleven he had tried to make an electric organ, from scratch. While still in high school, he published a hardcover pictorial book about trains called *The Train That Ran By The Sea.* He experimented with fermenting beer and wine, puttered around a distant, played-out gold mine inherited from his father, and built showroom-quality furniture. In the engineering department, he was as much of a meddler as I was in the marketing area. He always wanted to see things done right. Unnecessary compromises made him break out in hives.

Behind his back, some executives said he walked around in a dream world pondering "Why is there air?" and other great questions of life, but John was a genius-caliber inventor who had turned his talents to computers. And Commodore was benefiting from his achievements long after these executives had vanished.

On the way into Disneyland, we came across Bill Seiler, Chuck Peddle's number-one engineer. Bill was distinctive-looking because he wore an unkempt beard and a long blonde ponytail that trailed down his back. He joked that he was too lazy to get it cut and smiled to himself whenever anyone stared. His ponytail was a statement, and no one begrudged him that.

He was standing near the Disneyland Hotel, playing with an aluminized balloon and a laser, so engrossed in his experiments that he didn't notice the light, misty rain. The laser had been set up between several buildings, several stories up, and you could see the thin, straight beams of blue light slicing through the air. Bill had discovered that flying a helium-filled aluminized balloon in the laser's path created an explosion of deflected laser beams. He and another engineer were having terrific fun, and four hours later when we left Disneyland the last thing we saw was Bill Seiler, still standing there in the rain, playing his own three-dimensional, laser-based videogame.

The NCC left me with lots of impressions. For example, it was obvious that Commodore made great computers and the customers loved them. Even the hostile press loved our computers, but they needed someone to talk to them from the company once in a while. Wall Street loved Commodore because sales (about $100 million in calendar year 1979) and stock price were aimed straight up. But dealer support and marketing were pretty poor. "How could we invent such terrific computers and not market them?" I kept asking. The answer was all too clear. The Jack of Clubs had already cut the deck.

When I went to talk to Jack about the firings, he waved off my questions and said, "I want you to help Dick Sanford and Dick Powers." Then we talked a bit about what should be done in marketing. I told him one of the things I wanted to do was make friends with the computer magazine editors.

He agreed, but reminded me that I was still in a learning mode.

"Don't *do*," he said. "Learn!"

"I can't help it," I replied. "I keep finding things that are all screwed up and I have to try to fix them. Besides," I asked, "can't I learn and do at the same time?"

Jack shook his head.

In those early days in Santa Clara, Jack often said to me, "You're a consultant. You like to tell people how it should be done."

"Give me the chance," I thought to myself. "Just give me the chance and I'll show you how it should be done!" But I had to keep my thoughts to myself because in Jack's eyes I was a pretty good consultant when it came to generating ideas, but when it came to putting those ideas into action I was still an apprentice.

Once again, he looked at me, shook his head, and said with pity in his voice, "You're so green!" But before long he noticed that I was sticking my nose everywhere, trying to find out how everything was done, which management techniques worked, and which didn't. Eventually, he gave me my label: *tumler.*

"I finally figured out what you are," he told me. "You're a *tumler.*"

"A what?"

"A *tumler.* Someone who stirs things up." He made a tumbling motion with his hands, like stirring a large pot. "You like to go around always stirring something up. If you see something wrong you can't keep out of it. That's a *tumler.*"

I grinned. It wasn't a bad nickname, although I found out later that *tumler* could also be interpreted as troublemaker. Maybe that was right, too.

Jack liked to put labels on people so he could keep them compartmentalized in his mind, and perhaps chart their progress up or down. The ones who went up—in other words, who learned The Religion and weren't intimidated by his confrontational style—seemed to lose their labels and simply became members of the family. The ones who went down kept their labels, lost their jobs, or fell like rocks before being crushed. I wondered if *tumler* meant I was going up or down.

But Jack's labels didn't mean you were going to be executed. Jack used labels to help his managers identify and overcome their weaknesses. "Shake that label," he was really saying. "Prove to me and to yourself it isn't true, or that you're better than your label."

Well, if I was going to get stuck with a label, I figured I should at least have a better label than *tumler,* so I invented a new term: *Commodorian.*

"I want to be a Commodorian," I told Jack. "I want to learn The Religion."

I told everyone else, too. Some people, especially the non-Commodorians and heretics, started throwing knives at me, mostly at my back. I think some people were beginning to think Commodorians were some sort of secret society, like 32nd-degree Masons or Rosicrucians or something.

Commodorians were more like disciples. We believed in what Jack was doing. We had faith in his leadership, even when the whole world said he would fail. We studied his business religion and felt like a family or like war comrades. We were bitterly disappointed when someone with talent had a chance to become a Commodorian and messed it up. A lot of people were simply too nice. They didn't belong in a war zone.

"You want people to like you," Jack would tell them, intending it as a criticism. Being honest was better than being liked.

"People are afraid of confrontation," he said. "There's nothing wrong with confrontation. We need more, not less."

He set a good example, because *all* of his meetings were confrontational, even when he was giving fatherly or personal advice. In 1982 when I told him I was going to build a house, he exploded. "Interest rates are too high, you don't have a pot to piss in, and you're building a house? Don't do it."

"But—"

He slammed his fist on the table and growled deep in his throat. "You can't afford it. *Don't do it!* You want a house? You can rent one for a thousand a month."

I bought the house anyway, got 11.5 percent interest, and the value of my house went up before it was finished (Jack admitted he'd been wrong).

I ping-ponged back to MOS and wound up sitting in a conference room, discussing the new $300 computer with Dick Sanford and several other key players. Evidently, Bob Yannes, the MOS chip-designer, thought he could have a prototype finished in time for the Consumer Electronics Show in Chicago, less than one week away.

"Jack said he wants the prototype at the show," Sanford said. "He wants to judge the reaction."

It was decided that the new computer would be shown in a small private room inside Commodore's booth. Two engineers—Yannes and his boss Charlie Winterble—would take the prototype to the show.

"We want to be careful who we show the computer to," Dick Powers cautioned. "We've got competitors there, the press, dealers—"

"Someone has to be able to figure out who gets in and who doesn't," Sanford said.

"It has to be someone who knows all the players," someone echoed.

"Someone who can run interference."

"Someone who can talk well."

"Someone Jack won't kill."

"Who's the best bullshit artist?" someone suggested.

All eyes turned toward me.

FIVE

One of the smiling young geniuses stepped forward, holding the contraption in his hands. His hood was pulled down over his eyes, like a monk.

"Careful, it might go off," someone said.

We could all hear it ticking like a clock.

No one dared to move.

Tick...tick...tick...

"It's going off!" someone yelled.

"Nonsense. It's only a computer," grumbled the Dormouse.

"You're wrong," someone said. "It's a time bomb! Can't you hear it ticking?"

"Don't worry about them," the Dormouse whispered. "They're just a deck of playing cards."

The young genius grinned and tossed the contraption high in the air. It hung there for several seconds, suspended in time and space until, quite suddenly, the plastic flew apart in slow motion and the air was filled with chips and wires and circuit board fragments, and pieces of playing cards.

The concussion knocked some people off their feet, but there was no sound, no explosion. Just the fluttering of cards.

The genius shrugged and went back to the lab.

The Dormouse closed his eyes and started snoring.

The Jack gave me a wink and said, "Come on, don't just stand there. It takes all the running you can do to keep in the same place. If you want to get somewhere else, you must run at least twice as fast as that!"

He grabbed my sleeve and everything around us was a blur, and the only thing in focus was the Future.

Chicago CES:
The War Starts Here

"You know," Jack said wistfully, "when I went to the Board [in 1976] and asked them to give me the money to buy MOS, I had to be totally committed. We were just a weeny beany company then. But I knew I was right. I knew it."

That was back during the Calculator Wars. Texas Instruments had conquered. Dead calculator companies were lying everywhere. Bowmar, the inventor of handheld calculators, had flipped over and died like a turtle in the sun. Commodore struggled to stay solvent, but lost $4 million on $56 million in sales in 1976. Jack refused to pay vendors. Why should he? He was losing his shirt. Lawsuits flew in all directions.

Jack woke up one morning and realized he was slip-sliding away. He had to decide: go ahead or go backward. There could be no wavering. Jutting out his jaw, he shouted, "Go on, hit me again!" and scrambled the company off to Europe. Maybe he could capture the European calculator market while TI busied itself with the U.S.

He was right. Commodore survived. The company was still broke, though.

It wasn't the first time he hit ground zero and bounced back. Jack himself had survived six years in Nazi concentration camps. After World War II, he joined the U.S. Army and was stationed in New York City, where he learned to repair typewriters. After his military tour, he started a small typewriter repair business in the Bronx, then branched out into new technologies such as mechanical and electro-mechanical adding machines. In 1955 he moved the company to

103

Canada and went public in 1962. Three years later, disaster struck. Commodore's first chairman was a financier named C. Powell Morgan, president of Atlantic Acceptance Corporation. In 1965, Atlantic Acceptance collapsed when it was unable to make payment on a $5 million short-term loan. The default set off a chain reaction of failures of small companies it had financed. A Canadian Royal Commission conducted an investigation, and it was reported that Morgan would have gone to jail for his business practices, if he hadn't died of leukemia before the investigation was concluded. Jack was tainted by the scandal, by association, and suddenly could no longer get credit to run his business. He turned to Canadian financier Irving Gould for help.

Irving had the money, and the connections. Jack offered him his stock—every share—and told him, "You give me the money to keep going, give me the money to buy MOS Technology, and I'll give you all my stock. If I succeed, you give me back some of my stock. How much you give back is up to you."

Irving gave him the money: over three million dollars. Jack bought MOS Technology.

Commodore climbed back to its feet and put on its boxing gloves. Within a few months, Irving returned 8 percent of the stock to Jack as his reward.

Now, four years later, we were standing on the floor of the 1980 Consumer Electronics Show in Chicago. A lot of people saw the PET computer start its decline and said we were a one-product company. Others saw the CBM and figured we were moving into business micros, where the competition was already red hot.

Jack said, "We have to be a mass-market company. I want to bring down the price of computers, like we did with calculators. It means we have to sell more volume and make less money. But we're spoiled. We have to learn to live on a diet—" he arched his eyebrows to see if I gathered his meaning, then said, "We have to sell to the masses, not the classes!"

If anyone ever says he's going to whip down, hop over, or pop into the CES in Chicago, he's lying, because nobody whips, hops, or pops in on the CES show. What you do is take a grueling overcrowded flight to O'Hare International Airport, make your way to a bus or taxi, ride half an hour to the hotel, wait in line for fifteen minutes to get your room, and wait ten minutes for the bellhop. Then you overtip the bellhop because you're so grateful to see him.

The Conrad Hilton is a venerable convention hotel, massive in size, elegant in reputation, but a bit old. We didn't see our rooms much, anyway.

The morning began at 6:00 a.m. with the *flap, flap, flap* of magazines thrown against our door. At least half a dozen show dailies were piled outside our rooms every morning. These ranged from *Home Furnishings Daily* (then an oversized tabloid) to glossy magazines like *Consumer Electronics Daily* and the *CES News*.

Once up, I made a mad dash to get breakfast (I never ate it myself, but other Commodorians liked to hold meetings with scrambled eggs in their mouth). The hotel lobbies were jammed, and out front on Michigan Avenue where the morning sun was always yellowish orange, the taxis and limousines rolled by on an invisible conveyor belt.

Twenty minutes later at McCormick Place, there was a tedious wait to pick up my exhibitor's badge (can't get in without it), then a long walk to the Commodore booth, which was on the back-lot portion of the convention hall, near Texas Instruments and Casio.

The convention itself was immense, with annexes and escalators and multiple levels, and whole buildings based on the hottest industrial themes of the season. A Mardi gras atmosphere prevailed. The displays were gaudy, attention-getting, and electronic—a sprawling potpourri of colorful signs, banners, TV camera crews, live demonstrations, amplified music, videogames, burglar alarms, satellite dishes, sexy models, fast-talking salespeople, hawkers, hustlers, givers, takers, buyers, sellers, and not many bystanders.

This was a convention where everyone was involved in some way. Nobody came just to look. It was too expensive.

Standard booths cost between $100,000 and $1 million, which meant the exhibitors couldn't afford *not* to do business, and lots of it.

As a trade show, the CES was just that, a show for the trade. In fact, it was the largest trade show in North America, so big they had to hold it twice a year, in Chicago in June and Las Vegas in January.

Behind the CES was impresario Jack Wayman, the snowy-haired, peripatetic organizer who drove the show hard and set exceptionally high standards, whether he was walking through the aisles with a walkie-talkie in his hand, lining up speakers or panelists, wrenching more hotel space for the overflow crowds, building an annex to hold more exhibits, or going to Congress to lobby for the Electronic Industries Association, which he chaired.

Wayman was a fast-mover who always had a grin and an idea and something to push for. He once talked to me on the phone while carrying on two other phone conversations at the same time. His imprint on the show was profound, and his character was reflected in the energy associated with every aspect of the show.

The complex was filled with thousands of booths and exhibits. A typical display was a two-story-high wall of television screens, all showing the same picture, or stacks of stereo amplifiers and speakers blaring some thump-thump-thump disco music. The largest booths had two floors, with the upper deck divided into meeting rooms and selling lounges.

Huge signs dangled from the three-story-high ceiling: Seiko, Sanyo, Sharp, Panasonic, names which Americans don't even think of as Japanese anymore. The Japanese domination of U.S. electronics industries was clear. Even U.S. companies like RCA and Zenith manufactured their products in the Far East.

Television sets. Stereo components. Appliances. Automobiles. Steel. The Orientals kept knocking over our industries, one by one, bolstered by cheap labor, government support, business cartels, and an industriousness that turned whole countries into beehives of capitalistic human endeavor. Hong Kong. Japan. Taiwan. Korea. The Philippines. Jack was right. The invasion was coming. It was only a matter of time before they took on computers.

Automobile electronics were hot, too. One entire building was dedicated to them. The area was worth visiting if only because Kraco staged a terrific live parrot show, and the models were the best in the show.

Many booths featured well-proportioned professional models clad in form-fitting T-shirts and silky shorts, a terrific lure for the mostly male dealers and buyers. Women with deeply scooped necklines stood in the aisles and pulled buttons or fluffy stick-on characters out of bins on the floor. When one model leaned over to get me a button, she leaned so swiftly that she released herself from her shirt. Lingering there, she made no effort to recover her modesty.

"Button?" she crooned.

"I have to run," I apologized, "uh—just give me fourteen—"

And at the back of the convention, about five aisles behind our booth, was a small pornography area. Videotape recorders had significantly boosted sales of explicit films and by 1980 about a dozen companies were selling pornographic movies on tape. Most of the booths were staffed by the stars of the films, with names like Desiree Cousteau and Seka. Some of the unknown actresses wore see-through blouses to attract attention (which they did), while the better-known stars like Marilyn Chambers signed pictures of themselves:

"Fred, darling, it was wonderful!"

"George, I'll never forget you!"

"Ralph, you taught me everything I know."

Most of the tapes were shown on large-screen projection TVs in special booths or closed tents, but the biggest attractions of all were the booths that let you pose with the actresses while a friend snapped your picture.

It was a ridiculous scene—long lines of middle-aged executives wearing dark vested suits (and bright red faces), waiting patiently to get autographs from their favorite porn star, or posing nervously with a busty actress while everyone watched nervously, and laughed even more nervously when the actress took the executive's hand and placed it on her bust. No one knows what they told their wives about the pictures when the prints came back from the drugstore.

I had to admit I was surprised how many executives in the consumer electronics industry knew the names of all the top porn stars, but I guess home pornography was becoming a booming business and this was a show that ran on trends.

You could see the ebb and flow of product lines growing and shrinking in the sun. Projection television sets were big. The first lightweight speakers (from Seiko) were there and they were ingenious—just a strip of wire attached to two tiny speakers, each wrapped in a pad of blue foam. Seiko had the headsets dangling in front of its display so passersby could try them out. We couldn't believe the quality of the sound coming from those two little pieces of foam. Jack enjoyed the music for a moment then took the headsets off, mumbled "Japanese," and walked away.

But in 1980, the hottest trend by far was the videogame machine. Atari was king of the mountain, with Mattel trying to compete with a machine that was better, but much more expensive. The Atari 2600 was around $200 and the Mattel Intellivision was $300. I said to Jack, "Imagine a computer that plays videogames, for the same price as a game machine. It wouldn't be hard to position. That's all you'd have to say: 'Now you can have a computer instead of a game machine, for the same price.' "

As hard as it is to believe today, computers were not then thought of as an item for the home. No one knew what they could be used for. Personal computers were still the special domain of businesspeople, schools, and hobbyists, mostly because the prices were too high and they were too difficult to use. Personal computers cost over $1,000 all by themselves, and the price tag topped $5,000 if you added a dual floppy disk drive and letter-quality printer.

And the machines were sold by specialized computer dealers or electronics chains like Radio Shack. In order for computers to become consumer items and achieve the hallowed status of an electronic *appliance*, they had to be sold through mass-merchandising stores like J. C. Penney, Sears, Woolworth/Woolco, Montgomery Ward, and even *discount centers* like K mart.

If indeed home computers were going to happen, the only companies that had a shot at doing it were Texas Instruments, Radio Shack, Apple, Atari, and Commodore. Texas Instruments had a strong reputation for their low-priced watches and calculators, and they made their own chips, but their TI-99/4 computer was really a mixed-up machine. Some of TI's own product managers told me the 99/4 was originally designed as a game machine, but the marketing people forced the engineers to rush and shoehorn a computer into the game machine, with crippling results. The keyboard was a calculator-style keyboard (as opposed to typewriter-style), the BASIC language ran slow, and at $600 the price was too high. Rumor had it that instead of taking advantage of their vertical integration, TI's semiconductor group made the computer group buy their chips at the same price as outside vendors.

Tandy Corporation had scored a tremendous success with its TRS-80, which was sold exclusively through its Radio Shack electronics stores. But the TRS-80 was nicknamed the Trash 80, and its nickname was indicative of its reputation. Because Tandy sold only through its captive chain of Radio Shack franchises, they didn't exhibit at the CES show.

Apple didn't come to the CES show, either, because they sold mostly to computer stores, not the retailers who attended the CES. And with the Apple II priced at $1,300 (not counting peripherals), they weren't really in the home consumer market. Apple very wisely chose to stay in the high-priced range, and over the years this strategy paid off because it allowed them to sell fewer physical units than other companies, but make higher revenues and profits overall.

Atari had the best chance of all to break into the home computer market, but they blew it. To begin with, their lower-priced model, the Atari 400, was overpriced at $600 and had a cheap-looking, hard-to-use, flat plastic membrane instead of a real typewriter-style keyboard. Their higher-priced Atari 800 was well designed, even in the thousand-dollar price range. Their engineers had designed a special electronic bus with plug and socket connectors, which they patented. This system made it easy to connect their computer system, like a modular stereo system; and the uniform bus made it easier for programmers to write software using printers and disk drives.

Unfortunately, Atari neutralized their own advantage. To everyone's shock and dismay, they decided to keep secret vital technical information like memory maps and bus architectures which programmers needed to write software. They then tried to blackmail programmers by indicating that they could get technical information only if they signed up to write Atari-brand software. This alienated the fiercely independent hobbyist/programmer community, and as a result many serious programmers started writing software for other machines instead. By the time Atari realized their mistake and started wooing the serious programmers, it was too late. The only programmers who remained loyal were game programmers.

That was their other disadvantage. Who would buy a serious computer from the world's most successful videogame and arcade company? Many customers thought the Atari 400 and 800 were more expensive versions of the Atari 2600 videogame machine. Some people even doubted whether the Atari 400 and 800 were real computers.

There was ample precedent for such confusion. Did you ever buy or receive a toy that pretended to be something it wasn't? The real motion-picture machine that turned out to be a series of cartoons painted on a paper scroll you have to wind by hand to make the movie? The toy construction set that showed giant motorized doodads on the package, but neglected to mention that you got the motor only if you bought the bigger, deluxe version? Many young adults who were in the right age group to buy computers still didn't trust all the advertising because they were raised in the 1950s before truth in advertising began to be enforced. They carried their childhood skepticism into the 1970s and 1980s.

Atari fueled the suspicion with their own game machine. Their Atari 2600 videogame machine was truly the gadget of the year, and Atari's exhibit featured wall-to-wall games that attracted huge crowds. But Atari called their game machine a VCS for Video Computer System. Some of us at Commodore were genuinely angry at what we considered Atari's false advertising. A game machine is not a computer, we maintained. But since there wasn't anything else in the same price range that called itself a computer, who was to say what was a computer and what was not? I kept thinking of that movie machine I got for Christmas in the early 1950s, the one that looked so electronic on the package but was only a paper scroll. My childhood disappointment—and anger—welled up inside.

Which brings us to Commodore. Here we were, tucked in like a loose thread among the crazy-quilt fabric of the CES show, barely noticeable in our little booth filled with digital watches and calculators.

It's hard to believe that the long-awaited, slow-starting Home Computer Revolution would catch fire and start burning here. But loose threads sometimes have a way of starting huge fires.

Our booth was staffed by a thin crew of salespeople from the Consumer Electronics Division. The division sold watches, calculators, and a new product called an electronic digital thermostat, which let you regulate the temperature in your home or office for up to seven days at a time. The division had dribbled down from favorite-son to poor-cousin status as Commodore moved from watches and calculators to computers, and while the division didn't show up on any formal organization charts, Jack kept the group active for several key reasons:

- Commodore watches and calculators continued to generate revenues (if not profits).
- We never knew when we might need to combine watch or calculator technologies with computer technologies.
- It was hard to let go of the products that had formed the backbone of the company for more than half a decade.

The people who ran the division included Ken Hollandsworth, an erudite, professorial executive, formerly a topflight consultant to companies like Timex; Dave Navarro, a longtime associate of Jack's who came through the Calculator Wars and who seemed to hold the Woolworth retail account in his pocket; and a small group of salespeople, administrative clerks, and manufacturers' representatives. (These reps sell a manufacturer's products in return for a small commission. A network of reps can serve as a company's entire sales force if the company can't afford salespeople of their own. Or they can supplement the company's internal sales staff.)

Commodore's booth was like most convention exhibits. In addition to the product displays, we had an information desk with brochures and price lists, and a couple of meeting rooms for signing up new accounts or closing deals with mass merchants like Woolworth. Our booth was tiny compared to the two-story booths of companies like Atari, and I didn't like what I thought was Commodore's lack of marketing flair. Our booths never had proper signs explaining what we were showing, and the Commodore name above the booth was never attention-getting or prominent enough for me. The sign was always hard to read or placed where no one could see it. It took about a year of constant complaining before we finally fielded a booth that put Commodore's name up in lights, with nice-looking signs next to the products we were displaying.

Since the CES was attended by dealers, distributors, and mass merchants—the people who buy the products that get sold in stores to consumers—the booth was aimed primarily at dealers and buyers for major accounts. If you were a buyer and you showed up at the booth, you were either invited to our hotel suite to discuss your needs in a more relaxed atmosphere, or if you were in a hurry, you'd be taken to a closed-door meeting in one of the two small rooms at one end of the booth. If you were here to see Jack or someone who wasn't at the booth when you came, the person at the information booth would take your business card and later give it to the appropriate person. Typically, a dozen or more business cards were left every hour.

In addition to dealers and buyers, we usually attracted

a few journalists doing stories for electronics magazines or show dailies, and inevitably the competition dropped by to look over any new products or technologies. Unearthing new technologies was a major activity at the CES.

My job at the booth was to sit in a glass-enclosed fishbowl office at the corner of the exhibit and screen out the competition (most of whom I recognized on sight). I also had to give a quick spiel to any major dealers Jack invited in to see the computer, and arrange a few discreet interviews with press people I could trust to run complimentary stories.

Before coming to the show, one of my jobs had been to prepare some red, white, and blue handout sheets, which I got hastily printed up in Valley Forge, in case we wanted to make a formal announcement at the show. Instead, we decided against any formal announcements, although a few of the handouts slipped out.

On the sheets, we called the new computer the MicroPET and billed it as the first color computer which consumers could afford. We hinted that there would be several different models, at different price points. We even listed the potential features, which included 5K of memory, eight separate colors, and built-in music; and we pushed the fact that it worked with any color TV set. Of course, MicroPET was only a temporary name and we knew it. Even the features weren't finalized yet. We were lucky to have prototypes at the show.

I accompanied Bob Yannes and his boss Charlie Winterble to the show. Working against incredible deadlines, and under strong political pressures, Yannes spent a marathon week of all-night engineering sessions to put together a computer we could show at CES. The result was nicer-looking than most people expected, especially considering it was a Frankenstein monster thrown together from old spare parts and obsolete products that Yannes literally cut apart and put together in a different form.

The No-Name Computer (alias MicroPET) was a very simple system, assembled by hand and stuffed in an old Commodore desk-top calculator housing. The housing was two-tone plastic, cream-colored and black, and was shockingly compact: about five inches by nine inches, and about three inches thick.

For a keyboard, the engineers used the cramped red-and-blue square metallic keys from the original PET computer. The keys were all squeezed together, even closer than the keys on a typical pocket calculator. Teachers liked the old PET keyboard because it was easy for children to use, although touch-typists hated it because there was no space between the keys. In any event, it was only a prototype.

At the heart of Yannes' prototype were MOS Technology's 6502 microprocessor and the Video Interface Chip (VIC). Although this was the first time the chip was used in a functioning computer, the VIC had been demonstrated in public before, way back in 1978. The original VIC chip was shown at the 1978 Consumer Electronics Show, with the intention of attracting a manufacturer who wanted to use it in a videogame or similar device. To show what it could do, the chip was programmed to bounce a colored ball around a TV screen. But no manufacturer wanted to use it. Now, two years later, the VIC chip resurfaced, this time not as a chip but as a computer.

Jack's attitude was clear. If nobody wants to use the chip, we'll use it ourselves.

At first we all thought the prototype from Valley Forge was one of a kind, but then the engineers from Santa Clara brought a prototype, too. Bill Seiler and John Feagans brought their own version of the computer, which they'd assembled in a few days when it was learned that Yannes would bring a prototype to the show. It turned out they'd been discussing the project with Yannes on their own and in quasi-secrecy all along.

Yannes only put the prototype together to prove it could and should be done. He always expected the systems group to assume responsibility for completing the engineering. Personally, he was just eager to get back to designing computer chips. But the systems group still wasn't ready to pick up the ball and run with it. Seiler and Feagans worked on the computer without consulting Chuck Peddle, their boss, and according to one of them, Peddle was furious when he found out they were working on the small computer. He forbade them to work on it, but Jack found out and overruled Chuck.

"It will be done," Jack said.

The rest of the show turned into a jam session between the East Coast chip designers and the West Coast systems engineers. The real importance of this show was not that we were previewing the first inexpensive color computer in the world. Rather, it was that our engineers had a chance to meet and brainstorm in a neutral corner and make the computer happen.

There were many issues to be decided. The chip had to be revised, memory maps determined, and the keyboard designed. John Feagans put together a special chip called a Kernal (similar to the BIOS in larger computers).

To understand the Kernal, think of a car engine. Let's say Ford Motors decides to improve one of its car models. They change the exterior to make it look more modern and design a more efficient engine, but the dashboard, steering column, and pedals remain the same. If you'd learned to drive the previous model, you wouldn't have any trouble driving the new one. The engine and outside appearance are radically different, but the driving (that is, the commands) works the same.

The Kernal was originally designed to provide upward compatibility among different generations of computers. Future computers would always require different, more advanced ROM chips and microprocessors, but presumably the Kernal would stay the same. Unfortunately, in practice the engineers kept changing the Kernal over the years so Feagans's dream of upward compatibility at the machine language level didn't quite materialize. Meanwhile, anyone who peered in at us got an unexpected glimpse at a revolutionary new computer in the process of being invented.

The glass walls of the meeting room were tinted, but passersby could still look in and see what was going on. Two prototypes were set up on a high counter inside the room. The two outside walls which formed the corner of the booth looked out on the junction of two heavily trafficked aisles, so there was a constant flow of people outside the windows. Those who peeked in saw two little computers hooked up to two small color television sets, placed on a four-foot-high counter. One screen showed a simulated shoot-em-up space videogame, with lasers firing at space rockets; and the other showed large birdlike creatures on the screen being shot down, one by one.

Although we were slightly paranoid about anyone getting a look at our new computers *inside* the booth, we didn't mind people pressing their nose against the tinted glass windows to get a look from the *outside*. I told Jack I thought it was a great idea to have people literally pressing their noses against the *outside* of the booth. Those who peered in would get a peek at the new computer actually being born at the CES show.

Jack agreed.

It was a unique phenomenon. Here we were, debating and reviewing the features of a new computer, in plain sight of anyone who happened to wander by. As more and more people stopped by and bumped their noses trying to see what we were up to, the rumors spread across the floor, and soon we were besieged by people asking, pleading, begging, and even demanding to get in to see the new computer.

At one point, some Japanese engineers managed to slip in while everyone was out of the room. They actually tried to unscrew the case and get a peek inside, but were shooshed away in time. They wouldn't have seen much, just a tangle of hand-soldered wires and shoved-together components on a skeleton circuit-board. Nevertheless, we were much more cautious after that.

That first day of the show, several of us went with Jack and his son Leonard to the cafeteria for lunch. Jack was beaming. It was as if until he'd seen it with his own eyes, he didn't really know if we could make a computer cheap enough to sell for $300. Now he knew. He was already thinking about the bill of materials, the list of components that would go into the computer.

We talked about what we should call it.

"Why not VIC, for VIC chip?" he asked, looking around the table for some reaction.

"We could say it stands for Video Interface Computer," I said. "Not bad."

"We can come up with something more creative," someone else said.

Jack turned to me and said, "Talk to your friends in the company. See what everybody thinks."

I said I would. My head was already buzzing with ideas, but it was too soon to broach them.

"Where will we sell the VIC?" I asked.

"We'll sell the VIC to anyone who wants to buy it."

"Just computer stores, or retail stores too?"

"Anyone."

"Mail order?"

"*Anyone.*" He grinned and said, "For the masses. We will sell this computer to the masses!"

The next few days of the convention floated by like clouds. Talking, planning, screening, debating, learning, absorbing, creating—

I was the gatekeeper, Jack was the keymaster, and there were unseen spirits lurking everywhere. The spirits of new computers and ghosts of technologies to come were lurking in the air. We hadn't even begun to consider the importance of what we were doing here.

Imagine children in ghettos being able to afford computers for the first time. Poor school districts and elementary schools could buy them (until now only high schools used computers on a large scale). Maybe the onscreen interaction of the computer would allow younger children to grasp abstract concepts like algebra. This thing could amplify the intelligence of a whole generation.

Some educators have maintained that certain concepts can only be learned at a certain minimum age. They are wrong. I remembered my first-grade teacher pulling my ears when she caught me with my head buried in my desk reading fourth-grade books about dinosaurs and the universe. It was torture. After a while, I developed a technique for snapping open my desk, pretending to rummage around for

117

something, reading a quick paragraph, and snapping the desk closed before she could get over and pull my ears. I *hated* having my ears pulled. But I loved reading more.

Today I keep wondering how many kids should have been reading two or three grades ahead but stopped short because their first-grade teachers pulled their ears. I wonder how many kids would find algebra more fun if they knew that much of BASIC programming is really an easy, entertaining kind of algebra in disguise. I wonder if some teachers will revise their questionable theories about how old you have to be before you can learn certain concepts.

Our computer would help, if not by helping more schools put them in classrooms, then by helping parents circumvent the school system and put computers in their homes.

Today, I know a Pennsylvania school system with a policy that requires students to be in the eighth grade before they can take BASIC programming, while in some school districts, children learn programming in first grade. And some children of engineers and programmers I know can do some simple programming before they start kindergarten.

The underlying question is: Why home computers? Because computers make us think differently and often make us think more clearly. They involve us in a new, powerful kind of logic. And they also teach our children faster and better manual-dexterity skills. The same skills required to play a shoot-em-up videogame will be required in the future to fly a space shuttle or maneuver an ocean-going mining rig at the bottom of the sea, or handle nuclear material used in medicine.

These thoughts weren't as obvious in June 1980 as they are today, but the importance of what Jack Tramiel and Commodore were doing by bringing computer prices lower becomes clearer with every passing moment. Nevertheless, the impact of the consumer computer will not be fully realized perhaps for another generation or two when someone sits down and analyzes how computers changed and improved our ways of thinking and moving and solving problems.

SIX

"Okay guys, let's go," George said.
"But we're cold," they complained.
"We're hungry."
"We're tired."
"And it's snowing!"
"Don't worry," George told them. "A little snow never hurt anyone. Besides, they'll never expect us. Who expects company on Christmas? Look, you'll go. You'll fight. You'll win. You'll feel terrific in the morning. Trust me."

A few hours later they were slowly making their way across the ice-clogged river, with George standing poised (or frozen) on the bow like some heroic statue.

"Hey, sit down!" the rowers yelled. "You're rocking the boat!"

George just smiled and said, "Keep rowing. We're almost there."

Crossing the Delaware

With the CES behind us, I was going to be asked to move east, to Valley Forge, Pennsylvania. Valley Forge gets cold in the winter. We all know that from biographies of George Washington.

"You'll hate it," my friends assured me.

"That's okay," I rationalized, fighting off involuntary shivers. "If Washington could do it in a tent, I can do it in a car. Besides, I'm from Wisconsin. It hits thirty below zero in the winter. No problem." But it was a problem.

Luckily, it was only July, or I might have turned around and got back on the plane as soon as I saw my first snowflake. Despite my Eskimo-like upbringing, a few years in Asia and three years in California had turned me into a Sunkist orange. Give me that sun anytime. I'd served my time in the Gulag. Now my blood froze at the same temperature as tomato plants.

The first clue I got that I was going out East to work permanently was when Dick Sanford started hinting that he wanted to hire an assistant—someone with an M.B.A. and some strong marketing experience, perhaps. Did I want the job?

"No, thanks," I replied. "I'm already Jack's assistant. Thanks anyway."

I wasn't good at reading clues. A few days later, he tried again. "You'd be in on all the decisions."

"To tell you the truth, I'm trying to get into marketing," I told him. "If I go anywhere that's where I'd like to be. Maybe I could be the VIC product manager—"

"No way," Dick said, shaking his head. "Jack doesn't believe in product managers."

"Oh." Then I have to convince him, I thought to myself.

I began by firing off a series of ten-page memos to everyone in sight, suggesting features for the new computers, marketing ideas, names, product numbering schemes, and software ideas. Don't forget the typewriter-style keyboard. How about programmable function keys, or a keypad on the console? We need a nice user's manual with a friendly introduction to BASIC. Who's writing it? What about box design? Shouldn't we start thinking about an ad campaign? Above all, think *user friendly*.

My first memo to Jack had a giant caricature of myself on the cover—a happy face with a beard and mustache. I usually drew this cartoon when I signed letters or birthday cards to friends. Putting a full-page cartoon on the front of my first memo to Jack was daring and frivolous, but in character. I didn't want to be lumped in with all the other memo-writers, and I wanted to make sure my user-friendly message was clear: If we were going to introduce a home computer, it had to be user-friendly.

My memos to Jack were received well. He'd known I was crazy when he hired me, so happy faces didn't surprise him. He did like my ideas, though, and began to encourage me to share my advice around the company, as a marketer and user advocate.

"Everybody wants to make computers friendly, but sometimes they don't know how," he told me. "I want you to show them how. You understand the consumer, what he wants."

"And if they choose not to take my advice?"

"Who wouldn't take good advice?"

He didn't understand corporate egos. I had learned that many smart executives will make a wrong decision rather than the right decision and admit they got the idea from someone else. Some people left the company with Jack's footprints on their trousers, and my good advice, which might have saved them, still ringing in their ears. They just couldn't accept The Religion, and they passionately despised zealots, disciples, missionaries, and true believers. Even some senior Commodorians warned me off the crusade.

Chuck Peddle, who was one of the people I respected most in the company, cautioned me not to get involved in the VIC, especially in the marketing aspects.

"But that's exactly what I want," I said. "I want to make sure the VIC turns out right."

"That's fine," Chuck said, "but do it from the sidelines. Look, let me give you some advice as a friend. Stay away from the VIC because you can't win. The VIC won't succeed, and frankly, you're getting in over your head. I mean it."

By this time, however, Chuck was beginning to have some open disputes with Jack over the VIC versus the ColorPET, and part of his dispute involved marketing. He would stand in Jack's office and try to tell him how to position the VIC in the marketplace, and Jack would turn red and explode and tell him to stick to engineering. A lot of us wondered if Chuck was a masochist, the way he kept going back to Jack again and again with the same arguments that he knew would cause Jack to blow up.

More importantly, Chuck wanted to go up-scale and take on Apple with a professional color computer, and Jack wanted to go down-scale with a low-priced home computer. Both men were right, but Jack's will prevailed, not just because he was the boss, but because the home computer filled a niche where nobody was selling computers, and where no one could compete with us on price because of our vertical integration. In time, Jack would want the up-scale computer, but first he wanted the small one.

"I want to make a splash with this computer," he said. A me-too version of the Apple wouldn't do it. The first home computer would.

Faced with Chuck's continuing resistance, Jack began to consider sending the whole project over to Japan, which had a small engineering group capable of handling the project. They were also close to the manufacturing contractors who made plastic cases, keyboards, and other parts of the computer. And Japan's general manager, Taro (Tony) Tokai, was a trusted Commodorian and samurai warrior first class, having worked with Jack for more than a dozen years.

He had an excellent blend of marketing and manufacturing knowhow, and he moved smoothly between Western and Oriental cultures.

One day early in July, Jack looked up from his desk and said, "This will be a Japanese computer."

"Huh?"

He smiled. He loved to shock me. Me, and everybody else.

"We can't make enough right away to sell in the United States." He was remembering that everyone got mad at Commodore when there weren't enough PETs to go around. "So we'll sell it in Japan first. And if we sell it first in Japan, we might as well let them engineer it."

The decision was made.

Chuck Peddle was furious. Several people predicted disaster.

Jack said, "You will *help* Japan."

Of course, much of the talent needed to finish the computer was based in Valley Forge and Santa Clara, but Jack wanted to make sure that Japan controlled the engineering. He didn't want to leave the project in the hands of engineers who didn't believe in it.

But almost no one believed in it, anyway. At one point, it looked like the only people in the whole company who believed in the VIC were Jack, Jerone Guinn, Bob Yannes, Tony Tokai, Yashi Terakura, and me. Everyone else seemed to think it was a toy. In fact, if you'd told anyone you were going to market a 5K computer with a 22-column screen, they would have laughed you out of the industry.

In truth, I believed it would sell not because of the features or price or positioning in the marketplace. I believed it would sell because Jack told me it would.

"You can market anything if you do it right," he said. And I believed him. I was too naïve to realize that what we were doing really couldn't be done. It was irrationality versus rationality. Faith versus common sense. In this way, Jack was very Oriental. *Impossible* is a word invented by people who don't want to strain their potential.

There were plenty of strong arguments.

"5K of memory is too small."

"Then we'll make it so you can expand it," Jack said. Presto! The VIC became expandable.

"But you can't use it for serious applications like word processing."

"Then we'll write a program that just teaches word processing. If they want something fancy, they can buy a PET."

"But serious users won't buy it."

"Then we'll sell it to beginners!"

His eyes twinkled brightly as he laughed deep in his throat. He had an answer for every complaint, but his basic argument was solid and consistent. We would not try to stretch this computer into something larger. We would sell it as something entirely new, a *starter computer*.

It was an entirely new phrase: starter computer. Who would imagine that the first true home computer would also be a computer for beginners? Until now, everyone had thought it would be something larger and more sophisticated, and higher priced.

Then the computer disappeared. It was as if it had become a taboo subject. The only person who discussed it in the open was Jack.

"Jack, I've got some ideas here—"

"Send them to Tokai-san in Japan."

"But—"

"Yes?"

"Nothing."

Jack's eyes bulged, and he hissed through his teeth. "How many times do I have to say it? This is a *Japanese* computer." Then he laughed. He was loving it.

What he did was create so much panic among our U.S. engineers that they started working like crazy with the Japanese contingent headed by Yashi Terakura. Participants in the project included the same engineers who'd worked on the PET, plus several others including Bob Russell and Shiras Shivji. Shiras wound up settling in California. He had been with Commodore during the calculator days, left for a brief hiatus, then returned in time to help lead much of the systems engineering work after Chuck Peddle left.

Commodore was also carrying on its other activities. We had to keep selling the PET, launch the new CBM line, restore good relations with computer store dealers, replenish our marketing group, and get ready for the new baby computer.

By the end of June, I was involved with some actual marketing. Jack had said "Learn!" but my conscience said "Do!"

One day I came to Jack and suggested we revive our tape software program. By this time, most people were using disk drives instead of tapes; tapes took several minutes to load a program into the computer, while disks took only seconds. Still, I felt we'd need some tape software for the VIC. It was simple logic. To begin with, there weren't enough disk drives for the PET/CBM, much less for the VIC. Besides, disk drives cost over $1,000 for a dual drive and about $600 for a single drive. The $89 Datassette was a more affordable alternative. Tape-based programs were still selling well in the United Kingdom, and I knew they'd sell in the U.S. if properly marketed.

I mentioned to Jack that we used to sell a lot of software on tape cassettes and we were still selling Datassettes with the PET. Several companies were selling software on tape and doing reasonably well, but Jack was against it. Commodore tape sales in the U.S. were zilch.

But tapes sold well in the United Kingdom, I argued, and the only reason they did poorly in the U.S. was because we tried to sell tapes one at a time. That piecemeal approach simply wasn't profitable. We had to sell tapes in six-unit packs, like gum or popsicles. Six programs for the price of five. Buy five and get one free.

Jack gave me the go-ahead to investigate, and I discovered that there was only one major tape vendor who specialized in computer tapes and was reliable. When I told Jack who it was, he almost hit the ceiling. "They're crooks!" he exclaimed. Apparently, Commodore had worked with them before and had had some disputes. I said I'd already talked to the owner and we discussed some pricing.

"What do you know about pricing?" Jack challenged.

"Uh—if we buy it at the price we discussed, we can make almost 100 percent profit," I said, expecting him to be impressed with the percentage.

Instead he shot back, "How do you know that's enough?"

"What?"

"You have to buy at the lowest price, not just to make money," he said, then went on to explain that if I bought a product for twenty-five cents because I knew I could sell it for a dollar, that was wrong thinking. I had to find out what the product cost the manufacturer to make, then tack on a reasonable profit, and I might come out with a cost of ten cents instead of a quarter.

"If you don't knock off that fifteen cents, someone else will do it," Jack said. He was right. Conventional marketing says: Take the price you think you can sell something for, figure how much margin you need to cover your overhead and make a reasonable profit, then get the cost down so you make the profit.

I called it the price-down method because it starts from the price and works down to the cost. Jack said it was completely backwards.

"I guarantee you'll lose money," he declared.

The cost-up method was safer. Under the price-down method, a tough competitor who used Jack's method and worked from the cost-up would always reach a lower cost. He could make the same profit as you and still lower the price and steal the market away from you.

I insisted that I still wanted to do the deal with the tape manufacturer, at which point Jack stood up, came around his desk, and grabbed the sleeve of my suit. "Come on," he said. "You're going to learn something."

He headed off toward the accounting department, literally holding the sleeve of my suit, as I dragged along beside him trying to keep up. He stopped in front of an accounting clerk's desk. The clerk looked up and started trembling.

Jack said, "This is Mr. Tomczyk. I want you to give him all the invoices for tapes which we bought in the past."

"All the invoices?" the clerk asked.

"Yes."

"But—" he opened a long file drawer stuffed with thin, paper invoices. "They're organized by date. It'll take hours to find all of them."

"Good. Then we'll leave so you can get started."

As we walked away, I shrugged over my shoulder at the clerk, who seemed slightly nonplussed by the cumbersome task at hand.

Jack continued the lesson, telling me to use history. If we had bought tapes in the past, I should find out how much we paid, who the vendors were—in short, everything we knew about buying tapes from our own records. That way I at least had some ammunition if I went to negotiate.

He said the price today should always be *lower* than it was before.

"What about inflation?" I asked.

He just glared at me and growled, "Lower!"

"Yes, sir."

Our suppliers have to be partners, he said. They have to work with us on the money. If they sell us a lot of tapes, they should knock our cost down on the next batch because they'd already made a lot of money. Then we can reduce our price and sell even more, which will make more money for both of us. That's how a vendor and marketing company (he always said Commodore was primarily a marketing company) should work together.

At the end of this lesson, we concluded that the tape prices I was negotiating were indeed lower than before (I made sure they were). Jack grudgingly let me do business with the company I'd chosen although he had his doubts about their reliability. But it became a moot subject when I agreed to hold off on tapes until the VIC came out.

In the meantime, we tackled another marketing problem: documentation. The manuals that came with the PET and CBM were pretty bad, both in content and appearance. One day Adam Osborne, then president of Osborne/McGraw-Hill, the computer-book company, approached us wanting to sell a new reference book on the PET/CBM, the

128

PET/CBM Personal Computer Guide. Jack and I discussed it, and Jack negotiated a deal to buy the books. To everyone's surprise, he agreed to include the 430-page book free with every computer. He saw it as a short-term (one or two years) solution until we could get some proper documentation written. Also, he felt that until we had a strong selection of software, hobbyists would be the first customers to buy our new CBM system, and they needed a solid reference to help them write software.

The manuals were the best books ever included free with a personal computer. However, systems kept slipping through manufacturing with books missing from the box, which meant some of us had to keep calling the manufacturing people to remind them to include the books.

At that time, Adam was an industry pundit who, like many editors, loved to chide manufacturers in print. But Adam went beyond punditing and invented his own computer, the Osborne Portable—a well-remembered, gutsy achievement which flared like a firework, then dissolved in midair and fluttered back to earth, snuffed out by an industry that couldn't wait for an encore.

The first VIC project I got actively involved in was naming the VIC-20. For some reason, the decision fell into my hands. The first names we considered were related to the VIC chip. Jack had suggested VIC at the CES show. A few people wanted to call it Vickie, but that name was never seriously considered. Most of the engineers liked the name Vixen. I even doodled some sketches using a cute little fox as a logo, but the name Vixen was ruled out because *vixen* had lurid sexual connotations and Russ Meyer's *Vixen* was a semiclassic porno film.

I favored the name Spirit because the full name of the computer would be Commodore Spirit. It made a lot of sense to me, and I kept pushing it. I made a list of all the foreign words for spirit, and even Jack started joking about the Duch computer (*duch* is Polish for spirit).

Unfortunately, the Japanese claimed Spirit translates as

ghost and has very unpleasant supernatural connotations. I guess it's like the Exxon tiger, a cute symbol all over the world—except in a few spots in Southeast Asia where tigers eat people and are more feared than friendly.

The name CX-22 was suggested, but Eastman Kodak had a CX color-film series. We probably could have used it, but we wanted to be unique. Jack liked SX-22 because it would have been a nice inside joke. He kept saying "business is like sex." ("You have to get involved. Each time is different. Watching it on TV is not the same as doing it.")

Finally, we decided to name the computer after the Video Interface Chip—VIC, which became Video Interface Computer. VIC sounded naked by itself, though. Besides, VIC by itself sounded like a truck driver. I insisted we add a number, but the only meaningful numbers were 22 (22 columns) or 5 (for 5K bytes of memory). For some reason, the number 22 didn't seem very friendly, so I told Jack I wanted to call it the VIC-20.

"Why twenty instead of some other number?" he asked.

"Because twenty sounds friendlier."

He shrugged and that was that.

Ironically, we originally vetoed the name Vixen because it had undesirable connotations both in the U.S. and Germany, but VIC later turned out to mean something even worse in German (V is pronounced F in German).

As a result, the German model was called VC-20 and was advertised as Volks Computer (People's Computer). For a while, the name Volks Computer was so well-liked that we considered using it world-wide, but the only U.S. tie-in was Volkswagen and Volkswagens were no longer being made in the U.S. Except for Germany (VC-20) and Japan (VIC-1001), we stuck with VIC-20. In the end, the short, snappy name VIC-20 turned out to be easy to remember, convenient for magazine headlines, and very user-friendly.

One day late in the summer, Jack said, "I'd like you to come up to the ranch on Saturday." Uh oh. That meant something serious was brewing. Was I going to be fired? Promoted? Given a nasty assignment? I had visions of a gold-plated hatchet with my name on it—but on the handle, or the blade? My worries were groundless. All Jack wanted to do was formalize my ping-pong status.

At the ranch, we had one of Helen Tramiel's marvelous meals which Jack affectionately called peasant food. We sat and discussed a wide variety of topics, culminating in a cordial invitation to go East. It was explained to me that eventually the entire management team would be headquartered in Pennsylvania, including Jack. He reminded me that I'd said I didn't mind leaving California when he hired me.

"I'm really not sure I want to work in Pennsylvania," I confessed. "Three years in California have made me a Californian. I like scuba diving. It's nice in California, but the ocean's like a sewer on the East Coast. Besides, it's *cold* out there, and the lease on my apartment isn't up until December."

"Don't worry," Jack said. "Keep your apartment. We'll rent you an apartment in Valley Forge. You'll still be going back and forth, and if you really don't like it you don't have to stay there."

So there it was. Some people live like golf balls—putting distance from the eighteenth hole, and some people live like ping-pong balls—close to the net and always in the air. Supposedly, all this was going to result with me coming to rest on the pong side of the table.

Since Jack was staying in California awhile longer, he suggested I report to Dick Sanford, who ran Commodore in the U.S. I said I didn't mind, and we talked about what kind of title I should have. I told him, "Titles aren't important. How about something simple like marketing strategist?" No problem. It was a rare title that didn't ruffle the feathers of any vice presidents or directors. My business card was printed with the title marketing strategist, and it was flattering to know that both Jack and Dick Sanford felt it was an accurate reflection of my job.

It was good also to know that I wasn't the only migratory bird in the company. Sam Tramiel, Jack's oldest son, was being spun off from the company into his own business in Hong Kong. His company began by manufacturing digital watches and later expanded into electronic subassemblies and miscellaneous components for computers and peripherals.

131

Sam and Jack both knew Sam wasn't going anywhere inside Commodore. He kept trying to flex his authority, but many executives still saw him as Jack's son and deferred to him only because they had to. It was important for him to earn his stripes. Some people felt he wasn't capable. Others cried nepotism.

Personally, I thought Sam was extremely likable, shrewd, hard-driving, and effective. He knew The Religion well and wielded it like his father, but always in his father's shadow. This gave way to a certain amount of bitterness, which he carried on his shoulder. It's tough to cast your own shadow when you're standing in someone else's.

Few people knew that Sam had been toughened and sensitized by various tragedies in his life. His move to Hong Kong changed his outlook and made it easier for him to deal with his father and other people on his own terms.

In the next three years, Sam's effectiveness, leadership, and savvy would be proved on alien battlegrounds, in the Far East where you either develop close and reliable working relationships with Chinese and Japanese vendors, or you come home and forget about it. Sam did not come home. After a few years of running his own successful company, he was pressed back into service to fill some gaps in manufacturing. He came back into the company on his own terms and became part of the executive glue that held together the extremely delicate connections between the Far East manufacturing centers and the rest of the Commodore world.

There were other migrations going on in July and August of 1980. Bill Wade, an Oklahoma native with tremendous hands-on experience in retail sales, was put in charge of Mr. Calculator stores, the Commodore-owned retail centers that once numbered a dozen stores. Mr. Calculator started out as a test in the late 1970s to see if Commodore should get into the retail business—the stickiest part of any vertical integration. But retailing was not in the cards for Commodore, so the stores were eventually sold and cut back to one location which Jack wanted to use as a market research barometer.

By selling our own products first through a store which we controlled, we could theoretically gauge the popularity of new products, spot problems and bugs before we hit the mass market, and gain a better understanding of the problems associated with retailing computers. That, at least, was the theory.

Unfortunately, our Mr. Calculator stores had the same problems dealing with Commodore that our computer dealers did. Trouble getting products, poor factory service, tangled paperwork, and shortages of literature and other marketing tools were only a few of the problems experienced by Wade and Randy Hain, who together ran the stores. It was disgraceful, and no wonder that Wade was constantly complaining. When your own family doesn't support you, it's pretty rough.

Chuck Peddle also migrated. By late summer 1980, Chuck and Jack were reaching the end of their patience with each other. Finally, Chuck was asked to move East to Valley Forge. He really wanted to stay on the West Coast, though, partly because this was where all the free-lance engineering talent was, and partly because he liked living there. He did come East for a few short visits, but insisted on keeping his residence in California where he was more at home. In his last weeks at Commodore he seemed to be doing more speech making than engineering.

A few executives took advantage of his weakness and pounced on him—a typical reaction in Commodore's higher echelons. If you stumbled and fell, they were on you like wolves. Even the father of the PET wasn't immune to the politics, except he didn't have to put up with it.

One or two executives called him Chuckles, and he began to get no respect. There was even some pressure to move Chuck out of engineering completely. If things kept going the way they were, Chuck would keep his title and work with the engineers, but his primary job would be public relations. The theory was, "Let him go out and talk to people—he's good at that—but don't let him near the computers."

It was the wrong thing to do to Chuck Peddle, one of the premier chip and systems engineers in the country. He promptly proved it by leaving Commodore in October 1980, and several of Commodore's young engineers went with him, including Glen Stark and Bill Seiler.

A short history of Chuck Peddle after Commodore begins with the formation of Sirius Software, which was promptly sued by another company for infringing their name. Then Chuck and his engineers designed an excellent business/professional computer which was built and marketed by an established business machine company named Victor, where Chuck became president.

In the meantime, Chuck was in possession of some stock certificates which Commodore maintained he hadn't really earned under his option plan. Chuck countersued for the stock and other benefits, including royalties on the PET computer line. He lost the suit. Then Victor sued Commodore, claiming the name VIC-20 infringed on the name Victor, which they were using for the computer Chuck Peddle and his engineers had designed. But Chuck was at Commodore and was one of the people who had approved the name VIC-20. I didn't think it made sense for him to come back and sue for infringement on a name he helped approve. In any event, they lost the lawsuit.

Finally, the Victor computer caught on. Bill Seiler cut his ponytail and started wearing vested suits to conventions. Chuck ran some ads featuring a picture of himself standing next to the computer. Victor Technology made a lot of sales ($65 million in 1983), but had trouble maintaining profits. In February 1984 Victor Technology consented to an involuntary petition filed by six creditors under Chapter 11 of the Bankruptcy Code. Under a subsequent reorganization, Chuck retained the rights to continue selling his popular computer in the U.S., and continues to sell it today.

Chuck's departure was followed in short order by the resignation of Chris Fish, Commodore's vice president in the Bahamas. The way I heard the story, Jack was starting to chip away some of Chris's responsibility for international sales. One day Chris called Jack from overseas, felt Jack was discourteous to him, and subsequently quit.

By the time Chris left the company, his stock options

were either exercised or exercisable, and with Commodore's stock still rising, he was financially well off. After leaving Commodore, Chris was reported to have gone into business with Chuck Peddle. Later, Chris and Sue Anzel, Jack's executive secretary, surprised everyone by divorcing their spouses and getting married.

All this wasn't especially traumatic for those of us who hadn't worked long or closely with Chuck or Chris, but it was significant that two members of the inner circle, two family members, would leave so abruptly. One of the reasons Commodore had trouble keeping disciples in top management was because the true disciples made the heaviest sacrifices, and felt most bitterly insulted when Commodore cut back on their power or authority. They took it personally, even when the growth of the company required the pie to be divided into smaller pieces. Virtually every true disciple who made it into Jack's inner circle and subsequently left the company, did so because Jack was reining in their authority. They felt embittered, insulted, or fed up.

Also, and perhaps equally important, the true disciples got the best stock option deals. In the late 1970s and early 1980s, it took about seven years to become a Commodore millionaire under the stock plan. Virtually anyone with stock options before 1980 had a good shot at becoming a multimillionaire, and many disciples who left seemed to time their departure with the maturation of their stock options.

Their departures had a profound impact on Jack, but it was indicative of his personal idealism that he kept grooming new disciples, kept preaching his business religion, and kept placing faith in every member of the inner circle, the samurai princes, knowing all the time that any one of these adopted sons was liable to turn ungrateful and leave the family without warning, without thanks, and without ever contacting him again.

Thus it was against a background of anticipation and change, with company politics flaring up, top executives leaving and shifting positions, that I headed east to Pennsylvania.

For me, going East meant staying in the Sheraton Valley Forge, a twelve-story, cylindrical hotel with a magnificent view of Valley Forge National Park, the sprawling site of George Washington's famous encampment. I was given my own car, sort of, a blue 1980 Toyota Tercel with no luxury features whatsoever. The car was technically Jack's, for use in Valley Forge, but he let me use it when he wasn't in town, which was most of the time. I took dinners in Chumley's, an elegant continental restaurant at the Sheraton, where I developed a taste for roast duck and prime rib. It was a long way from mooching pizzas on Clement Street in San Francisco. After three weeks of marvelous but boring decadence, I found an apartment about twenty minutes from MOS in the countryside, and filled it with cheap rented furniture. The company picked up the tab.

It didn't take long to see why Jack wanted to move to Valley Forge. Dick Sanford ran a tight ship there. Like Kit Spencer in the U.K., he had a talent for attracting talented young managers and manager candidates. They worked long hours, stayed late every night, and often came in on weekends. Bonnie Wilson, Dan Bliss, and Sam Chin were just three of the diehards from those early days. Most of Dick's staff worked with finance, accounting, and sales administration, although operations, shipments, deliveries, and warehousing were also part of his domain.

Our legal counsel was also based at Valley Forge. Richard Blumenthal, Commodore's in-house attorney, was constantly harried by a series of lawsuits and countersuits involving charges of infringements, contracts, contractual disputes—much more work than most corporate counsels receive. Commodore used lawsuits like weapons. We weren't afraid of being sued, ever, and weren't afraid of suing.

Backing up Blumenthal was Leonard Schreiber, Commodore's veteran trial counsel. Lee had been a member of the board of directors since 1978 and a special friend and confidant of Jack, since the typewriter repair days, in the 1960s. Schreiber was tough, knowledgeable, and extremely likable, both in and out of the courtroom. After seeing him in action for several years, I wouldn't want to wind up in court with him on the other side. Lee was as wily as a fox, and used every trick and trap in his considerable legal arsenal.

Dick's right-hand man and protégé was Greg Pratt, considered to be future president material in the making. For most of the years that I was with Commodore, Greg was the man you had to see if you wanted to spend money, place an order with an outside vendor, or get Commodore products released from the warehouse. Greg joined the company in the late 1970s after working with Commodore as an outside auditor. At 32 he was possibly the highest-ranking black executive in the personal computer industry. As a manager, he was tough, mature, serious, hardworking, unflappable, and always fair and thoughtful in his approach to management problems and decisions. He was a marathon workaholic, given to late-night sessions and six- and seven-day workweeks. More than anything else, he had a unique ability to slice through to the heart of an operational issue. Because of this, he was one of the few young executives entrusted with the authority to approve purchases, sign checks, and work directly with Hong Kong and Japan.

Being allowed to work with Japan was a significant honor and a symbol of trust, because Jack kept contacts with the Orient to an absolute minimum. At one point he went so far as to forbid everyone except one person to communicate by phone or telex with Japan. Experience had shown that when it came to Japan, too many cooks spoiled the broth. If too many people talked to Japan, they wound up issuing conflicting instructions and creating confusion.

I was lucky to be the person allowed to telex Japan, mostly in conjunction with product planning for the VIC-20. Tony Tokai and I began a lively telex correspondence, and before long he was directing most of his VIC-20 questions to me. Jack was copied on all telexes, and when he saw the volume between Tony and me, he gave me a mild kick in the pants.

"Do you know how much it costs to send a telex?" he asked, threatening, "If you send one more telex to Japan I'm going to make you pay for it!"

137

It was an excellent example of Jack making a forceful point—in fact, an outright threat. But he didn't expect me to take his words literally and stop sending telexes. What he was really saying was, "Don't waste money on unnecessary telexes, and keep the words to a minimum." As Kit Spencer often said, Jack expected his top executives to do what he wanted, not what he said.

In response to Jack's complaint, I started abbreviating the words in my telexes to make them shorter. For example, the word *with* became *w* and *information* became *info.* A few weeks later, Jack took me aside and said, "If you have to send telexes, don't abbreviate anything. Write it all out. Some people overseas might not understand your abbreviations."

Of course, I kept sending telexes, and Tony and I started putting together the strategy for the VIC-20. Tony supervised the product design, production, and marketing in Japan. I started developing a marketing strategy for the United States, not because anyone told me to, but because nobody else was doing it. Most people still thought the VIC-20 was poison, a toy computer that wasn't worth bothering with. Even Dick Sanford wanted to use the VIC-20s as premiums and give them away to dealers who bought PET and CBM systems. There were also fears that the low-priced VIC-20 might kill sales of the PET.

Jack's response was, "So what? If our customers want VIC-20s instead of PETs, then we'll sell them VIC-20s." His unspoken argument was always the same: If we don't do it, someone else will.

In addition to my VIC-20 promotional activities, my main job at Valley Forge was to get out the 1980 Annual Report. The fiscal year ended June 30, and the report was supposed to be printed by the end of September. It seemed like everyone got excited about the annual report because it was inevitably a political and conceptual hassle. As Jack had seen in my résumé, I had spent two years in Wisconsin and California as an investor-relations consultant and had edited more than two dozen annual reports. I had also done some annual report photography myself, so I knew how to stand over a photographer's shoulder and get a good shot.

Doing the annual report wasn't as hard as finding a place to sit. Since there wasn't enough office space, I camped out at a desk in an open alcove behind Josephine Marinello (Dick Sanford's and later Jack's secretary). I didn't have a phone, a file cabinet, or a permanent desk, and I carried my file folders around with me in an oversized black leather camera bag. I picked up that bag in 1971 while in Vietnam. During two years of traveling around East Asia, I fell into the habit of carrying a collapsible black bag instead of a briefcase, like many Asian businesspeople.

During those hectic weeks, I also spent a considerable amount of time plotting U.S. marketing strategy with Dick Powers and doing special projects such as filling out ten-page questionnaires for bankers and brokerage firms.

"It'll give you a good chance to learn about the company," Dick Sanford said with a sarcastic smile. He loved seeing young executives tackle difficult challenges, like an airborne drill sergeant who likes to see troops run three miles in combat boots on an empty stomach, singing in cadence:

Soldier, soldier, don't be blue
One more mile and you'll be through
When we're done with our last mile,
We'll do another one, just for style!
Sound off! (One, two)
Once more! (Three, four)
One, two, three, four. . .one, two. . .THREE-FOUR!

I began to see questionnaires in my sleep. We were all surprised, Jack and Dick included, that nobody could answer some of the most basic questions, like how big was our market share, how many computers had we sold since 1977, and so on. A lot of our answers had to be educated guesses, while others required detailed research. Often when I asked someone to help me make a guess they'd reply, "Put down what you think. Your guess is as good as anyone's."

While doing these projects, I made an important discovery: Research houses are unreliable, and their reports are overpriced. When I compared the estimates in market surveys and so-called research reports to our own calculations,

I was appalled how far off some of the reports were. They almost always rated us much lower than we were, and I learned that industry research—like many other things in life—is about one-third popularity contest, one-third educated guess, and one-third reality.

Often, researchers would call and ask me where I thought Commodore ranked in relation to the other computer companies. It was obvious that since we didn't have a department to answer such inquiries, most of the researchers were getting their data from Apple or other companies that had better public relations or marketing staffs to answer questionnaires or phone calls. And, of course, other companies might well offer data which was less than thoroughgoing or optimistic about Commodore.

It surprised us when the numbers revealed that Commodore microcomputers were used in more schools worldwide than any other computer, including Apple. This was due mostly to our two-for-one and three-for-two school donation programs. We began to stress this point in our advertising.

After that, when anyone called asking us to pay up to $8,000 for research reports or surveys, I said to them, "Look, I'll make a deal with you. You pay *me* $8,000 and I'll tell you what's really going to happen in the industry, because nobody, not the consumers or dealers or anyone else, knows what's going to happen next year. Only those of us who are inside the computer companies know what it's like to feel the pressure and the pull of the marketplace. The personal computer market is a vacuum and we're all being sucked into it. What happens tomorrow depends on what we, Commodore, do to make it happen, not what somebody thinks might happen based on last year's numbers, or what they saw in a dream somewhere off in the blue sky above the clouds. We're still working *below* the clouds—" At which point the researcher would usually say, "Uh—thank you very much," hang up, and go off in search of some insecure marketers who felt they had to rely on industry surveys instead of their own originality.

By the end of August, I had most of the annual report

written and had gathered photographs from around the world. On the cover, we used the photograph of the lab technician removing a tube of wafers from an oven. In August I also had my first real meeting with Irving Gould, the man who'd rescued Jack from the brink of bankruptcy, major stockholder in the company, and chairman of the board. Irving was a handsome, sixtyish, cosmopolitan executive who was undoubtedly a world-class businessman. He owned his own container leasing corporation, called Interpool, which was similar to Sealand. He was perennially tan. His longish, light brown hair was stylishly swept back on both sides and on top. I always thought he had the calm, pleasant demeanor of a professional golfer, with a touch of royalty thrown in.

In addition to Toronto, where he was born, Irving maintained residences in New York across from Central Park, and in the Bahamas where he kept a seventy-foot yacht complete with captain and crew. He was an avid diver and prided himself on diving for his own lobsters. I was once told he was so rich, he had trouble spending the interest. His personal wealth was figured variously at between $100 million and $250 million.

He was a serious collector of Oriental art, and was one of the first collectors to begin accumulating Japanese netsukes before their value started skyrocketing. Netsukes are small, distinctive carvings in wood or ivory (presumably, no two are alike), which were used in samurai days by Japanese men to hold their purse-bags inside their sashes. The drawstring of their money bags was threaded through the netsuke, and when the string was drawn tight the purse was closed and the netsuke could be wrapped around their sashes, for easy carrying. All this because once upon a time the Japanese didn't have pockets.

Anyway, I once saw the netsukes when I spent some time with Jack at Irving's home. They were displayed in four small vertical cases that took up hardly any space at all. I have to admit I was surprised when Jack said they had an estimated value of over a million dollars. Irving also collected Oriental vases and other *objets d'art*.

I had first met him at the Consumer Electronics Show in Chicago, but only briefly. I next saw him at a special event I'd set up in New York, a donation of Commodore computers to the United Nations School. Irving made the presentation at the school, and we shot photos for the annual report, then had lunch at the United Nations with Mrs. Sylvia Fuhrman, special assistant to the Secretary General of the United Nations.

Irving was gracious, cordial—you might even say democratic. I never saw him flaunt his tremendous power and wealth.

Irving Gould was a mystery to us at Commodore. He had an uncanny knack for knowing more about the company than you'd ever expect, considering that we almost never saw him at Commodore offices. He must have memorized briefings from Jack (and from a few special sources he maintained inside the company). In analyst briefings he deftly fielded questions that included marketing strategy, technical issues, expansion plans, and financial results and projections. He was what a chairman should be: well-informed, approachable, charming, businesslike, concerned, interested, and smooth.

When he asked me how the annual report was coming, I told him it was pretty much on schedule and that I would be having a final meeting with Jack and Steven Greenberg in a week or so. Steven Greenberg was Commodore's investor-relations consultant and a personal friend and consultant—a flamboyant *consigliére*—to both Irving and Jack. He was also a major shareholder of the company, and wanted to be in on, or least briefed about, major decisions, sometimes to the chagrin of Commodore managers. He resembled a middle-aged Ben Franklin, with a bald pate fringed all around by a flowing shock of shoulder-length light gray hair. He even had Ben Franklin's nose.

My personal impression of Steven Greenberg includes a long list of adjectives: mercurial, moody, prying, invasive, dogged, flamboyant, colorful, temperamental, charming, creative, annoying, and many more. He had élan. He bragged about being a multimillionaire (partly from investing in client companies' stocks). He once invested in a disco roller-rink. Socially, he would probably be classed as a middle-aged jet-setter.

Steven was so intense and temperamental that he could be seen as either complicating or facilitating, depending on what he was involved in (and on your point of view). He was always fun, and sometimes dangerous. For example, on more than one occasion when we were chatting, I innocently let drop some piece of information he wasn't supposed to know about or be involved in. He would go running back to Jack or Irving to make a fuss, and then Jack would roar at me because I'd talked to Steven. On the other hand, not talking to Steven could result in an even bigger fuss and possibly some criticism from behind closed doors.

Around the company, some people called him a meddler. Jo Marinello nicknamed him Noodge. He had a habit of calling managers and demanding information. Once he created such a flap calling around the company that Jack issued a memorandum forbidding anyone in the company to talk with him or accept his phone calls, and directed that any incoming calls from Steven be referred directly to Jack.

Steven's main job was to interface with securities analysts and members of the financial press such as the *Wall Street Journal*. His company, Anametrics, was located in Rockefeller Center and what he did for us was promote our stock. In some circles, investor relations is seen as a sophisticated type of public relations. The target audience includes individual and institutional shareholders, stockbrokers, financial journalists, and most important, the securities analysts who follow certain companies or industries. Analysts are important because they're the ones who issue buy or sell recommendations, which stockbrokers and institutions rely on to make investment decisions.

Investor relations consultants have to conform to the rules and regulations of the Securities and Exchange Commission (SEC), which regulates the activities of publicly owned companies. These regulations also determine the format of company annual reports, which is why all annual reports contain essentially the same financial information.

Working with Steven wasn't the hardest part about doing the 1980 report, nor was it gathering the research or writing the report. The hardest part was getting Jack to approve the photograph for the cover. We met in Steven Greenberg's office in New York, and after about an hour selected a moody picture of a woman technician removing a cylinder of silicon wafers from a red-hot oven.

Writing the report was fairly straightforward. I just kept track of everything that was going on and wrote it like a journalist. The inside of the report included research, product and news photos, and our European friends contributed some excellent photos of the new CBM system in use. (Harald Speyer was a magician; he had full-color brochures with pictures of the CBM before the product was even off the assembly line.)

The financial figures came last, and they were outstanding. Our net income was $16.2 million or about 13 percent of net sales, with a gross profit margin of over 40 percent. Our sales had topped $100 million while I was with the company, reaching $125 million in fiscal 1980 compared to $71 million in 1979. Return on shareholders' equity exceeded 57 percent—giving Commodore one of the highest equity returns of *any* publicly owned corporation.

Commodore's stock reacted well. It soared to over $90 a share during September and was the darling of the American Stock Exchange. This was particularly significant, considering that Commodore stock had already split three-for-two twice during fiscal 1980, and was still climbing. It was estimated that 100 shares of Commodore stock purchased for $565 in 1969 were worth more than $100,000 by the end of 1980.

Commodore's 1980 Annual Report was published in September. Most people, including Jack and Irving, said it was Commodore's best annual report, in terms of writing and design. Of course, the numbers weren't so bad either, and this was only the beginning. While there was no way of knowing it at the time, it would be my privilege to serve on the management team that would take Commodore from under $100 million in sales to over $1 billion, in less than four years. This growth was anything but orderly. It was drastic, sudden, and filled with trauma.

Throughout the summer and fall of 1981, we had some more major changes in the U.S. organization. Commodore was growing up. We were moving away from the entrepreneur-managers and mavericks Jack had always favored to professional managers with experience in large, organization-bound companies. Jack approached these professionals with extreme skepticism and found himself giving long lectures over and over to bring them in line with The Religion.

Many of these new managers were brought in from the minicomputer industry. Several managers in their late thirties and forties came to Commodore from a minicomputer division which was disbanded at BASIC/FOUR, a Philadelphia area computer company. I called them the minicomputer gang. Bill Robinson, who later became president of Digilog (with much success), was hired as vice president in charge of marketing and sales, and Dick Powers was put in charge of national sales. Other middle managers included Dieter Ammon, the fast-talking, laugh-a-minute, German-born software director; and Frank McCullough, a stone-faced former salesman with a military demeanor and a wry sense of humor who fired off one-liners without cracking a smile.

About the same time, Dick Barton, who had been running manufacturing from Santa Clara, left to join a major semiconductor company, and Jerone Guinn was put in charge of manufacturing. Elton Southard took charge of semiconductor operations.

If I had been forced to gamble on which new vice presidents were going to make it big at Commodore, I would have said that Bill Robinson looked like a sure winner. He had piercing blue eyes and was an all-American manager in appearance, personality, and philosophy. His background included considerable experience in the minicomputer industry, as well as a stint with the CIA in Europe. He knew what intrigue and danger were all about, and he had a trait I can only describe as an extreme calm. Most people who've faced death and survived develop that calm. It's something in their eyes and in their attitude.

I've experienced it myself. If an older executive tried to intimidate me, just because he was older, I found myself thinking, "You never felt the hot steam of combat, or lay on your belly in the jungle, suddenly realizing the only thing between you and a bullet was a bunch of green leaves. You didn't parachute out of the sky, or sit on a stump in Vietnam and have a six-foot-long pit viper crawl out between your legs. You didn't risk your life." Thoughts like that give you an edge.

In high school I had a friend named John Ndavu, from Africa. Sometimes he laughed and told us about the time he killed a lion, with a spear. It was a manhood test. I think it was this characteristic that Jack could read in people's eyes. A quality. A calm. A type of fearlessness that comes from close brushes with death. He saw that quality in Bill Robinson. Everything about Bill suggested he would succeed.

There was only one problem: His marketing approach ran head-to-head against Jack's.

It was really a question of timing. Bill felt strongly that we should be taking the CBM to Fortune 500 companies and major corporations, but Jack felt that was premature. Our service/repair organization wasn't in place yet and couldn't support sales to corporations. We didn't have a networking system. Corporate customers need special support and we're not ready to give it, he said.

"You're a year too soon," Jack told Robinson, and told him to aim at the small business and professional market first. Maybe it was his experience selling business computers, but Bill kept returning to the corporate market. He maintained that a $5,000 CBM system could easily replace functions performed by systems costing $13,000 to $20,000 or higher. He was right, but Jack felt we weren't ready for that market. He wanted to aim at consumers, at individuals. He wanted to make sure we could handle word processing and electronic spreadsheets before we went into regression analysis.

Bill left the company after several months. As I understood it, he was asked to stay on but refused the terms.

Personally, I think Jack and Dick Sanford would have liked to keep him on ice until we were ready to follow through with our business marketing ambitions. However, the minicomputer gang stayed in place after Robinson left, and gave the company a business computer emphasis, at least for a while.

When Robinson left, Dick Sanford took over his sales and marketing responsibilities, with Dan Carter serving as second in command in the sales area. Dan was an excellent senior executive who later left Commodore to become president of Pertec.

We started selling *WordPro* for a while under an interim agreement, but *WordPro* was too expensive. So we switched to a British word processor called *Wordcraft*. We also sold *VisiCalc* briefly, but our software effort was kept to a bare minimum. Jack said, "We're a hardware company, not a software company." We would sell only enough software to support the machines.

Besides, we had to get our distribution working first. That was Commodore's next challenge in the U.S. The strategy was a radical turnabout. We were going to establish our own distribution network, with seven fully staffed regional centers located in major cities throughout the country. And we would do it like we did everything else—fast.

The plan was to move organizational functions to the East Coast and to set up regional warehouse distribution centers all around the United States. The regional centers would handle regional sales, warranty repairs, dealer relations, training, product warehousing and shipping, minor repair of defective units, and more. These regional support centers would be set up in seven locations: Boston, Valley Forge, Atlanta, Dallas, Chicago, Santa Ana, and Santa Clara.

It was a military-style approach. In the Army you have a brigade, several battalions, then companies, platoons, squads, and teams. We were doing the same thing. Company headquarters would function like a military support brigade, and the regional centers would be like tactical battalions. In theory, this would shorten and speed up the lines of communication and support between Commodore and its dealers.

Jack wanted to divide the United States into six or seven distribution regions and put a separate manager (a czar) in charge of each region. Each czar would run his region like a separate country and would theoretically control everything that went on there. The parent company (called Commodore Business Machines, Inc. in the U.S.) would be a service organization and provide such services as marketing, accounting, and other consolidated activities. The regions would get billed for their share of the cost of providing these administrative or creative functions.

"The regional managers will be czars," Jack explained. "Each region will be like a separate country." The country concept had worked internationally: set up a sales company in each country/market, put a local national manager in charge, and tailor marketing and support to each country.

In theory it sounded great. After all, it was working in Europe—which was why Jack wanted to try it in the States. In practice, when it finally got put into action in 1980 and 1981, it half worked and half didn't.

To begin with, it was difficult to draw hard and fast boundaries between regions because a large dealer in one region's territory might have stores in several states that covered different regions. To conform to the new distribution scheme, it was suggested to some dealers that they should stop expanding into other regions' states, or change their way of doing business. This didn't please them.

Also, some regional czars who were more aggressive than others encroached on neighboring regions that weren't doing such a good job helping dealers, and some dealers who didn't like working with their regional manager went to other regions. Above all, the cost of setting up and running seven different locations with seven different offices and warehouses meant products had to be shipped twice, once from the factory to the regional warehouse and again from the region to the dealer/store.

The way it was supposed to work, the regional warehouse would always have products in stock for quick 24-

hour delivery to local dealers; but since demand exceeded Commodore's manufacturing capacity, the warehouses were often out of stock and animosities developed. This was especially bad when a dealer sold a complete system (computer, disk drive, and printer), but the disk drive or printer was back-ordered for up to six months. The customer had to wait and wait, and the dealer had to stall and stall. Or when a dealer sold several systems to schools under Commodore's three-for-two giveaway policy and the free units couldn't be delivered until after school started, it created difficulties with the school's curriculum planning.

Sometimes, products which were available at the factory didn't get shipped to a region. Then we had a regional manager screaming for more products and a factory manager crying that he had too many products. The result was paralysis. Allocating products from the factory was always a major problem at Commodore, since demand invariably exceeded supply.

On the positive side, the regions provided close support, and the regions' sales representatives visited individual dealers on a round-robin basis to provide training, discuss problems, and demonstrate new software.

Jack and Dick Sanford were just beginning to put this network together in the fall of 1980. Setting up a total Commodore distribution system meant they had to cancel contracts with existing independent distributors who had been carrying the Commodore line. Some distributors were quite angry. All this compounded Commodore's dealer-relations problem because several large distributors also owned computer store chains or franchises.

Another consideration was Computerland, a franchise operation representing one of the largest groups of computer-store dealers in the U.S. Computerland wanted favored pricing because they purchased for their dealers. The only way they could sell Commodore equipment to their dealers at Commodore's standard dealer price, and still make their profit off the top, was if Commodore gave them favored pricing. After an uneasy relationship of several months, Commodore and Computerland finally parted company and

Commodore invited individual Computerland dealers to buy directly from Commodore if they wanted.

Unfortunately, the distributorships were canceled before the regions were up and running. Many dealers were waiting to find out how and where to get their Commodore computers, so they started stocking Apples instead. Over the years Apple had had its share of problems with distributors and dealers, but in 1980 Apple was doing well in dealer relations. In the personal computer market it was difficult to win back an inch of ground once you'd lost it. It was far easier to forge new ground than to try to take a bite out of Apple. And forge new ground was exactly what we were going to do.

PHOTOS

Author Michael Tomczyk, who spent more than a year in Vietnam, felt that his experiences in a real war gave him a definite edge in the Home Computer Wars. Here he is in a Viet Cong bunker complex near the end of the war in 1972.

The many faces of
Jack Tramiel

"Computers for the masses,
not the classes."

"The Japanese are coming, so we will become the Japanese. We have to compete with ourselves."

"Business is like sex: you have to be involved."

(Photos by Eisenberg. Photo lower right corner courtesy of hfd/The Weekly Home Furnishings Newspaper.)

Clockwise from top right: Tony Tokai, with Jack more than a dozen years; Jack with his son Sam a few days before leaving Commodore in January 1984; two "VIC Commandos," Neil Harris (left) and John Stockman; British marketer Kit Spencer; and a conclave of Commodorians at the January 1984 Consumer Electronics Show.

Clockwise from top: Bob Lane, President of Commodore for six months; Sig Hartmann, President of Commodore Software; the author showing the VIC to TV spokesman William Shatner; and the author and his wife Kim—married at a computer convention. (Photos of Bob Lane and Sig Hartmann courtesy of hfd/The Weekly Home Furnishings Newspaper.)

Jack Tramiel always saw business as a kind of war. In this 1982 caricature, Jack is shown as a smug naval commodore, blithely slashing prices of home computers. (Photo courtesy of hfd/The Weekly Home Furnishings Newspaper.)

SEVEN

"What's that?" someone asked.

"The VIC-20," I replied.

"The what?"

"The Gizmo of the Year."

"You mean Lemon of the Year! Har, har, har!" they all laughed. "Let's give it away to sell PETs!"

"Vixen!"

"Spirit!"

"Volkscomputer!"

"Wait a minute, wait a minute, we still need someone to launch it."

"Who?"

"How about the Little Red Hen?"

"No way. She only does bread."

"Hey, let's get Mikey!"

"Mikey won't like it. He doesn't like anything. Besides, he's a tumler!"

"He'll love it," said the Jack.

"He's right," said the Dormouse.

With a tumleresque shrug, I crawled to my feet and started to reach for the scroll.

"Beware the Jack Attack," warned a playing card. "He'll tear you to shribbons."

"Beware the shribbons," came the echo.

"Shribbons? What's that?" asked I.

"That's what's left after a Jack Attack."

"Don't worry," said the Jack. "You'll love it."

"He's right," said the Dormouse.

"A motto! You need to choose a motto!" they chanted.

"User friendly!" I heard myself say.

"Benutzefreundlichkeit," spoke the German.

They handed me the sacred scroll, laughing in the background. I gulped and scrawled my motto on the parchment.

"He likes it!" someone yelled. "Mikey likes it!"

"He's right," said the Dormouse.

Suddenly, a live grenade landed at my feet.

"Now it begins," warned the Dormouse.

In the distance, I could hear the sound of shribboning.

Grace Under Pressure:
The Real Story of the VIC-20

VIC-20 is a magic name today, but not in 1980. Back then, it was a threat. A joke. A toy. Something you find in a Crackerjack box. At Commodore, the minicomputer gang made great fun of it.

I was about to learn the true meaning of the childhood nursery rhyme about the Little Red Hen. That's when a bunch of executives poke fun at you for tackling a project and refuse to help in any way. But later when the project succeeds, they all want to claim credit and take it away from you. That's the Little Red Hen Syndrome.

In 1980, there were only Jack, myself, and a handful of others going around the barnyard asking, "Who will help us pick the wheat? Mill the grain? Bake the bread?"

"Not I."

"Not I."

"Not I."

The VIC had great significance to me; it was part of a lofty goal that went beyond personal or even corporate values. We were coming from behind with the world's least-likely dark-horse computer product. We had the chance to launch the world's first affordable home computer, to define the phrase *home computer* once and for all. If things went well, we might be able to turn computers into electronic appliances and sell them in the same places where real appliances are sold and, thereby, to enlist the entire world in the march of technology.

I didn't know that the VIC-20 couldn't succeed. Jack said we would succeed, and I believed him.

"Okay. I want to make sure the VIC turns out right," I told him. "Make me the VIC-20 product manager."

He shook his head no and said, "I don't believe in product managers." Then he went on to explain that his definition of product manager meant being totally in charge of a product from manufacturing—even the cost of components—to sales. I replied that if that was his definition I had to agree I couldn't fill the role. And the main reason was that half of those things he expected a product manager to do couldn't be done, because he forbade it.

By closing off the marketing staff from engineering and keeping us ignorant of cost-price information, Commodore made it difficult if not impossible for a marketing person, especially a young one like me, to fit Jack's definition of product manager and shepherd a major product.

Still, perhaps it was a test. Maybe Jack was trying to find out if I could overcome or sneak around the barriers. Or maybe my sheer chutzpah would convince him to make an exception and promote me from the rank of marketing strategist and *tumler* to VIC product manager. I vowed to keep pushing.

It was *Star Raiders* all over again. Jack would let me rise to Captain (never Commander), but if I slipped and made a mistake, or let an enemy ship penetrate my defenses, I'd be immediately relegated to the rank of Ship's Cook, which was no rank at all. And a fall would be breathtakingly fast.

Working at Commodore, or most computer companies for that matter, was like a real-life videogame. Make one mistake, lose one game, get shot once, and you're back to the beginning. Start over at Level 1.

I was going to have to fight my way past the playground bullies, survive a demotion, do battle with a corporate assassin, and experience the most dangerous Commodore experience of all, the dreaded Jack Attack.

My girlfriend Kim gave me a memento that carried me through these chaotic days. It was a gold bracelet inscribed with my favorite motto: *Courage is grace under pressure.* That was the best line Hemingway ever wrote. To me, it means smiling when someone shouts at you. Not flinching when the bullets (or computer chips) come zinging past your head. It means putting forth ideas (like the VIC) when no one believes in them but you. Making the right decision when being right means being scorned or ridiculed. It means Jack slaving over a half-built road with the Nazis yelling "Scheisskopf!" in his face, but always knowing and preserving his sense of self-worth.

"Scheisskopf!"

Jack once awoke in a hotel room in Berlin and heard two Germans yelling "Scheisskopf!" at each other. For a minute he imagined he was back in the camps. The cold sweat beaded on his forehead, and he was trembling.

"I thought I was over it," Jack later told me, "but that moment I really thought I was back in the camps." He smiled and there was a sudden soft poignance in his smile that only a few people have ever seen, or understood. The poignance is what Jack Tramiel was really all about. The fear of slipping back. Of repeating history. Of letting down a loyal comrade or losing the sense of family.

"You know," he once said, with a faraway look in his eye, "if I thought it would do any good, I'd take the money and buy food for the poor and hungry, but the food would be gone and the people would be hungry again. We have to do something more."

So he lowered the price of calculators and digital watches and computers so everyone could afford them and use them to make the world a little better, and he shared and set in motion a business religion that makes it possible to keep providing the newest technologies "for the masses, not the classes."

Making the best and latest technology so everyone could afford it is what he chose to do, and keep doing. That's why he insisted on the VIC-20. It was a computer for the masses, and it was one of the reasons I personally wanted to make sure the VIC-20 turned out right. I wanted to live in the future, too—not to forget the past, but because it's an exciting place to live. Making future technologies happen today—that's our only real Time Machine. We can't go to sleep and wake up a hundred years from now (at least not yet), so we have to compress those hundred years into a decade, and stay awake while it happens.

The phrase *user friendly* was seldom heard in 1980. Who'd ever heard of a friendly computer? Friendly computer? It seemed to be a contradiction in terms. Most magazine articles talked about user-friendly features, but when it came to computers, the word *friendly* was reserved for features the editors, hobbyists, and educators hoped would be developed *in the future.*

By September 1980, I was involved in a continuous communication with Tony Tokai over the future of the VIC-20. At the end of August I was asked to meet with the engineers and finalize the keyboard. It was an interesting meeting. To begin with, I knew practically nothing about engineering. We met in a small office in Santa Clara, located diagonally across from Jack's. There was a large greaseboard covering the wall, and as soon as the engineers had gathered I scrawled in large letters on the board: USER FRIENDLY.

"Any idea, any concept, any technical jargon or discussion or recommendation that does not conform to this phrase will not be discussed," I declared. "User friendly, user friendly, *user friendly*! That's our law."

The engineers shrugged their agreement, and we began to talk about the various features of the VIC keyboard. Almost immediately, one engineer launched into a long technical discussion arguing in favor of expanding the VIC along the lines of the ColorPET, which would have complicated the computer and delayed its introduction.

I pointed to the phrase on the wall and said, "That's not user friendly. We're here to define the VIC keyboard."

By asking some stupid questions, I found out that the numbered keys (0 to 9) could be used with the CONTROL key to change the color of the characters being displayed on the television screen. There were eight colors (white, black, red, light blue, purple, green, navy blue and yellow; but the full names of the colors wouldn't fit on the keys so we abbreviated them to WHT, BLK, RED, CYN, PUR, GRN, BLU, and YEL. CYN was my contribution; it stood for cyan

164

and was a carryover from my photography days, when blue filters were called cyan. We used cyan because it was the only short word we could think of that stood for light blue.

When I found out there were a couple of undefined keys, I insisted on including an English pound sign. I knew this was important to selling the VIC in Britain, Canada, and other countries. It meant we wouldn't have to change the keyboard to sell the VIC in countries that used pound currency. One of the things I always hated was the slowness with which computer companies introduced foreign keyboards for large overseas markets. Here was a chance to make a multiple-market keyboard, simply by adding the pound sign. Later, even Jack thought I was overdoing it by insisting on the pound sign, but Englishman Kit Spencer thought it was a great idea (naturally).

In that keyboard discussion it was also decreed that the VIC keyboard would be more like a real typewriter than the PET keyboard, which had an awkward programmer's keyboard minus the period. Our brilliant engineers even found a way to add upper- and lowercase letters, too (most computers, even Apple, had only capital letters). And of course there was the famous PET graphics character set, and a complete reverse character set as well. That meant the graphics on the computer could be displayed in color as either positive or negative images, which made it easier for users to design pictures.

There were also four programmable function keys—a real first for a low-priced computer, but there wasn't enough space in the VIC's ROM circuits to define the keys. The function keys were not predefined, but could be programmed in BASIC or machine language by users. To their credit, Tony Tokai and Yashi Terakura tried to define the keys to change colors and include a SOUND command, but they ran out of space and couldn't do it.

Not long after that meeting, someone came into my office and said, "We need someone to sign off on the keyboard." That meant me. I corrected an error or two and initialed the blueprint, but I was starting to get frustrated.

Except for Tony Tokai in Japan, there really wasn't anyone in charge of marketing the VIC. It rankled me that Jack wouldn't make me the VIC product manager, and it seemed like he and the others preferred having no one in charge to having me in charge. Over the coming years I would learn that it wasn't something to take personally. Commodore often left no one in charge of such things. It was part of the lean-staff philosophy. It was also part of the politics.

Understanding this kind of politics was still beyond me in 1980. I was having enough trouble keeping my shoes from wearing out. It was on one of my frequent trips to New York that I met Jack at the Helmsley Palace Hotel and mentioned that I had a small problem. In his characteristic way, he curled his lips into a pleasant smile, cocked his head in slow motion, looked at me sideways, and drawled in that Baltic baritone of his: "Ye-e-e-e-s?"

"I'd like to get a little more money. I know we agreed on a salary when I started, but I didn't think I'd be doing this much traveling and it's tough to keep up with—"

Jack exploded.

"We have a deal!" he yelled, half-shouting and half-spitting the words. The anger flashed in his eyes. (Boy, was he mad!)

"But—"

"A deal!"

I shrugged and persisted. I had to. My American Express bill was paid up but the little extras were killing me. Paying off my bills didn't leave much money for extras, and my ping-pong traveling was wearing holes in my wallet, and other things, too.

"But my shoes are wearing out and my suitcase is broken!" I blurted.

Jack sighed a huge exasperated sigh, shook his head, laughed scornfully, and said, "Then go buy some shoes and a new suitcase!"

"Okay!" I shouted back. "That's a good idea!" Then, more meekly: "I didn't think of that."

I grinned at my own foolishness, and Jack laughed, too, although his eyes still rebuked me for being so silly. We both realized I was still pretty green. I honestly didn't think

166

I had the rank to go out and buy something as presumptuous as a pair of shoes and a suitcase—after all, The Religion kept teaching us to be frugal—but Jack had assumed I had the rank and figured I would buy what I needed.

I left that meeting feeling for the first time that Jack's image of me and my authority was a bit higher than my own image of myself, in spite of the minor beating I got for asking for more money. I was still thinking of myself as a protégé, but Jack was thinking of me more as a functioning executive and expected me to behave accordingly. I had moved from learning to *tumlering* and now I was on my way to managing, and that meant becoming a real Commodorian. It was a grand realization.

But there was more to come. Much more.

The Japanese were coming, and we were going to outsmart them. We would do the unexpected. A surprise attack. An ambush. Guerilla warfare on a grand scale. We would take the battle to Japan before they could bring it to America.

Jack knew we didn't have to worry much about U.S. competition because no U.S. computer companies were as vertically integrated as Commodore, and we could beat them hands-down on manufacturing costs. But the Japanese were another story, not because they were vertically integrated, but because Japanese companies had a nasty (and successful) habit of pooling their resources before they attacked a foreign market, often with government support.

That's why we never referred to any single Japanese competitor. We just lumped them together and called them Japan, Inc. It wasn't unusual for several Japanese companies to get together under government sponsorship and form a cartel to attack a foreign market, sort of like the dukes of old England getting together to raise an army and attack France.

But we weren't going to wait for that to happen. Do you know what to do if you're hiking in the woods and a bear looms up in front of you? While he's standing there, snarling, all ten feet of him, waving those mauling claws, you take off your backpack, and *throw it down at his feet*. The bear stops to see what it is and you run like blazes for the nearest tree. While you're sitting in the tree admiring

167

the view, pretty soon the bear gets bored or frustrated and goes away to find a more cooperative dinner.

That's what we were doing in Japan, but instead of a backpack we were throwing down the VIC. We hoped to succeed because of a flaw in the Japanese business philosophy. They don't move quickly. They study, they analyze, they meet in committees, and only when they've reached a consensus and everyone agrees, do they finally move. And that's where Jack could run circles around them.

We knew there were several Japanese companies planning to introduce low-priced home computers in the $600 to $1,000 price range. Their target date was January 1981, at the Consumer Electronics Show in Las Vegas. By introducing the VIC first in Japan, we would cause the Japanese planners to screech to a dead halt, while they studied the impact on their competitive position. Clearly, they could not afford to manufacture a color computer, ship it to the States, pay customs duties as well as massive advertising and distribution costs, and still compete in the under $500 market, much less as low as $300.

Their reaction was predictable. They would stop and analyze. They would hold committee meetings. They would push back their timetables for at least six months. They would choose to fight the Computer Wars on a higher level where the profit margins are safer—in the $2,500 to $5,000 price range. At least that's what we hoped. We really didn't know if our plan would succeed. We were just arrogant enough to think so.

Know your enemy. Think like your enemy. Fight like your enemy. Patton studied his enemies inside out. When he defeated Rommel's army in North Africa, he yelled on the battlefield, "I read your book!" *I read your book.*

As the *unofficial* VIC product manager, it was logical for me to go read the enemy's book in Japan, and to be there when Commodore Japan introduced the VIC-1001. It was the opening volley of the Home Computer Wars and I was actually going to be there. But I resisted the temptation to be smug, for in business Japan is a large and clever bear, and a worthy international adversary.

168

I was told I was going to Japan with just a few days' notice. Tony Tokai said, "Come on down!" Dick Sanford informed me it was official; and Jack told me why—to confer with Tony and gauge the Japanese reaction. He also told me to use my nose to pick up any ideas I could about how the Japanese are designing and marketing computers.

"Use your nose," Jack instructed me. By this time, he was talking a lot about my marketing nose and was beginning to tease me about being able to smell what a consumer wants in a product. It was a terrific compliment because, prior to this, the only person he said had a nose for the future was himself.

So off I went to Tokyo. It was a nostalgic return. I'd been to Tokyo several times in the early 1970s while stationed in the Far East so I didn't have much trouble getting around. However, most of the signs were still in Japanese characters only, not in the English (Roman) alphabet. On the way to the Hotel Okura, I relaxed while waiting for the time zones and my jet lag to catch up with each other.

"Bee-ee-ee-eep!" The horn woke me out of a daydream.

The taxi driver zipped neatly to a halt and told me we were there. I paid him and slammed the door as I got out. It was my worst faux pas in Japan. Japanese cab drivers can close the door from the front seat and don't like it when you do it yourself, but I kept forgetting and trying to slam the door.

Commodore's Tokyo office was hidden deep in the recesses of a small unassuming building that looked to me like a four-story Philadelphia apartment house. To economize on space, there was a special garage located underground which you reached by driving your car onto a car elevator which took the car downstairs. The elevator floor was a motorized pedestal which rotated to let the car in or out at the right angle. Space was tight in Tokyo.

Inside, I met Taro (Tony) Tokai, the influential czar of Commodore Japan. He had been Jack's friend and business associate for more than twelve years, and was more like an adopted son than anyone in the company. He was in fact the linchpin in the Far East negotiation, contracting, and manufacturing process.

He shared Jack Tramiel's love of classy cars, had the driving habits of a race-car driver, and owned a shiny black Datsun 280Z in 1980 (later discarded as passé).

Physically, he looked a little like Nguyen Cao Ky, the stylish Vietnamese general. He was so thin he looked gaunt and everyone was constantly worrying about his health just because he was so slender. He had a long, sober face, expressive eyes, a thin mustache, and long hair with a tinge of gray just beginning to appear. You leaned toward him because he spoke his fluent colloquial English in a soft, deep voice. He had the ability to sit in a meeting for long periods of time without saying a word, then offer, in a single sentence, an impressive synthesis of the problem.

Periodically, Tony would turn out new product reports, the only documents in the company that summarized what new products we were planning to purchase, subcontract, or manufacture. These reports were highly confidential, but I was privileged to receive them, either from Jack or from Tony, and in this way kept up on most new product developments.

Tony was to become a terrific friend and confidant who helped me—even from the other side of the world— through some rough political times over the years. He was cosmopolitan, quick to laugh, and the kind of friend who would blink once and step in front of you to take a bullet if the occasion demanded.

That day, we discussed various aspects of the VIC with Yashi Terakura, the glib engineer I'd met at Hanover Fair in Germany. Yash was in charge of Japanese engineering and was coordinating VIC development between U.S. engineers and his own group. We discussed a wide range of VIC-related topics, including such things as how to number the function keys (we settled on f1 through f8), the color of the case (ivory), keys (chocolate brown), and function keys (mustard).

I kept stressing user-friendliness. Tony teased me about my obsession, but he shared it too, and we vowed that we

170

marketers, east and west, would carry the user-friendliness banner. When Tony and I, in a moment of friendly euphoria, descended on Yash Terakura to tell him the VIC *had* to be friendly, Yash cocked his eyebrows, smirked, and looked up from his workbench with a marvelous innocent expression and said, "Of course the VIC will be a friendly computer. I am a friendly engineer!" Yashi kept his word.

That evening, we went to a terrific dinner and I was introduced to a special delicacy called *Saza-e*, which is made by removing a conch from its shell, boiling it in a soup, putting the concoction back in the shell and serving it that way. Now, sea worm in the conch-shell isn't quite as elegant as oysters on the half-shell, but it is delicious. The multicourse meal continued with several other seafood dishes, and afterwards we went to a *pachinko* parlor, the Japanese equivalent of a video arcade. The spirits were with me that night because I won lots of chips at video poker, but the chips are only good for videogames (you can't cash them in for anything), and I wound up giving most of them away when we left.

The next day, Tony took me on a tour of a fabulous vertical shopping center which was several floors high and specialized in computer stores. There I was shocked to discover nearly a dozen low-priced Japanese personal computers all in color, all impressive, and all potentially targeted at the U.S. marketplace.

Every time I gasped at a new computer, Tony would give me a sidelong glance and say, "Ne?" which is sort of like saying, "Oh, yeah?" It was obvious that Tony was already fighting hand to hand in the trenches, while those of us in North America and Europe were still unscathed.

Most impressive among the small computers was NEC (Nippon Electric Corporation), which in a few short months had become the leading personal computer in Japan. It was widely expected in Tokyo that NEC would assume a similar leadership position in the U.S.

Ironically, Tony told me Commodore once had had over half the personal computer market in Japan. Our market share shrank rapidly to 15 percent and below as more

Japanese computers were introduced and companies like NEC captured the home market.

Luckily, NEC—which did sell a terrific computer—would have extreme difficulty penetrating the U.S. marketplace. Like most Japanese companies, they just couldn't get the right mix of product, price, software, advertising, and retail distribution. Part of their problem was cultural, part was a difference in business styles. But I think most of NEC's problem came from not having talented U.S. marketers on their staff, marketers who understood the home computer market and knew how to help them break into it. Of course, there weren't any experienced marketers in the early 1980s, so it wasn't the fault of the Japanese. Those of us who would pioneer the market were still learning how to do it.

There were other computers, too. Sharp was impressive. So were the Apple clones which were already being sold in Japan. Those Apple-compatible copies, really illegal rip-offs, later gave rise to several lawsuits which helped define and strengthen U.S. patent and copyright laws as they apply to computers.

The launch of the VIC took place at Seibu Department Store in downtown Tokyo, a huge, prestigious store comparable to Bloomingdale's or Bamberger's, with classy merchandise displayed on several floors all connected by elevators and escalators. What surprised me was how busy the store was on a weekday.

Most of one floor had been turned into a computer show (modest by U.S. standards but large for Tokyo), and about a hundred companies had exhibits. Right across from the Commodore booth was the Okidata booth. They were showing a stunning, full-color printer which I predicted would eventually become popular in the states. Commodore was showing the VIC-1001 which was (besides NEC) the only computer in Japan which could be used in either English or Japanese. Instead of upper- and lowercase letters, the VIC-1001 keyboard had uppercase English letters and a separate Japanese alphabet, along with most of the other features of the VIC-20. I could almost hear the Japanese computer companies gasp when they saw the VIC's low, low price.

The booth was crowded but not overwhelmed, and the response from dealers was excellent. Tony received orders for over a thousand units the first day, which was fantastic in 1980 when the entire world population of personal computers was only a few hundred thousand. Jack was reassured long distance that his winky-dinky 5K 22-column color home computer was a hit.

When I arrived back in the States, I had a pleasant surprise. It was almost time to review my compensation. Jack was beginning to tease me about how little he was paying me (I guess he thought he was getting his money's worth), but we both remembered his promise to "make it up to me in six months" if I worked hard and fulfilled what we both felt was my potential to become a major or colonel in Jack's eccentric army.

My six months were almost up—October 14 was the magic date. By now I was a full-fledged member of the Commodore team. I had one whole annual report under my belt. I had survived one staffing purge. And I was deeply involved with the VIC-20, the world's first true home computer. I wanted desperately to be the VIC product manager, and everyone was treating me like I already was (even Jack), but I wanted Jack to make it official.

I didn't want to mention salary until we reached the magic date, because Jack, among his other talents, had a good memory. He never forgot a personal promise or commitment. Months and even years could pass, but if Jack made a promise he always strove to keep it, and he had some sort of internal alarm clock that started ringing when it came time to keep the promise.

One day he casually said to me, "Michael, we have to do something about your compensation. Tell me, which is more important to a young executive, the present or the future?"

"What do you mean?"

"What I mean is you can have stock, which is the future, or you can have cash, which is today. I want to give you $50,000 every year for five years, and I'll give it to you in a combination of salary and stock, but you have to tell me which is more important to you. Think about it," he advised. "But you have to tell me this week."

I nodded and went off to do my homework. By now I'd learned to do homework when dealing with Jack because to deal with him in the blind was like choosing curtain number three on "Let's Make A Deal." The curtain would open and you'd either win a trip to Europe or ten cans of fruit cocktail.

Negotiating a compensation package at Commodore was tricky. Typically, Jack asked what you expected to make, and if you asked for too much, he was apt to make you a vice president and give you a three-month honeymoon. If you survived, fine; but if you stumbled, or tripped, or stammered in a meeting, or developed a nervous tic in your eye, Jack would think to himself how much he was overpaying you and come swooping down out of nowhere exactly three months later—to the hour—and oversee your hasty departure, or, on rare occasions, give you a lower job.

Many executives thought Jack was kidding when he said, "I'll give you six months" or thirty days or whatever. They seldom felt he meant it, because at most companies when you're in, you're in, even if you screw up and lose money and fall asleep at your desk every day.

On the other hand, if you didn't ask for enough money, you found yourself working 16-hour days, coming in on weekends, going without vacations, bickering with your wife, neglecting your children, and generally sacrificing your life to Commodore without getting paid to be a bond slave.

So there it was. I had a chance to be a honeymooner, a bond slave, or a Commodore millionaire. It was a unique opportunity, especially the part about stock options. In 1980 about thirty Commodore executives had stock options, world-wide. It was one way of identifying who was a Commodorian and who wasn't, although not all Commodorians received options.

As part of my homework, I went to the best two compensation experts in the company, Dick Sanford and Greg Pratt. Both were extremely open and generous when it came to coaching new disciples. They had already welcomed me into the Commodore fraternity and always gave me the respect and autonomy I needed to make things happen.

They told me Jack likes young executives to go for stock instead of salary. Stock is where the real money is because if everyone works hard, the company succeeds and the stock goes up. Also, taking stock made a young executive an owner of the company and made him work harder to make the total company succeed.

I remembered that an early mentor of mine, O. John Haering, had said, "If you ever have the chance, go for equity. Equity, equity, equity. That's where you make money. Nobody gets rich just on salary."

I heaved a deep sigh and sharpened my pencil. The Commodore stock plan was crazy. I'd read about it in the annual report and SEC 10K filings. Under the plan, Commodore would grant me an option to buy stock, say a thousand shares, at a certain price. That meant I could buy 200 shares every year at my special option price. The only catch was, I had to wait one year before I bought my first 200 shares, then I had to wait another two years after it was registered before I could sell it. This would happen five times because it was a five-year plan. It meant I wouldn't be able to sell my last 200 shares for seven years.

As if the waiting time wasn't long enough, the Commodore plan required us to *pay taxes* on the difference between the price we bought the stock at (the option price) and the price of the stock on the day we bought it. That meant we had to buy the stock, pay taxes on our paper profit, and then wait two years before we could sell it. The taxes alone could amount to tens of thousands of dollars. To soften the blow, bank loans were arranged to help buy our stock and pay taxes, and of course we had to pay interest on the loans.

Supposedly, there were fortunes to be made, although you had to look hard to find out how. Over the years, the splitting and rising of Commodore stock gave option holders the right to buy thousands of shares for as little as five dollars, or in some cases, less than a dollar a share. In September 1980, Commodore topped $90 a share on the American Stock Exchange. Some old-timers already had options to buy stock at under $5 a share.

I met Jack in Santa Clara later that week and flew back to the East Coast with Jack and Sam Tramiel on a commercial flight. Jack insisted on flying coach because he didn't like to waste money on first-class tickets. He expected his employees to pinch pennies when traveling, and he practiced what he preached.

It took the whole trip for us to negotiate my compensation formula. Basically, it boiled down to this: I could take a large salary and a five-year option to buy 1000 shares of stock at $90 a share, or I could take a smaller salary and the same amount of stock at a lower option price.

I decided to take a medium salary and a medium price. The Golden Handcuffs snapped shut around my wrists. That's what the top executives called Commodore's executive compensation plan: The Golden Handcuffs. They were generous by anyone's standard—especially with Commodore's stock going almost straight up. But it took seven years to collect all the benefits from the stock plan, and if you lasted that long, it locked you into the company. Not many lasted that long. Me, I was an optimist.

A week later, I was back in Santa Clara and Jack walked over to a nearby restaurant with me. The sun was bright and Jack was wearing a short-sleeved knit shirt. He was beaming a lot and there was a Polish gremlin lurking in his eyes, hiding some secret mischief, perhaps. Contrary to what some people write in the press, Jack's eyes gleam more often with mischief than with rage.

"Well, Michael, you now have three thousand shares," he said, arching one eyebrow. "We just tripled your options."

I was startled, but still wary. Jack sometimes rewarded people on the spur of the moment, but I knew he wouldn't just give me three times more options because when he made a deal he never changed it, up *or* down.

"What do you mean?" I asked.

"The board of directors just voted a three-for-one split, effective October first. They also approved your options."

It was terrific news, but I wasn't counting any golden eggs yet because I still had a year to wait before I could buy my first stock, and two years after that to register it. Still, it was reassuring to know the stock was on a fast track, splitting and rising again and again.

We had lunch sitting on stools at the counter because there weren't any booths (Jack ordered chili). There, munching our lunch, I asked him about pricing. "How do you determine the price of a product so you make a suitable profit?"

"As a rule of thumb, the retail price is three times the cost. That should cover the cost of making the product and all the extra costs like customs, shipping, warehousing."

It was an important guideline, but Jack made it clear that it wasn't cast in stone. If the home computer market took off, everything would change.

"We have to learn how to live on low margins," he predicted. "The PET and CBM are making us lazy. It's nice to sell five thousand dollar systems but we have to sell to the masses, not the classes. We have to learn how to sell in volume—*big* volume—and that means we have to learn to make money on lower margins."

He talked about the need to cut costs and to move into new channels of distribution.

"How do you think I'm doing?" I angled. "I know you just gave me stock options so I must be doing okay, but how about the business side? Any advice?"

"Just keep doing what you're doing," he said, taking a spoonful of chili. Then he smiled with his eyes.

With Jack's blessing, I continued to bombard him and everyone else with memos about the VIC. Most of these memos referred to the VIC as Vixen, its engineering code name. I wrote memos on every aspect of the VIC. Memos on names, memos on features, on design, accessories, marketing, advertising, staffing. Memos on memos.

In one lengthy marketing report, I described the VIC as a bridge between hobbyists and home users. Until now, hobbyists and educators bought most of the personal computers that were being sold, but in thousands instead of millions. We needed to jump into the home market if we wanted to make the home computer revolution happen. Unfortunately, there was a huge gap between the hobbyists who liked to get inside and *understand* the machine, and the home users who just wanted to *use* the machine like a typewriter or calculator. The VIC would bridge the gap.

At this time, Commodore was the second or third leading computer company (behind Radio Shack and Apple), with over 150,000 computers sold. Atari and Texas Instruments hadn't caught on yet. The winners were still undecided.

The first company to break out of the pack and sell a million computers would be the winner, and getting computers into the mass market was the key. If Commodore could capture the mass market, even with a starter computer like the VIC-20, we could capture the personal computer market, too, because most VIC-20 owners would automatically move up to larger Commodore computers when they outgrew their VIC. But how could we break open the home market?

There were three reasons why home users weren't accepting computers:

1. The price was too high. $600 was the lowest price of a home computer, and we at Commodore felt $300 was the price barrier we had to break before consumers would start buying computers in large quantities.
2. Computers were perceived as unfriendly and hard to use. This was a function of design and promotion. The VIC-20 scored well on friendliness.
3. Computers were not being marketed or distributed as consumer items. To become a consumer item or an appliance, a product has to be sold where appliances are sold.

We had to overcome these obstacles, and we were already on our way with the $300 price point. Overcoming reasons two and three would be more difficult, but it had been done with similar products in the recent past. At one time, calculators were expensive, hard to use, and not aimed at general consumers. Now calculators are part of our culture. We could do the same thing with computers.

The videogame craze could help us, too, because videogames were getting people used to connecting electronic gadgets to their television sets. Without videogames, I doubt that computers would have caught on as fast as they did. In this sense, the VIC would be a bridge between videogame machines, which were enormously successful, and personal computers, which were still just beginning to catch on.

In 1980, videogame machines were sold in the millions, but personal computers were still being sold in the hundreds of thousands. I started pressing for an advertising theme that would position the VIC-20 head to head against the videogame machines.

"Nobody will buy a videogame machine if they can get a computer for the same price, because computers can play games, too!" I said. "All we have to do is ask the consumers, 'Why buy a game machine when you can get a computer for the same price?' " This later became our VIC-20 advertising slogan.

My memo bombardment wasn't limited to marketing and design issues. I suggested various types of product-marketing organizations we should develop to support the VIC-20—software programmers, technicians, advertising people, and a user hotline. I slyly asked Jack to let me know which of these functions should *not* report directly to me.

I also started drawing diagrams of what a complete VIC *system* would look like, and made a strong point that we weren't just selling VICs. We were selling whole systems, because as soon as someone bought a VIC they'd also buy a joystick, Datassette recorder or disk drive, printer and—possibly—a relatively new device called a *modem*, for connecting their computer to a telephone. This meant we weren't really selling a $300 product. We were selling $1,000 home computer *systems*.

As early as June 1980, I proposed using the VIC for telecommunications, telling Jack: "We need a low-priced modem to go with the VIC but most modems are priced over $400. I'd like to get one developed that we can sell for under $100." This was a premature and (some people thought) frivolous suggestion. But I was thinking in the future. I was doing what Jack said and using my nose. A year later, Jack would remember my suggestion when I took the idea to him again.

By the middle of October, most of the U.S. executives were talking about *my* product. Tony Tokai was treating me like the unofficial product marketing manager. Dick Sanford had become a believer and was saying we would sell VIC-20s "like popcorn." Even Jack was expecting me to act like a product manager. But I still wasn't the VIC product manager, *officially.* And that's what I wanted most. Jack surprised me again.

By early October, our regions were all in place, located in Costa Mesa and Santa Clara, California; Atlanta; Chicago; Norristown, Pennsylvania; Dallas; and Boston. Among our regional czars were John Gould, Al Ciaglia, Jerry Ziegler, and Tom Priestley. (Tom later defected to the Japanese and became general manager for NEC in the U.S.)

Bill Robinson was in charge of sales and marketing. After Robinson's departure in December, Dick Sanford assumed the sales job, with Dan Carter serving as second in command in the sales area. Dan was an excellent senior executive who later left Commodore to become president of Pertec. The always-capable Ethel Burkhart ran sales administration, along with Bill Crouch. Jim Scarduzio handled credit administration.

In October, Dick Sanford held his first conference to get the U.S. regional czars up to speed. I went over to the meeting, held in the basement of the Valley Forge Sheraton, to hear Jack's opening address. The next thing I knew, Jack was standing at the podium saying something like, "Gentlemen, there is a young man named Michael Tomczyk who many of you have come to know especially in the area of marketing. Michael probably knows more about the details of what's happening in the company today than I do, because he looks at things like a journalist, and he had to find out the details of how the company works when he did the annual report." He said a few things about my background in marketing and then I heard him say, "And so, I want to announce today that Michael is becoming director of marketing for the United States."

My head dropped straight down on the table, and by the time I straightened up, all the managers were swarming around congratulating me while I was still trying to figure out what had happened. I leaped to my feet to ask Jack what was going on, but he just breezed past me and said, "I'll see you in two weeks." Then he was gone and I was director of marketing.

That's the way it happened at Commodore. One day I was assistant to the president, next marketing strategist, and soon director of marketing.

Dick Sanford told me to "Go get 'em." Bill Robinson was a trifle more wary of me, because he knew I was close to Jack, and he and Jack were having philosophical differences.

During the next few months we were under great pressure to drive ahead toward our various military objectives, and we all had to cope with extraordinary hour-by-hour change. We weren't growing like a normal company. As soon as we formed a new skin we had to break out of it and grow a new one; and as tough-skinned as we all were, there were constant pressures and politics.

Dick Sanford, Bill Robinson, Dick Powers, and their troops were all working overtime to bring our new Commodore regions up to speed. Their problems ranged from paying bills and collecting receivables (which becomes increasingly difficult the faster you grow), to allocating products from the Far East and stocking enough equipment at each regional warehouse.

Dieter Ammon and Paul Goheen were putting together a fledgling software licensing effort for the PET/CBM, and Frank McCullough was working training and sales support.

The regional managers struggled to consolidate their territories, get enough products to sell, and hire competent staffs. Their day-to-day problems involved keeping their dealers happy, trying to sell computers without disk drives (or vice versa), placating disgruntled dealers, signing up new ones, and providing fast technical service and training support across several states.

In marketing, it was like starting over from scratch. We already had an ad campaign underway, but it was a weak campaign. We experimented with regional Commodore computer shows. We attended at least one national computer convention *per month* from September to January. We reconstituted our marketing staff. We got ready to launch the VIC-20, a massive undertaking by itself.

I hired several new young people to help support our marketing effort. Sheila deSimone became my administrative assistant and, later, a marketing assistant. Cheryl Wilhelm also joined as a marketing assistant, along with Joe Devlin, who edited our Commodore magazine. We started off calling the magazine *Interface*, but in deference to our friends at *Interface Age* we changed the name to *Commodore Microcomputing*. I also hired John Stockman, a bright young student from Drexel University, to serve as my assistant under a six-month internship.

Everyone was hired within a month. Most of the marketing people were in their twenties and thirties. No one was overpaid, but everyone was excited to be involved with personal computers. Everyone got my standard briefing on what it means to be a Commodorian, and what it means to work at Commodore—a quick capsule of Jack's management philosophy and a strict warning that anyone who hates change or turmoil shouldn't work at Commodore.

About this time, a senior sales executive was fired. The executive had been newly hired by Bill Robinson and was on a fact-finding trip to Santa Clara when he made the mistake of dropping in to see Jack. Jack started grilling the executive on what he was doing at Commodore and the executive stuttered and stammered around, then beat a hasty retreat. Jack later labeled him a *shlub* and he was gone in two months.

Also someone hired a high-level manager without consulting Jack, and Jack reversed the decision. The poor manager showed up to find out he didn't have a job, after all.

Both events were examples of Commodore no-nos. You don't add new managers unless you can justify them, and even then, the managers themselves had better be able to explain what their job is and how they contribute to the organization. My young staff was concerned about these goings-on, and about the precipitous departure of the last marketing department. I assured them their jobs were secure and said they shouldn't worry.

"Look," I joked, "when you come to Commodore, they throw you a champagne party if you last thirty days, your pension plan gets vested in six weeks, and at the end of a year they give you a gold watch!" That line soon became a standard response for new employees who asked old-timers about such things as fringe benefits and pension plans.

Before long, we were all too busy to worry about such goings-on. I turned my attention to advertising, public relations, conventions and special events, and of course, the VIC-20.

By the end of 1980 we were strongly promoting the CBM (strongly for Commodore, that is) with print ads in most business and computer magazines. The ads were in color but weren't sophisticated. They showed a CBM system and bore the slogan "The Great American Solution Machine" with the name Commodore bannered across the bottom in red, white, and blue letters ringed with silver to make them look metallic. Jack pointed out that it didn't make any sense running color ads showing the CBM system, since the CBM colors were black and white. As a result we wound up paying for full-color ads that looked black and white. "If you're going to pay for color," he said, "use color. Otherwise run black and white ads."

Public relations and conventions were being handled by the inimitable Marge Jillett, a spritely Irish leprechaun who exuded personality and enthusiasm. During 1980 and 1981 she was a ubiquitous and effervescent presence, arranging everything from brochures and news releases to seminars and conventions. Working closely with Dick Sanford, she set up Commodore's experimental computer fairs, which attracted more than 16,000 people in Philadelphia on December 13 and 14, 1980, and drew the same attendance in Boston during February. Speakers included Al Rosen, a long-time PET supporter and president of MicroPhys; Dr. Ludwig Braun, another PET booster from Stonybrook University; and Bob Crowell, president and founder of one of the nation's first and most successful computer retail operations. Larry Bowa, shortstop for the world champion Philadelphia Phillies, was there to sign autographs.

The hardest part of those shows was uncrating and setting up the CBM systems. We all pitched in, from the highest-ranking managers to the lowest-ranking plebes. It was a rare time at Commodore. In those days we all had to set up and take down convention exhibits. Later, as we grew larger, an elite group of top managers developed. You could tell who they were because they stood around in suits or sports jackets watching everyone else *do* the work. It was the opposite of Jack's admonition that everyone, especially managers, should get *involved.*

Marge Jillett's most shining hour came in November 1980 at the COMDEX Show, when more than 80 people died in a tragic fire at the MGM Grand Hotel in Las Vegas. It was the second deadliest hotel fire in U.S. history, and it struck at the height of the convention when the hotel was packed with computer professionals.

As news of the fire spread, calls poured in from concerned relatives and friends. Marge organized a Commodore Command Center in the East Hall of the Convention Center, where vital information for the evacuees, their relatives, the police, and Red Cross could be gathered and processed. With the consent and encouragement of Jack Tramiel, the Commodore staff worked through the night. They took seven computer systems from the COMDEX booth to use at the command center, leaving only one person and a hand-scrawled sign to represent Commodore on the last day of the convention.

Marge recruited volunteers to enter information about the condition and whereabouts of the victims and to answer the countless phone calls. Everyone pitched in.

The fire itself was a horror. Stu Martin, who owned the

rights to *WordPro* software, told me how he leaned out his hotel room window, trying to catch gasps of fresh air between the billowing green clouds of poisonous smoke. More than once he tried to reach the stairway, knocking out two teeth while groping his way through the smoke-filled corridor. Once, he reached the stairwell and found someone sitting upright against the wall at the top of the stairs. The person was dead, suffocated from the smoke and noxious fumes. Stu made his way back to his room and waited there to be rescued.

In 1980, fire seemed to be haunting the computer industry. A short time after the MGM fire, a similar fire occurred at Stouffer's in Boston and one of the speakers at our Commodore fair was killed.

But almost no one knew about the most harrowing incident of all. It wasn't reported in the press, it wasn't even widely discussed in the company. It was the near-fatal crash of the Commodore PET Jet. It happened in midair on a freezing night in September 1980.

Jack, Dick Sanford, Dick Powers, Ken Hollandsworth, and two software authors from Chicago were on their way to California. They were flying the software authors to California to negotiate a contract, and they thought it'd be more impressive to give them a ride on the corporate jet.

The jet caught fire in midflight, at twenty thousand feet. The wiring that led to the coffee maker was faulty, and over many flights it had worn away and finally shorted out. They didn't smell the smoke until it was too late. They grabbed the fire extinguishers, but they didn't work. Within minutes, the entire right side of the jet was engulfed in flames. The jet shot through the sky like a Roman candle. The fire licked and danced in the windows. Only the thin air and altitude kept the whole thing from exploding in midair. Smoke began to fill the cabin.

Most horrifying of all, no airports in the area could handle their landing. They needed a long runway because the electrical systems were shot, and they couldn't brake by reversing the engines. Stranded in the sky, the pilot and co-pilot struggled to control the craft, and to find an airport before they burned alive. By all accounts the fire should have hit the fuel tanks and exploded. They were in the air and on fire for a total of forty-five minutes.

Before long, the entire cabin was filled with dense black smoke. The passengers huddled on the floor and tried to breathe. Dick Sanford noticed Jack wasn't handling the smoke well and made him stand up and breathe through the air from one of the air vents.

Dick later told me he'd noticed that some of the light metal trim on the right side of the jet had started to melt, and he thought to himself, "That's all I need. It's bad enough I'm going to die, but I have to die listening to all these men screaming when that hot metal starts falling on them." Dick was as tough in a crisis as he was in the office.

The two pilots manhandled the small jet onto the runway at Des Moines and rammed down the manual brakes as they skidded, still in flames and filled with smoke. The jet reached the end of the runway and kept going on the grass. The electrical systems were shot.

The pilots looked up, saw a post sticking up out of the ground. If they hit it at this speed, the post would slice the jet in half. At the last minute, they veered to the right and skidded to a stop. Everyone piled out as the emergency teams rushed in to extinguish the fire. They were shaken, but alive.

After the crash, they headed for the lounge. Drinks all around. Commodore had almost lost its founder and three vice presidents. The passengers handled the crash very differently. Dick Sanford was the most stoic of them all, although to me it seemed he began to ponder his own mortality and lifestyle more deeply. Ken Hollandsworth refused to fly on the PET Jet anymore. Dick Powers was the most philosophical of the group. Ironically, later in 1981 he developed an ear infection which minimized his flying and precipitated his departure from Commodore.

Jack took the experience as a message from God. A week later I saw him in his office. He still had a large red bloodspot on his left eye from the smoke. "It was a message," he said with conviction. "God was telling me, 'Don't fly so high.' "

He was talking about the value of his stock in Commodore, which had risen to over $50 million when the stock topped $90 a share. By the late summer of 1980, it seemed that Jack was struggling to come to terms with the vast fortune that was suddenly his. Being a millionaire and then a multimillionaire was not strange for Jack because he'd been there before, lost it, and got it back. But being a fifty-million-aire was something different. It was as if it was too much to count, or spend, or even too much to conserve. For someone who'd pinched pennies his entire life, for someone who'd hit hard rock bottom more than once, for someone like that, becoming a fifty-million-aire was in some ways disorienting. For Jack it was a challenge to keep everything in perspective and keep moving toward the higher ideals he'd established.

I think there must come a point in every wealthy person's life when they've got all the money they need, and suddenly the money seems like an end in itself. Then reality sets in. For Jack, the reality was the near-fatal crash of the PET Jet.

The PET Jet wasn't completely destroyed in the crash. They were able to take what was left and rebuild it. Then they flew it for a few months, until they traded it in for a larger model.

After these various brushes with death, we regrouped and made some strong progress in the U.S. market with our older computers. However, it was becoming clear that we had more than enough managers to handle the various PET/CBM marketing chores. We needed someone to handle the new VIC-20 full-time and make sure it happened.

There was still laughter in the halls over the VIC. It was a toy. It was a premium. It wasn't even big enough to run word processing software. Or so they said. The mini-computer gang wasn't wrong; they were just more interested in minicomputers and business computers and 32K teaching machines. They were not consumer-product people. I told Jack and Dick Sanford I was more worried about the VIC-20 than about U.S. marketing. In two months we put most of the support functions in place and hired some excellent people.

Then one day a few months later, without warning, one of Dick's assistants came into my office and said, "I'm here to help you develop your business plan."

"Huh?"

"Your business plan. For the VIC. You have to write a three-page summary for the board of directors, describing what you plan to do with your product."

"My product?"

"Yeah. The VIC. How are you going to launch it? What's your timetable?"

I told him thanks but I didn't need help writing the summary. I already had several reams of old memos describing exactly what to do with the VIC. Now I was going to get my chance to make these plans come true. I put together a quick plan of attack (no cartoons on the cover of *this* memo), and the next thing I knew I was assigned full-time to the VIC-20. Dick Sanford let me print business cards for the January CES Show designating my title as VIC-20 product manager. Jack didn't object.

It didn't bother me that I was being shifted to my fourth job title since joining Commodore, all in less than one year. I used to joke with Greg Pratt that we were constantly riding the surf into shore, paddling back out to catch another wave and riding back in again. What made us different, what made us Commodorians, was that we kept paddling out to catch the next wave. Non-Commodorians either washed up on the beach and gave up, or tucked their surfboards under their arms and refused to go out again. I didn't mind catching the next wave, and the next, and the next. The ride back to shore was always worth it.

The January CES Show loomed up in front of me like a huge swell about to break, but in the distance you could just barely see the dorsal fins of the sharks—friends and foes alike—circling and circling and waiting for mistakes to be made. January 6 found me in Las Vegas for the Winter Consumer Electronics Show.

The most surprising thing about the January CES was the absence of any Japanese home computers. They simply didn't come. The lesson of the bear and the knapsack kept running through my mind. We had thrown the VIC-1001 into their laps and now they were puzzling over what to do next. It looked like Commodore had singlehandedly stopped the Japanese in their tracks. Hooray for us!

Like the last CES, the booth was again mostly given over to watches and calculators, and responsibility for the exhibit belonged to Ken Hollandsworth, who ran the small consumer products division. Ken was an erudite consultant-manager with considerable experience as a top-level consultant in the watch industry.

By the time the CES Show arrived, he had picked up on the VIC as a potential hit that could plump up his division sales and give him something to sink his teeth into. He began to lobby, very subtly, to get the VIC-20 product transferred to his division. That meant getting it away from the computer systems division, and from Dick Sanford.

I had to admit it made sense. The consumer division was already selling to stores like Woolworth's, and they had more experience dealing with mass-merchandising chains, most of whom weren't even carrying home computers yet. Besides, the systems division had its hands full with the PET/CBM, and they could still be allowed to sell VICs to computer dealers. This argument was bolstered by the systems division's lukewarm response to the VIC. "Why sell VICs for $300 each and have to spend the money for product support when we can sell $5,000 professional systems?" I've heard that argument again and again during my marketing career. It's the first warning signal of complacency, and complacency in marketing is what gets people buried in the sand.

The VIC was a hit at the show, but expressions of interest from major retailers were spurned for the time being. We couldn't gear up to make enough VICs to feed the mass market for several months yet, and we still planned to introduce the VIC through our existing computer stores first.

The VIC exhibit at the booth was relatively small. We

used Japanese VICs with U.S. keyboards and VIC-20 nameplates, and demonstrated mostly Japanese games which had been hand-carried to the states by Tony and Yash. For literature, we handed out a comprehensive eight-page newsletter which I wrote covering the features of the VIC-20. I figured with all the literature being flapped against people's doors at the show, they might be more inclined to read a brochure that looked like a newsletter. I was right. The newsletter described "How The VIC Was Born" and gave "A Tour Of The VIC-20 Keyboard." It also listed "VIC System Peripherals" and made a point-by-point comparison against our nearest rivals: Atari and Radio Shack.

The biggest breakthrough was price: $299.95. We had broken the $300 price barrier, less than nine months from the day Jack had told us in Europe that he wanted a $300 color computer. It was an amazing speed record for an industry that had previously moved in 18-month cycles. Nobody in the industry could beat us on price/performance.

The Atari 400 was priced at $600. We beat them hands-down on price. The Atari had 16K memory, but it had a flat plastic membrane instead of a real keyboard and it looked more like a toy than a computer. It was no contest.

The new Radio Shack Color Computer was being highly touted, too, but the Color Computer had only 4K to the VIC's 5K memory, was less expandable, and had a calculator-style keyboard. Again, no contest.

Even the TI-99/4 at $600 had a cramped calculator-style keyboard. Later, TI's product manager Bill Games would confide that the VIC-20 forced them to upgrade the TI keyboard. But that only made things worse: Instead of enlarging the case to make room for the larger keys, they cramped all the keys together and the keyboard was harder to use than before. No contest.

The keyboard was one of our biggest advantages. In the April 1981 issue of *COMPUTE!*, columnist David Thornburg wrote that the VIC-20 "is about the smallest size a computer could be and still have a full-sized keyboard."

Thornburg tested a five-line BASIC program on all three computers and found it executed on the VIC-20 in 77 seconds, compared to 103 seconds on the Color Computer and 159 seconds on Atari. (Later we also discovered that Commodore's BASIC ran up to five times faster than Texas Instruments's BASIC.) "VIC will create its own market, and it will be a big one," Thornburg predicted. He was right.

Our engineers had done a splendid job and we marketers had a good product to sell. Now all we had to do was to get the product to market. That meant producing the VIC-20 in quantity, getting a box designed, writing a user's manual, developing a line of software, producing more peripherals, launching an ad blitz, getting our dealers lined up, and more.

But there were more things going on at the CES Show than the VIC-20. To begin with, we had a new *president and chief operating officer*: James H.E.J. Finke. He came to Commodore from a distinguished career with Data General, most recently as vice president–general manager in Europe; and before that, he was general manager of international operations for General Electric's medical divisions, and a vice president with Motorola's semiconductor division. Jim was the same age as Jack, and it turned out Jack had tried to woo him over to Commodore for quite some time. Jim was soft-spoken, likable, authoritative, and courtly, almost chivalrous.

Though an American, he was European in his management approach, and displayed a conservative style brandished by diplomats at the rank of ambassador and above. He would have made an outstanding U.S. ambassador. Sam Tramiel would later say of him, "Jim Finke would make a good king." It was a sincere compliment as well as a mild criticism, for most people genuinely liked Jim Finke.

As king, he had the personality, temperament, and probing intelligence suited to a monarch. He tended to hold court, which was slightly different from holding business meetings or combat planning-sessions. Talking to him was always a treat. It was like talking to an international scholar and linguist, which he was.

Jim Finke was a world-class executive, akin to Irving Gould in temperament and calm. But there are world-class executives and there are world-class executives. One drives the army forward with guts and fist-banging resolution, and the other leads the diplomatic corps.

In calmer times he would doubtless have made an ideal president for Commodore, or any other corporation. However, what we needed in 1981—and what the general managers insisted on—was a Pattonesque president cut more in the pattern of a tactical combat general than a secretary of defense. Unfortunately, he didn't have the ruthless edge which was needed to control the independent-minded mavericks who ran Commodore world-wide at the general manager level. It was said he wielded a scepter instead of a sword.

The appointment of Jim as president placed him, technically, between Jack Tramiel and the rest of the company. His appointment was greeted with blatant skepticism by many Commodorians. Several key general managers saw him as a threat to their autonomy and power, and openly chided him just to see how he reacted. To make matters worse, they kept going to Jack for decisions, which made it tough for any president to succeed.

Within a month or so of his appointment, Jim was pictured in *Newsweek*, holding an Apple with a bite taken out of it. "We compared the CBM to the Apple and Commodore ate the Apple!" he professed. We used that line in our advertising, too, at least till Apple threatened a lawsuit. Jim was excellent at garnering publicity, and by the time he left Commodore in mid-1982, he was operating more and more in a public relations mode.

But while Jim's influence was slowly eroding, another force began to be felt. One of the nicest things I witnessed at Commodore was a brief scene between Sam Tramiel and his father. It happened at the beginning of the CES Show. Sam had just arrived from Hong Kong and met his father at the booth.

"I've booked a room for you at my hotel," Jack told him.

Sam smiled and replied, "No thanks. I've got a suite at the Desert Inn."

"A suite?" Jack challenged, and began to chastise him for spending too much money.

"Wait a minute, father," Sam interrupted. "You're forgetting I own my own company. I can stay anywhere I want. If I want a suite, I'll stay in a suite."

Jack stopped cold. It was one of the few times I ever saw him genuinely startled. He flashed me a sidelong glance, then slowly arched his eyebrows as the discovery, and admiration, sunk in.

"You're right," he told his son. Then he nodded, laughed heartily, and touched his son on the shoulder. It was the moment when Sam became truly emancipated from his father, the moment he stepped out of Jack's shadow and began building his own career.

In the coming months and years, Sam would continue his informal schooling in the Far East and would learn a lot of difficult business lessons which no one can teach. You have to experience them firsthand. As a result, when Sam came back to Commodore a year later, it was on his own terms as a consultant whose services were both needed and valued.

Later still, he would join his father in a unique coming-together of the Tramiels that would surprise the computer industry, and the world.

In January, just after the CES Show, there was enormous pressure on us and on me in particular to launch the VIC-20 immediately. The first few thousand units were coming over from Japan in plain blue and white boxes. For manuals, we'd get by with English translations of the Japanese user's manual. In Japan Tony came up with some very good game cartridges which became the first VIC software. But I still had to Americanize and *consumerize* the VIC.

Jack requested an update a week or two after the CES, in a large office reserved for him at MOS Technology. The timing was lousy. To begin with, I had a severe case of pneumonia. My head kept wobbling on my shoulders, and I guess I should have been home in bed. But there were too many important things to do.

It was a terrible mistake for me to meet Jack while I had pneumonia, and I learned a valuable lesson: never meet with Jack when you're sick. He's likely to mistake the head-wobbling, stammering. and bloodshot eyes for indecision, lack of conviction, or even fear. I kept thinking about the bear and the knapsack. If you slump down in a heap on the ground, the bear attacks. You have to throw him your knapsack and run like hell toward the nearest tree. Unfortunately, I was too weak to run. Too weak to climb trees. Too weak to fight back when he attacked. And too dumb to throw him a knapsack.

I made other mistakes, too. For example, I met with him all by myself, one on one. If there's one thing I learned about business meetings, it's never present an important proposal without several allies or subordinates in the room. There really is strength in numbers, and trying to go it alone inevitably begs the question, "Why aren't there others here giving their support and approval?"

Since I was presenting creative projects like VIC packaging and advertising, I should have had the ad agency there to back me up, either to make the presentation or to suggest alternatives if he didn't like our presentation.

To make matters worse, there were already invisible explosive gases lingering in the air, since the first executives in the company had started to smell that the VIC-20 was going to be a success—and made their political moves to take over the project.

The result was that I almost singlehandedly set myself up for a massive two-day Jack Attack. It began with me showing Jack the new packaging and ad theme. We decided to play off our success with the PET. The ad copy went something like this:

LIGHTNING STRIKES TWICE!
In 1976 Commodore introduced the PET, the first self-contained personal computer.
In 1981 Commodore introduces the VIC-20. The features speak for themselves. (Then we listed the features.)

The box was black with a color photo (shot from outer space) of Earth, shown as a semicircle at the bottom of the box. Above Earth was a large photo of the VIC-20. A streak of lightning split the box and electrified the VIC.

"It's not friendly!" was Jack's first reaction. It was the most cutting insult he could make. "What's friendly about lightning?" he asked. "People get struck by lightning. It's not friendly. Also, I want to show people on the box, enjoying their computer. That, to me, is friendly."

I tried to keep my head from wobbling on my shoulders and sank down into my chair.

"What about advertising?" he asked. I showed him the ads which were based on the lightning theme. "That's not advertising," he declared. "I want something dramatic. Maybe we need a spokesperson. Who would make a good spokesperson for us?"

I said I hadn't given it much thought. Then he proceeded to beat the hell out of me.

"Okay, what else?" he asked. But it wasn't a question. It was a dare.

I had to make a tough—and dangerous—decision. I decided to clam up and not show him any more of my strategy. Not one thing. Not the back-of-the-box copy. Not the outline and schedule for the user's manual. Not the software plan. Not the proposed organization. Not even the news releases and brochures I'd already written.

I didn't tell him I'd given the VIC-20 a subtitle, "The Friendly Computer," or that I had had Rich Blumenthal, our attorney, trademark the phrase as part of the name of the computer. After all, Atari trademarked the phrase "Computers For People." If they could do that, we could trademark "The Friendly Computer." Reserving that phrase was a major coup.

But I didn't tell Jack. I just sat there and let him beat the hell out of me for two days. To complicate matters, we left the door open and his booming indictments echoed down the hall and around the corner to my marketing staff. But I didn't close the door. I really didn't mind that they heard Jack scorching my soul.

When I walked out of that meeting at the end of the first day, Jack was frustrated and incensed that I hadn't given him more answers on the VIC-20. He thought I didn't have the program together. I protested that I did have a program, but I simply refused to present more because I couldn't risk having the rest of the program canceled in the heat of my Jack Attack.

I believed so deeply in the VIC-20 that I was willing to sacrifice myself to save the rest of the program. Jack could knock me down, but I could always stand back up again. Good soldiers don't stay down when they're wounded, and neither would I. But if, in the heat of anger, Jack canceled my plans beyond the ads and box design, those plans would be gone forever. It wasn't fair to take a chance on losing the rest of the program just because he didn't like the ads, or because I was too weak to defend the ads and present alternatives.

When I came out of that meeting, we were both completely drained of emotion. In truth, neither one of us had wanted the Jack Attack to happen. Jack didn't want to beat me to a pulp and I didn't enjoy feeling like tomato puree.

As I slowly walked back to my office, several of my marketing people came up to me and asked point-blank if I was going to be fired. I remember smiling reassuringly and telling them, "No, I'm not gonna be fired. It's only a Jack Attack. It happens to the best of us."

I don't think they believed me. I mean, Jack was *roaring!* He attacked me from almost every angle, personally and professionally, but I knew I had *the plan.* You can't beat a man with a plan. I'd already thrown him one knapsack— the ads and box art—and he tore them to shreds. I couldn't throw him any more knapsacks. I had to climb the tree and wait for the pneumonia and Jack Attack to pass. It was all I could do. The next day, I had another meeting with Jack.

"I'm going to assign you to Ken Hollandsworth," he said. "He's going to make sure the VIC-20 happens."

I just wobbled my head in a half-nod and muttered, "Fine." There was no point in arguing. I needed to get home and collapse.

A day or two later I met with Ken Hollandsworth—a very nice, mild-mannered, sensitive and caring human being. Ken looked grim. He wanted the VIC in his camp, but he was a trifle upset that he'd inherited it under what looked to him like crisis conditions. He assembled his three most trusted staffers, all sales managers, in what looked like a war conference.

I presented my entire plan on a flipchart. It was the plan I had hoped to present to Jack. When I was finished, Ken shook his head in amazement and scrunched up his face.

"Have you shown this to Jack?" he asked.

"Nope. If I showed it to Jack in the mood he was in, he would have canceled the whole thing and I couldn't take that chance." I went on to explain what had happened. When I was finished, Ken shook his head and told me very solemnly, "It looks to me like you've got everything covered. I was led to believe the whole program was really screwed up, but what you're doing looks fine to me."

Ken was extremely supportive. After our meeting, he took me aside and said, "We need to rehabilitate you. This happens sometimes in companies but I think we can deal with it."

So Ken endorsed my plan, and I kept pushing ahead with it. The only problem was, I had to work in the cramped consumer electronics division offices, which had recently gotten squeezed when the East Coast regional distribution center was moved into the same building. I found myself sitting at a desk surrounded by sales order clerks, all busily chatting on the phone taking orders and typing up sales forms. It was hard to hear yourself think, much less negotiate deals on the phone with all that clattering going on, but I brought it on myself. It was one of the consequences of the Jack Attack.

There wasn't even space for the VIC staff I was hiring. John Stockman stayed with me as a marketing assistant, camping out here and there without even a desk and sometimes not even a chair to sit in.

In early February I hired Neil Harris as assistant VIC product manager, and soon afterward, a young programmer named Duane Later. Neil was a multitalented writer/ programmer/salesman who was one of the major hands-on contributors to the success of the VIC product launch. He was an honest and candid friend as well as a right-hand man, and his talents in the computer field were considerable. He helped plot and manage many of the details of our software development effort. He programmed some of our first software programs on tape. Together, we co-authored the *VIC-20 User's Manual*. Neil even helped build up our team by recruiting his friend Andy Finkel, fresh out of engineering school, to join our team as a programmer and technical guru.

Suddenly, I had three people working for me—soon to be four (Andy hadn't joined us yet)—and no place to put them. Luckily, the regional service manager, who had a small office in the same building, gamely volunteered to share his already cramped quarters with our group. They stacked up several computer systems on two tables next to the service manager's desk and worked literally elbow to elbow during the day, putting in long hours at home in the evening.

A typical assignment would be my stalking in and saying, "I want you to sit here and give me 21 sample sound effects for the user's manual. I want them by the end of the day and I want you to include the sound of a phone ringing, and the sound of ocean surf."

"Why ocean surf?" one of them asked.

"Because I used to live in California and I miss the ocean," I replied.

They agreed it was a good reason.

Creating a friendly user's manual was very important. My definition of user-friendliness in marketing means *giving the customer an item that requires little or no special expertise to use, apply, or enjoy.*

One way to do this is to include a really nice instruction book that lets you have fun and do interesting things without expensive peripherals or packaged software. You don't have to be an auto mechanic to drive a car, so why should you have to be a programmer to use a computer?

The user-friendly manual we wrote for the VIC-20

doesn't even *mention* the word "programming" until the last chapter. Our manual teaches people how to compute, which we interpreted as meaning to have fun. So we talked about cartoon animation, sound and music, color graphics, and other topics. We also wrote the book so users could turn to any chapter and start computing from that point with little or no experience. If you like music, you could turn to that chapter and start there. If you like to work with color and graphics, start with that chapter.

What we didn't say is that if you worked through the book, you'd learn how to program in BASIC, by osmosis, since our examples included a very subtle introduction to programming. It meant new VIC owners had a head start if they decided they wanted to learn computer programming.

This was only one of our VIC projects. There was only one problem. About this time a corporate assassin emerged, like a snake sliding out of a murky river. We called him Vito Corleone.

If you work for a company that's moving as fast as Commodore was in the early 1980s, you're bound to come up against a corporate assassin sooner or later. You can come into the office every day, point your face straight ahead at a piece of paper and do nothing but produce results all day long, but sooner or later a Vito Corleone will sneak up behind you and try to get you fired. Sometimes there's no reason for it whatsoever. It could be jealousy, envy, pure sadism, a power grab, a personality clash, anything.

If it weren't for the damage they cause, it's easy to see corporate assassins as cartoon characters. They twist and turn and change shape and float around making trouble— like a *tumler* with a poison dart—and like Wiley Coyote in the Roadrunner cartoons, they keep chasing their victim until a rock falls on their head.

The best way to react to a corporate assassin is to avoid him (or her). Stay out of the line of fire. If you don't fight back, the assassin has no target and may stop shooting. If the assassin keeps coming, however, you have no choice. You have to fight back—and prevail.

I tried avoidance at first. I tried to overlook what I saw

as rather clumsy attempts to discredit me. But my assassin refused to slither away. He kept throwing barbs at my back, tearing me down at every opportunity—but always behind closed doors and never to my face. I suspect that my recent Jack Attack might have inspired him. I didn't really get mad, though, until Vito started harassing my young troops. When Vito, a manager with a certain amount of authority, came around and tried to bully newly hired young creative talents, I reacted.

Vito tried to kick my VIC team out of the service manager's office. He literally ordered them out. I told them to stay where they were and they did. There was no reason for them to move. What's more, there was no place for them to go. Besides, the service manager wasn't complaining, and the only one who wanted them gone was the assassin.

He kept after them. Whenever I turned my back or left the building, he came over to harass them. Finally, I put my foot down. I went around the building and told everyone who had any contact with Vito that the next time he came within ten feet of my young staff, I was going to give him a free karate lesson. And I meant it.

I never threatened Vito to his face, I simply smiled charmingly, not even clenching my teeth, whenever he slid past me in the halls. Then Vito threatened the service manager and told *him* to get my team out of his office. Finally, one day, one of the guys asked me to show them some karate, so I did. But first I made sure Vito was standing where he could see it. Then I stood in the doorway of that cramped little office and showed them a few moves. Vito stopped harassing the troops.

Of course, some people thought the whole VIC team was crazy, but that was all right. Armchair critics and corporate assassins tend to avoid crazy people, and that's exactly what we needed to get our job done.

I still couldn't relax my guard against Vito. He hissed, he snapped, he moved in the shadows. It wasn't making my rehabilitation any easier with Vito slipping around making unpleasant comments about me at every opportunity. I finally decided it was time for Plan B.

200

In casual conversation, I chatted with a few senior executives above my assassin's level (not Jack) and mentioned almost as an afterthought that I knew Vito was trying to assassinate me and that it was kind of annoying to have someone in my own company working so hard to get me fired.

The executives didn't think much about my remarks until Vito next visited them and offered them a poisonous observation or two about me. Until then, they might have thought it was my imagination, or maybe even that I deserved it. But when Vito did his trick, it only served to confirm what I had mentioned in passing. Vito was trying to assassinate a fellow manager, apparently for no reason, and that wasn't just.

One day, Dick Sanford said to me, "You don't have to worry about him any more." Dick's word was always good as gold, so I stopped worrying.

Thirty days later Vito was out of the company. I didn't feel relieved, or overjoyed, just a bit sorry that the assassin had fallen on his own sword.

About this time it became obvious that we were making strong progress on the VIC, and both Ken and Dick made sure Jack knew. One day, Ken called me into his office and said, "You're working for Dick Sanford again."

Just like that. Almost overnight, we packed up and moved into a new building Commodore was leasing on Moore Road in King of Prussia, Pennsylvania. The entire computer systems division was being given its own office space to make room for several corporate functions which were being created or moved into the MOS building.

The VIC group was moved into an open bay partitioned into short countertops and shelves. The spaces barely held all the computer systems, but it was better than sharing the service manager's tiny office. You could see over the tops of the walls and there were no doorways. This created frequent crises because every time someone had to give a sales demonstration or collect equipment for a convention or show, they would cannibalize cables and sometimes even computers or disk drives from the CBM systems in the VIC area. This was extremely disruptive. Our programmers and writers needed their systems to write software, manuals, and literature, and the June CES Show was our next big deadline. We had to have the whole product line ready to go by then.

Since we couldn't get higher walls or doors installed, we had to take creative action. So we became the VIC commandos. The VIC commandos was something I invented as a nickname for our group, to instill some fighting spirit and help ward off those mysterious gremlins who kept spiriting away our computer cables and equipment.

I told our group that we were going to become commandos, just like guerilla soldiers. We would pretend there were doors on our office bays, and anyone caught wandering around in our area would be booted out with military efficiency.

"This is a research area," we started telling people. "No one is allowed here except the VIC group."

I told the managers the same thing: "We're working on proprietary software and manuals. What we're doing has to be kept secret. There are too many people wandering around, even visiting dealers and journalists." I also threatened to file a stolen equipment report if anything was found missing from our area, without at least a note explaining who took what and why. Again, a lot of people thought we were crazy, but our commando attitude paid off, and we started getting more work done with fewer disruptions.

One day John Stockman, whose family had a specialty items business, brought in some large brass coins, about the size of a silver dollar. On one side the coins said "Good Fortune Under The Wings Of The Phoenix" and on the other side they said "The Phoenix, Symbol Of Good Fortune." The phoenix seemed to be a perfect symbol for the VIC commandos.

Before long we were all standing around flipping our VIC coins like George Raft. It was something we started doing unconsciously while we were chatting, and pretty soon the whole team picked up the habit. I guess we must have looked like amateur gangsters, but it was part of the mystique of the VIC commandos. Although the minicomputer gang was laughing at us behind our backs, we maintained our commando posture because thinking of ourselves as commandos gave us a peculiar, but powerful, camaraderie.

Later, additional commandos who joined us included Bill Hindorff, an excellent machine language programmer; Rick Cotton, our next student intern/assistant, who wound up dropping out of Cornell University to stay with Commodore as a software programmer; Rick's friend David Street, who also joined Commodore as a programmer; and Sue Mittnacht, our cheery secretary who later graduated to doing packaging, artwork, and other media work for the Commodore Software Division.

Chris Morgan, editor of *BYTE*, gave us a slogan. He used to tease me about how rabid I was when it came to user-friendliness. One day he sent me a clipping in the mail about how long German words are formed. One of the examples in the article was *Benutzefreundlichkeit*, the German word for user-friendliness. I immediately had some brass plaques made with the word *Benutzefreundlichkeit* in large letters, and below it the slogan *Official Motto of the VIC Commando Team*. The VIC commandos ceremoniously presented them to various members of the company, including Jack.

By May, we were beginning to sell VIC-20s in some volume, and we had accomplished quite a lot by the time we reached the June CES Show:

• Commodore Germany's ad agency came up with a unique silvery box design with a shaped window and a VIC-20 logo with letters printed in rainbow stripes. Commodore U.K. translated the design into English. We collaborated on box copy with John Baxter (my counterpart in the U.K.), and the result was a distinctive new look in computer packaging.

• The entire VIC team worked with a local artist to design a poster that showed a picture of the VIC-20 superimposed over a colorful rainbow rising from the desert. They say a camel is a horse designed by a committee, but our group effort turned out an excellent poster.

- The VIC commandos rushed out our first six-pack of game software on tape, which included such titles as *Car Chase, Slither/Super Slither, VIC-21 Casino Style Blackjack, Biorhythm/Compatibility, Spacemath,* and the inimitable *Blue Meanies from Outer Space.* Subsequent six-packs featured home calculation and education programs. The six-pack concept was well received by dealers, who had the option of selling the tapes as value packs or splitting them up and selling them one at a time. Nobody at Commodore thought software on tape would sell, but I insisted on marketing the six-packs. Once or twice, U.S. managers prevented me from restocking tapes, but relented when huge back orders piled up. By 1983 we had sold over a million tapes.
- We took a programming tool developed by Andy Finkel and turned it into the *Programmable Character Set/ Gamegraphics Editor* on tape for use by VIC programmers.
- We adapted Hayden's *Sargon II* chess program to a 16K cartridge for the VIC. It was the best home computer chess program on cartridge.
- Commodore Japan provided a constant flow of animated cartoon videogames which allowed us to compete head to head with videogame machines like Atari.
- The 290-page *VIC-20 Programmer's Reference Guide* was well underway, written entirely by Andy, Neil, Paul Higginbottom (a topnotch programmer from the U.K.), and me. I established a policy that programmer's reference guides would be produced for all new Commodore computers, and these guides would have practical examples to try in addition to technical information.
- We hired half a dozen college students to form our first user hotline. Questions poured in from new VIC owners, especially concerning technical problems with the early models. To begin with, there was a color balance problem. Different television sets provided different color hues. Dealers and users had to be told to adjust a small screw inside the VIC to fix this. Certain television sets also didn't work with the VIC (or any computer), and as the home computer craze mounted, television manufacturers soon

abandoned certain circuits which made the screen flutter when used with computers.

There was also an overheating problem, caused by the heat sink coming into contact with the cartridge port. We worried about people burning their fingers on the warm cartridges. "Well, if nothing else you can always use the VIC to fry eggs," we joked, but it was no laughing matter. The heat sink was moved.

The most troublesome technical problem wasn't so much a problem as a change in FCC regulations. The Federal Communications Commission suddenly began to realize that home computers emit low-level radio frequency waves which can interfere with television sets and other electronic devices. This caused a real problem if someone in one apartment was using a computer and his neighbor on the other side of the wall was trying to watch TV. As a result, the FCC required home computers to be shielded to minimize RF interference. Apples, PETs, and other computers had been in use for several years without complaints about interference. In fact, business computers were exempted from the shielding requirement. But home computer makers had to comply.

The solution came in several forms. One way was to embed ferrite balls in the plastic case. Another way was to spray the inside of the case with a metal coating. But the best way was to encase the offending electronics in a small metal box inside the case, which is what was done with the VIC-20.

Getting FCC approval was a complex process. Shiras Shivji and Fujiyama in Santa Clara did most of the FCC work. Often, this entailed taking a sample computer or accessory to a certified FCC lab out in the middle of the desert, and measuring the radiation in all directions. Even when the product passed the lab tests, it still took quite a while to get certification. We had to put temporary stickers on the first VICs warning users that they could cause RF interference.

During the next year or two, more than one company would encounter costly delays introducing their computers or peripherals because they had trouble getting FCC certification. Nevertheless, these FCC regulations probably prevented a lot of unnecessary fights between neighbors.

When we finally got to the June CES, we felt good. For one thing, the booth suddenly got fancier. We had a five-sided pillar in the middle with working VICs displayed on all sides. Our software included several games from Japan including *VIC Invaders*, a version of the ever-popular *Space Invaders*, *Midnight Drive*, and *Rally-X*.

No sooner did we open our booth than Atari's lawyers descended on us, charging that *VIC Invaders* infringed their right to the name *Space Invaders; Midnight Drive* was too close to their name *Night Driver;* and *Rally-X* was a direct copy of their road rally game. Worst of all, we had the best version of *Pac-Man* for any home machine in the world, but we couldn't sell it.

It looked disastrous, until we did some investigating. While chatting with Atari's lawyers, I discovered that the game *Space Invaders* was apparently not properly copyrighted and the game itself had been so widely emulated that it was in the public domain. It was only the *name Space Invaders* that Atari owned. So we kept the game and changed the name to *VIC Avenger*.

For *Midnight Drive* the same rules seemed to apply, so we got written permission from Atari to let us sell out our remaining stock and promised to change the name later to *Road Race*. The rally game was something else. We couldn't use it in the form we had, but the game gave us an idea for an even better game called *Rat Race*, which has little mice running through a maze, picking up cheese and avoiding cats, while the tune "Three Blind Mice" plays in the background. It became one of our most popular games.

Even the *Pac-Man* game was salvaged. It was sold in the U.K. under the name *Jelly Monsters*. Atari and Commodore later went to court to settle infringement claims over *Jelly Monsters* and a somewhat similar game called *Cosmic Cruncher*, which was programmed by our VIC commandos and featured a chewing Commodore logo and animated satellites instead of ghosts.

We were off to a tremendous start, but it was only the beginning. The final phase, the price wars, was still to come.

EIGHT

We were waiting to go over the top, all of us huddled in the trenches—even the generals.

In the back of my mind, memories of real wars kept playing like a deep-throated violin. The sound of bombs falling. And rockets. Red lizards in the jungle.

"Break for snake" was jungle slang for stopping to have lunch. One day I was sitting on a log and a real snake—a pit viper—crawled out between my legs. I just watched it crawl away and kept eating my sandwich.

Back then, the snipers used real bullets. The Dormouse wore black pajamas. We all shared a familiar bravado and death couldn't touch us, even when it did.

The first time I went into combat, I had to go AWOL to do it. Everybody thought I was crazy, but no one said a word when I came back two weeks later smelling like a swamp and dragging my rucksack behind me. The general found out where I was and called me every day in the jungle, but we kept telling him I couldn't come to the phone.

At night we slept in the thickest patch of bamboo so no one could sneak up and cut our throats. Some people didn't care and slept in hammocks.

Everyone loved to hear war stories. Like when we slept in the Viet Cong bunker complex and the camp was overrun by rats in the middle of the night.

The playing-card managers never understood. They said, "This isn't war. This is business."

But the Jack understood. He said, "This is war, too."

I looked up from my foxhole and told them: "Business is the best form of war. Nobody gets killed. There's only winning and losing."

Commodorians:
The "Force" Was with Us

In 1981, the war began to heat up, both inside and outside the company. We all sensed it. The company was gearing up like a great army on the move. "Hang on!" we kept shouting to each other.

Commodore began to spin round and round, faster and faster, until the whole organization was whirling so fast it was hard to keep from being flung off. Some people thought I was on my way out after that Jack Attack. They didn't realize that Jack's philosophy was, in some ways, profoundly Japanese. When you make a serious error in a Japanese company, they put you in an office without a phone until you're rehabilitated. Then they bring you back with no loss of face.

In my case, Jack sent me to Ken Hollandsworth, and when I was ready he brought me back, with no loss of face. It was as if the whole thing had never happened. It was all part of being a Commodorian, for true Commodorians didn't get shell-shocked when Jack exploded. They took it in stride. Nothing personal. It's only business. Business as war, without death.

The rest of 1981 went by in a blur of conventions, shows, sales demonstrations, speeches, analyst presentations, product developments, software programs, books, manuals, ads, and meetings, meetings, meetings.

Moving to the new, leased building in King of Prussia was a big step for us. The computer systems division under Dick Sanford was housed on the second floor of a brand-new building at 681 Moore Road, a short drive from the building that housed the sales region and consumer division.

High-walled offices with wood-grained walls were installed at one end of the building for general managers and vice presidents, and the rest of the division lived in ivory-colored office cubicles or large open bays. The decor was Herman Miller Office Furniture—all completely modular, which meant whenever they needed more space they could take down your office, squeeze you into a smaller space, and put everything back together again. From now on, Herman Miller was to rule Commodore's ergonomics and space allocations, with both good and bad results.

On the good side, everyone could hear everyone else over the walls, so people stopped gossiping about each other so much, and the politics settled down to a mere quiet roar for nearly a year. On the bad side, there was little or no privacy. Trying to hold meetings was sometimes a challenge when you could hear other meetings on the opposite side of the partition.

I was invited to take one of the high-walled offices, but I chose the opposite end of the building so I could be close to the VIC group. Politically, it wasn't a wise move at all, but for getting more work done it was the right thing to do. My office was in the back corner of the building, just down the hall from the VIC group's large open bay. The Moore Road building was nice because it had windows all the way around it. My window looked out on a neatly trimmed meadow that sloped down toward a stream where two groundhogs lived. You could see them lumbering back and forth all day, quietly accomplishing groundhog tasks.

Things were becoming somewhat less hectic for those of us inside the building as well. Software director Dieter Ammon was my neighbor on the other side of the partition. Dieter was always joking and we made constant wisecracks over the wall at each other, always in fun. We often eavesdropped on each other's meetings (you had to wear earmuffs not to) and offered advice back and forth. Dieter was in charge of software except for VIC software, which was in my domain.

In essence, I was the VIC czar. Some people used to tease me by calling me Father of the VIC—retribution for my earlier teasing of Chuck Peddle as Father of the PET.

About this time, the organization settled into a kind of golden period. Office politics subsided through the spring and summer of 1981 and the calm lasted until autumn, mostly because of Dick Sanford's strong, steady leadership.

Morale in the VIC group was high, despite their being forced to work in a large bay where each person had only a four-foot counter and overhead shelf, all ergonomically determined to be the minimum comfortable working space. Comfortable unless you have to work with stacks and stacks of computer equipment. Each person needed a complete VIC-20 system, plus a CBM system. The bigger CBM was used to compile machine language listings of the programs we were writing or testing, and also to write manuals and other literature.

We usually worked late into the evening to create, fine-tune, complete, and launch our various VIC-20 products, but the results were worth it:

- The *VIC User's Manual* (called the friendliest manual in the industry).
- The first Commodore *Programmer's Reference Guide*.
- Programs on tape (recreation and math improvement six-packs).
- *Sargon II Chess* (licensed from Hayden, converted by Andy Finkel).
- Videogames from Japan (we tested and helped debug them).
- Our own videogames (*Cosmic Cruncher, Rat Race*).
- Programming software for use internally and for sale as products.
- A software development system for programmers under contract.
- Demonstration programs for conventions, shows, and sales pitches.
- Dealer materials (*Demonstrating the VIC-20*).
- Sales literature (the VIC-20 newsletter and catalog sheets).
- Press releases and interviews, and more.

During the day, Andy Finkel, Bill Hindorff and the other programmers spent long hours studying machine language printouts and doing hand-to-hand combat with a wide assortment of mathematical challenges. I could never understand how they could program directly in numbers and mnemonic codes—BASIC was hard enough—but they did it, and did it well. Andy and Bill carried the entire VIC group with their machine language skills, later passing on those skills to newcomers Rick Cotton, David Street, and Jeff Bruette, who became the next generation of VIC commandos.

It turned out that everyone in the group could write as well as program, so we all chipped in and wrote instruction sheets, manuals, and the massive *VIC-20 Programmer's Reference Guide.*

I started writing a how-to column for beginners in Commodore's magazine. It was called *The VIC Magician,* and I stopped being called Father of the VIC in favor of VIC Magician. There were a lot of magicians around in 1981. Dieter licensed a data base program for the CBM called *Ozz, The Information Wizard,* and Marge Jillett promoted it by hiring a magician to appear at those conventions where our business system was displayed. Our wizard and his magic were always a big draw.

Even though we had little time, between bits and bytes we tried to top each other's game scores at a funny little PET game called *Cosmic Jailbreak,* where little green men beep across the screen trying to rescue other little green men while you, the player, try to shoot down the little green rescuers.

Once in February I allowed myself the luxury of a same-day flight to Boston to address the Boston Computer Society. I was responding to a request from Jonathan Rotenberg, the extraordinary teenage founder and president of the society, and a real computer prodigy. The whole city was frozen solid. I took my VIC-20 and gave a sneak preview to the group, most of whom seemed to be Apple fans. I predicted that Commodore was going to become the number one name in home computers.

Neil Harris and I occasionally went to science fiction conventions, partly to scout new videogame ideas, but mostly to escape the real science fiction at Commodore. The commandos sometimes got together at someone's house and played board games like Diplomacy, but those sessions were few and far between.

The funny thing is, none of us knew exactly why we were working so hard. It wasn't bribery. Sometimes it wasn't even fun. The ceilings were too low. Our office bays were crowded. People kept borrowing our equipment. It was noisy. And there was always a low level of politics.

"It was us against the world," Neil Harris recalls. Us against the competition. Us against the press. Us against the non-Commodorians.

In the face of all this craziness, we had to admit that if it wasn't our job we'd be doing exactly the same things at home, or for some other company. Experimenting with software. Writing computer books and articles. And immersing ourselves in computing.

Not that we were immune to the craziness. But we were battle-hardened at an early age, and our youth made us resilient. At age 21 or 23 or even at my age, we were young enough to recover from emotional wounds, long sleepless nights, and the odd snap from an assassin. We cheerfully endured all these agonies and more. We believed in the home computer.

I don't think any of us thought much about it at the time, but our hobby had become our obsession, and our obsession had become an addiction. As computer warriors, we couldn't retreat into different lives anymore than Commodore could back away from the battles we seemed destined to fight.

In the midst of all this, it seemed like a good time to get married. I had proposed to Kim Tuyen Nguyen on Christmas Eve in Wisconsin. We had met in Los Angeles and had been dating for two years. Kim was beautiful, tolerant, intelligent, and spoke with a melody in her voice, but then I guess I'm prejudiced. She was born in Vietnam and came to the U.S. to get her M.B.A. at the University of Southern California. When the war ended she was stranded here, and became a controller for a travel agency in Beverly Hills, and later joined an accounting firm.

One day she asked me, "Michael, who is Vincent Price? He keeps calling me about his accounting."

Beverly Hills was an interesting place to work, but it wasn't as hard as we thought to give up California. I had moved permanently to Pennsylvania in November 1980. Kim and I were in love, we both had careers, and she supported my long-term goal to become a novelist and screenwriter.

The only problem was where and when to get married. Most of our friends were in the computer business, and it was going to be hard to get even a few of them together in one place at the same time. The obvious solution was to get married at a computer convention.

The National Computer Conference was being held the first week in May and would be attended by Commodore's international managers like Kit Spencer and Harald Speyer, as well as various magazine editors who were friends. It seemed absurd to be married at a computer convention, but also strangely appropriate. Besides, Jack Tramiel was going to give away the bride.

Commodore's regional office in Chicago made most of the arrangements for us, and they were supposed to schedule a minister as well, but when we got to Chicago we discovered they had everything set—even the band—but they had forgotten the minister. Pauline Nishi, a very kind Japanese-American woman who was one of the stalwarts in Commodore's Chicago office, graciously volunteered to help. Hesitantly, she said she knew a Japanese Buddhist monk who could perform the ceremony. It was the ultimate irony. I asked Kim what she thought. We were both very religious Judeo-Christians, but we were also ecumenical and steeped in Oriental philosophy. So we said as long as God knew we were married, that was okay. The next morning we met with the monk.

He was exceptionally kind, but when he showed us the ceremony he planned to read, I noticed there was no mention of God.

216

"Uh, this is fine," I said. "Just insert the word *God* here—"

He shook his head and said, "Sorry. I can't do that."

"Huh? What do you mean?"

"That's the only word I can't say," he explained. "I can say the Creator, the One-ness, the Great Awareness, or anything similar, but I can't say God."

"And that's the one word we have to have in our ceremony," we said. We agreed a Buddhist ceremony was out. But we still had to find someone to marry us, and fast. Half the computer industry was coming to our wedding.

That day we went to more than half a dozen churches, but no one could do the ceremony on such short notice. Two churches insisted we had to be members. A supervisor at another church said they could do it if we paid $600, but without even talking to anyone she told us there were no ministers available.

Finally, we were referred to a kind lady at a mission church housed in an office. After making several unsuccessful phone calls, she looked up, and without even calling on the phone to make sure, said, "Here's the address of a church down the street. I'm sure they'll help you."

Thirty minutes later we found ourselves in a large, century-old stone church with a grand entrance and high-ceilinged lobby. It looked like all the other large churches who'd turned us down, except somehow we felt this was a friendly church.

Kim and I and our best man Doug Daughaday went to the church office and explained our problem to the receptionist. She said she was sure the minister could help us; he'd see us as soon as he finished a meeting. While we were waiting, a woman came in and walked up to me and started speaking gibberish. Whether she was a deranged streetperson or an angel in disguise, none of us knows to this day. She spoke to me faster than a professional speed-talker. Kim and Doug heard her speaking, but didn't understand a single word she said. They claimed she was babbling unintelligible gibberish, but I understood every word clear as a bell.

She said something about my getting married, complimented me on my beard, and said something about angels in the church the last time she was here, but there were no angels this year. Then she went over to the receptionist, who also didn't understand what she was saying, but I heard her say very clearly, "I slept in the church the last time I was here and there were angels in there but this time there aren't any angels and the man told me I couldn't sleep there this time."

Then she picked up her purse and walked out.

We began to get impatient. The wooden pews in the lobby were uncomfortable, and we suspected that we were in for another letdown. Then I noticed a rack full of religious brochures across the hall. One whole row on the rack was filled with the same brochure, its title repeated over and over again. It was called *Wait Twenty Minutes for God*.

We decided to stay. Exactly twenty minutes later, the minister came out. He was distinguished, elderly, and kind. He said he'd have to rush back from a wedding in the suburbs to perform our ceremony, but he was happy to be able to help us.

The next night, the wedding went perfectly. The only kink was a family emergency which required Jack to leave the country on short notice and miss the wedding. He asked Jim Finke to take his place, which Jim graciously did, and from that evening on we've always viewed Jim as Kim's stand-in "wedding dad."

Following the wedding, most of the Commodorians attended the reception along with friends from the industry such as Jim Mulholland from Hayden, a contingent from The Source, and a few dozen friends and relatives from Wisconsin and California.

Jim Finke read a congratulatory message from Commodore's board of directors and announced they had voted us a cash wedding gift. My mother, Dorothy Davis, who had been a nightclub singer in the forties using the name Mickey Martin, crooned romantic melodies while everyone dined, danced, and chatted.

Wayne Green, who founded and edited more computer magazines than anyone else in the industry, surprised us by videotaping our wedding as his present. Despite his reputation as an industry curmudgeon, Wayne was only mildly irascible. His first magazine was called *Amateur Radio Frontiers* and was published in 1951. As technology changed over the years, he became one of the few people in publishing to keep up with all the changes. By the early 1980s, he had achieved guru status in half a dozen different technologies, and was involved in virtually every aspect of the personal computer industry.

The classic story about Wayne Green concerns *BYTE Magazine*, the computer industry's most famous publication. In one of the most bizarre episodes in the annals of publishing, Wayne founded *BYTE* and then lost it virtually overnight—to his former wife. Today Wayne laughs when he tells the story, but it's a slightly dry laugh. It was 1975 and he had just founded *BYTE*. He says that at the time he incorporated the magazine, he was embroiled in a difficult lawsuit, so he decided to put the magazine stock in his ex-wife's name. It made sense from a legal point of view.

One fateful night, she moved the magazine to a new location and *kept it.* Wayne never got paid anything for the magazine he had started, not a nickel—he didn't even recoup his start-up costs, which totaled $100,000.

Says Wayne: "The next day was not one of my better days—if you call almost having heart failure a poor day!"

He bounded back with a vengeance. In the ensuing years, he published a flurry of popular technical magazines and newsletters, including *Kilobaud Microcomputing, Desktop Computing, 73 Magazine, 80 Micro, Hot Coco, inCider, Digital Audio Magazine, The Pico Report* (on briefcase computers), and *RUN Magazine.* He published books and software, too, and became a consultant to third-world nations, helping them start computer literacy programs. Once when I had difficulty contacting him, he told me he had been in the palace of a king. In August 1983, Green merged his business with CW Communications Inc. in a five-year transaction valued at $60 million.

The day after our wedding should have been the first day of our honeymoon: Acapulco, the Bahamas, surf and sand, piña coladas at sunset, scuba diving. And bleary lazy mornings where nine o'clock only comes in the evening and no ones gets up before noon.

If I'd worked anywhere else, Kim and I would have had such a honeymoon, but the day of our wedding, Jim Finke sheepishly asked if I could forgo the honeymoon to attend an international managers meeting in Valley Forge. Kim and I talked it over and said okay, but only if we got something in return—like Commodore paying Kim's expenses the next time I traveled to Europe. Jim agreed.

At this time, I became involved in the development of yet another new product. It's hard to imagine what Alexander Graham Bell or Edison must have gone through until you help invent something yourself. I got my chance when we developed the VICModem. It started in early 1981 when I went looking for a company to make a small modem we could sell for under $100.

A modem is a device that lets you hook up your computer to a telephone so that two computers can talk to each other and exchange information. They also make it possible for computer users to call special computerized telephone services—like The Source and CompuServe, which offer sports scores, encyclopedia listings, newswire stories—and even do business accounting or chat with other users around the country. These services make a home computer an extension of the far larger computers at the other end of the phone line. That adds great power to consumer machines.

For a nominal charge of $5 an hour plus the cost of a local phone call, you could call a friend in California and communicate with him through the computer, or chat with several people in different states at the same time, or leave electronic mail messages in a large centralized computer that someone in a different time zone could read and respond to when it was convenient.

Unfortunately, none of the companies I approached wanted to tackle the job.

"You can't sell a modem for under $400," they said.

"It costs too much to make."

"There's no need for it. Why lower the price when we can still get $400?"

"We want to make modems for the classes, not the masses," I told them. "People won't start using home computers with telephones until they can buy a computer for $300 and a modem for $100. We've got the computer. Now we need the modem. I intend to have a hundred-dollar modem for the VIC-20 if I have to design it myself!"

After being turned down by every major modem company in the industry, I found a company who agreed to do the modem; but as we approached the deadline the president called and said it couldn't be done. "We just can't do it," he declared. I was furious. I felt they'd wasted my time—and the public's time—when I could have been looking elsewhere for the modem.

Soon after this disappointment I got an unexpected call from a sales executive who said he'd just left the modem company I'd been dealing with.

"Michael, don't lose hope. I think I can get you your modem. Just give me a little time." His name was Bert Weiss, and he plunged full-force into finding another company who could engineer the VICModem.

Within two months, Bert found a small company called Anchor Automation which produced modems used to control industrial processes in factories and food-processing plants. Bert teamed up with George Eisler, the owner/engineer, and together with George's staff they tackled the project.

I arranged a meeting with Jack as soon as Anchor had a working prototype to demonstrate—nothing fancy, just a modem that worked with the VIC so we could show Jack how telecomputing worked.

This was one of the best things about Commodore. Anyone who had a good idea for a product was free to take it to Jack and that's what I did. I expected him to tell me I wasn't an engineer and should turn it over to the engineers, but instead he thought it was a good idea and urged me to pursue it.

We met in Santa Clara, in the conference room next to Jack's office. Jack questioned Bert and George closely. After a while, Jack excused himself and I followed him into his office. I took a few moments to outline the terms I thought they'd accept, then went back and confirmed it with Bert and George, then went back and told Jack. I felt like a shuttle diplomat. In management terms, it was a classic example of a third-party mediator, me, greasing the negotiations. Of course, I wasn't neutral, but both side trusted me. A few minutes later, Jack returned and we all went to lunch, where we chatted about everything *except* modems, and wound up concluding a deal.

Over the coming weeks and months, we wrestled mightily with the challenge of designing the most inexpensive modem in history. We all chipped in with ideas. One memorable evening we even drew pictures on the tablecloth in a restaurant; and while I personally didn't know much about electronics, I managed to make a few contributions to the design, mostly by asking probing questions like Jack did, and pressing hard for answers and solutions.

For example, in 1981 almost all modems were acoustic. This meant the phone receiver was placed in a cradle consisting of two cups, but these cradles were expensive and notoriously unreliable. If someone dropped a book on the floor, that could easily disrupt the communication.

Our conversation went like this:

"Why can't we connect it directly to the phone?" I asked.

"You mean a direct-connect modem?" George said.

"I don't know what I mean but you probably do."

"Well, that would probably be cheaper," he admitted.

"Then do it."

The size of the case was another problem. Most modems came in bulky rectangular boxes about 10 × 4 inches. Too expensive. I suggested we put the modem on a cartridge and plug it straight into the VIC-20 user port. Again, they went back to the drawing board and somehow squeezed the circuitry into a case less than 3 × 6 inches. It was the first modem-on-a-cartridge. The best part was, our competitors couldn't duplicate it. Only the VIC-20 had the right combination of RS-232 interface and user port engineering.

The modem wasn't done, though. It still had to meet certain specifications, and be cheap enough to make so we could sell it for under $100. The breakthrough came at a computer convention in the fall of 1981. After a rough meeting the night before, it seemed like we just weren't going to make it, but that night one of Anchor's engineers flew in and they had an all-night session. The next morning Bert and George stalked triumphantly into the Commodore booth, smiling broadly. "Here's your VICModem," George announced. "I hope you can read our scribbling." He handed me a coffee-stained, legal-notepad sheet with the schematic for the modem.

The next challenge was how to introduce the product to the mass market. In 1981 not many people knew about modems. When I started collecting data on telecomputing services, I made an important marketing discovery: There was no sales connection between modems, telecomputing services, and customers. Modems were sold by manufacturers. Telecomputing services were sold by computer stores and by mail. Many modems didn't work right because the modem-makers and computer-makers didn't talk to each other. The solution was simple. We had to find a way to put the telecomputing subscriptions inside the box with the modem.

I contacted CompuServe, The Source, and Dow Jones and made them a deal they couldn't refuse. If they let us package free subscriptions and trial offers with our VICModem, we'd sell more modems and they'd get thousands of new subscribers. They agreed, and by the time we introduced the VICModem in March 1982, we were able to include $197.50 worth of free offers, including a free subscription and trial hour on CompuServe, a free hour on The Source, and a free hour on the Dow Jones information service. Where else could you buy a $100 product and get $200 worth of free services?

To encourage our participation, CompuServe offered to pay royalties on user access time, and we agreed to develop and maintain an electronic magazine which we called the Commodore Information Network. The network's first editor was Jeff Hand, and he was followed by Barb Karpinski. Before long the network contained over 1000 pages of information, and there was even a special hotline that answered questions addressed to a special electronic mailbox.

To help launch and manage the modem product line, I hired Larry Ercolino, a former math teacher and salesperson for The Source. As manager of telecommunications, Larry was assigned to follow through on the deals we had initiated with the telecomputing services and to develop the modem product line.

The VICModem went on sale in March 1982 and was officially priced at $109.95 although most retailers sold it for under $100, and later for even less. It was estimated that in 1982 and 1983 we sold more modems than any other company. The Commodore Information Network became one of CompuServe's busiest services.

It bears mentioning that when I went in search of a telecomputing service to include free with the VICModem, I contacted The Source first, but The Source managers couldn't bring themselves to forgo the $100 subscription fee. We settled for a free trial hour instead, and most VICModem users wound up going with CompuServe because they provided a free subscription as well as a free hour.

In the summer of 1981 Neil Harris proclaimed that he wouldn't admit that home telecomputing had arrived until he could dial up an encyclopedia, type in the word *manatee* and find out everything he wanted to know about manatees. Less than a year later, CompuServe put the *World Book Encyclopedia* on-line, and it was easier to use than the book version. All you had to do was type in a subject and the information appeared on the screen.

One morning Neil came into my office, shook his head and said, "It finally happened. I called CompuServe last night and checked 'manatee' on their encyclopedia. I guess home telecomputing has arrived."

In the fall of 1981, Neil was promoted and became the first commando to graduate out of the VIC group. He went on to help support Commodore's mass-market retail push and subsequently took over Commodore's two magazines, *Commodore Microcomputing* and *Power/Play,* and the Commodore Information Network.

We also witnessed a shakeup in the Commodore international management team about this time. Previously, the European command had been quite stable. General managers stayed in place for half a decade or more. The Europeans didn't play musical chairs like we did in the U.S., which was possibly why Jack decided to bring over the heavy artillery in the form of Kit Spencer, Commodore's best marketing executive.

Under Kit's leadership, Commodore U.K. captured between 60 and 80 percent of the U.K. computer market. His sales were consistently higher than sales in the U.S., much to the embarrassment of the U.S. systems division.

Jack had promoted Kit to vice president–international marketing and moved him to Switzerland in the summer of 1981. His replacement in the U.K. was Bob Gleadow, an iconoclastic Englishman in his thirties who had joined Commodore as an accounting clerk during the Calculator Wars. Bob quickly proved himself to be an instinctive, uncompromising manager who could handle a variety of top-level assignments from sales to manufacturing.

I first met him in Europe at the general manager's conference back in April 1980. Following the meeting, Jack and Bob had later rendezvoused in Santa Clara, where they had a series of tremendously vocal meetings that sounded like mini Jack Attacks. It appeared that Jack was expending a great deal of energy to hammer Bob into the mold of a Commodore general manager.

Believe it or not, there were times when having Jack beat the hell out of you was an enormous compliment—that is, if he was doing it to shape your character and prepare you for higher rank. The technique was no different than military boot camp.

He once told me after a minor beating, "I talk to you like this because I know we're friends." I laughed and was tempted to say, "I hope I survive the friendship!" But I knew what he meant. We all did. What he was saying was that Commodorians were tough enough to endure heated confrontations, raw passion, and blunt, undisguised criticism.

Confrontation was part of The Religion. Jack knew that truth is always buried and obscure. You have to dig deep to find it. Dig deep enough and you always find water or oil or treasure.

People often say something can't be done because they don't have all the facts, or because they're lazy, or because they didn't dig deep enough for the truth. Sometimes someone passes a project to someone else and assumes it's done; but in a lean management team, everyone's constantly overworked and you can't assume something gets handled just because you passed it on. You have to keep following through, just to make sure nothing gets overlooked in the heat of battle.

Corporate generals like Spencer and Gleadow seldom let projects drift away. Kit Spencer really didn't relish moving from Switzerland to the States. It was October 1981 and the cold weather was already starting to set in. Jack had just moved him from England to Switzerland a few months before, and now he had to move again. He was concerned about the effect on his family, but like any good general he went where his orders directed.

Explains Kit: "You have to understand it was a very difficult time for Jack. He was under a lot of pressure from the board of directors and needed to make things happen in the States. So he asked me to come over and help out. He wouldn't have asked if it wasn't important."

Kit did more than help out. He wound up staying in the States and took charge of all marketing activities. Jack placed him on an equal level with Dick Sanford, and although Dick got along well with Kit, it was clear he didn't relish sharing the power. In the meantime, Jack was beginning to talk about establishing an office of the president and began to treat Jim Finke, Dick Sanford, and Kit Spencer as an unofficial triumvirate.

I wound up working for Kit, which I thought was great because I considered him a good friend and mentor, and a lot of my own marketing successes were modeled on techniques I saw Kit use in Europe. Kit kept his title of vice president–international marketing, and during his first few months in the States, he was technically a consultant to the U.S. organization.

I was lucky to start working with Kit as soon as he came to the States. I now rose to the highest position I was ever to hold in the organization: My title was expanded to product marketing manager for Commodore International. I inherited a broad assortment of international responsibilities related to marketing and product development. Kit gave me almost complete autonomy as his second in command. My VIC-20 responsibilities continued as before and I still ran the VIC group, although by this time the emphasis was shifting from product development to product marketing, sales, and distribution.

There were fewer than 20 people in the marketing group, including half a dozen VIC-20 programmers, a small magazine staff, two documentation writers, a public relations director, some advertising and merchandising people, and a two-person telecommunications team. Kit fostered motion and creativity.

Kit's marketing reign lasted fifteen months, and his contributions ranged from handling the final negotiations with CompuServe to getting our Commodore magazines upgraded to newsstand-quality publications. But his most visible achievement was persuading Jack to authorize a multimillion-dollar ad campaign to introduce the VIC-20 in magazines and on television. The ads featured William Shatner, who had played Captain James Kirk on the "Star Trek" television show and in the movies.

In the commercial, Shatner stepped from out of a field of stars and proclaimed the VIC-20 as the Wonder Computer of the eighties. I was our on-site marketing representative when those commercials were shot in New York. The toughest part of the shoot was finding Shatner an alien-looking sweater he could wear to look trekkie without infringing on the Captain Kirk character, to which we didn't have the rights.

Jack was involved in this search for someone to be our television spokesperson, as he was in everything that affected the company. One day he asked me, "What do you think about Spock?"

I said, "He's okay, but he might come across too cold. I prefer Captain Kirk. I think he has a broader appeal."

Later, it turned out Leonard Nimoy, who played Spock, was representing Magnavox and there was a conflict of interest, but Shatner was available. He was a good choice. Not many people recall Leonard Nimoy in those Magnavox commercials, but a lot of people recall Shatner introducing the VIC. Our ad agency was Kornhauser & Calene.

One day Jack told me Steven Greenberg, our investor relations consultant who also represented Bally-Midway, had arranged a meeting with Bally in Chicago to talk about licensing Bally's popular arcade games for conversion to the VIC-20. We really needed some good software.

All we had was a handful of Japanese cartridge games like *Draw Poker* and our first six-pack of recreational programs on tape. With a little help from our friends, we licensed six excellent adventure games from Scott Adams, and Hayden Software came through with *Sargon II Chess*. But these programs required 16K cartridges and the larger cartridges had been delayed in manufacturing.

Jack, Irving Gould, Steven Greenberg, and I flew out to Chicago to meet with Bally. After I demonstrated the VIC-20 for the Bally executives, everyone adjourned to make the deal. A few minutes later—it was only a matter of minutes—Jack appeared, shaking his head in amazement. "Now that's what I call a straight deal! Those men knew exactly what they wanted. We told them what we could do for them. And we did the deal." I seldom saw Jack so impressed with a business negotiation. It was one of the straightest deals he'd done, he said, and was based on a handshake as much as a contract.

We chose several Bally arcade hits like *Omega Race*, *Wizard of Wor*, and *Gorf*, along with a few older classics like *Clowns* and *Seawolf*, and gave some of the games to Japan and did some in the VIC group. Before long, all the VIC programmers were converting Bally-Midway games, and started to be known as the games group. The only problem with programming games in an open bay was that other people in the company with more mundane jobs grew jealous. Some managers complained at what looked to them like a bunch of young people playing arcade games and spread rumors that the VIC group was playing more than working. It was true, of course, but playing games was part of the job, and was crucially important to the next phase of our product plan: positioning the VIC-20 head to head against videogame machines.

In November 1981, we were all shocked when Dick Sanford abruptly left the company. His departure was attributed to a dispute with Jack, but it happened gradually over a period of several weeks as the two men moved farther and farther apart. Dick seemed to want to do things with the organization that Jack didn't agree with. Dick called their dispute a misunderstanding, but it was apparently important enough that they didn't contact each other for the next three years, although they did eventually patch up their differences.

During those intervening years, I saw Dick once in a while and was always struck by how he kept referring to Jack, or quoting his philosophy. He clearly still counted himself in the family, even though he and Jack weren't in contact. I got the impression that Jack too was hurt by their breakup, but still considered Dick part of the family.

Over the years I've noticed that executives who leave Commodore seem to look over their shoulder as if Jack were standing there critiquing their performance. Some even believe that Jack has monitored their progress after they left the company.

At the other extreme, a few executives fell into a blue funk after they left the company and literally spent years carping in the press or anonymously attacking Jack's personality or his management style.

Dick Sanford remained a Commodorian after he left the company. I'm not sure if he looked over his shoulder, but it was clear that he carried The Religion with him when he went into business for himself. His company, Intelligent Electronics, was based in Lionville, Pennsylvania, and was a new type of concession business. The company specialized in the design and operation of custom computer centers for large department store chains such as Strawbridge & Clothier. Thanks to Sanford's aggressive leadership, and an excellent staff which included more than half a dozen former Commodore employees, his company's revenues quadrupled after his second year in business.

When Dick left Commodore, his departure created a serious power vacuum. Greg Pratt, vice president–operations, stepped in to fill part of the vacuum. Don Richard, who had been Jack's executive assistant immediately before I joined Commodore, returned to the company in the same capacity. But more was needed.

Our most important goal was moving the VIC-20 into mass retail stores. The VIC was sold mostly through computer stores, but many computer dealers used the low-priced VIC to trade up their customers to higher-priced computers like Apple and even Atari. We had to sell VICs in department stores if we wanted to sell VICs in large quantities.

To help get this started, Jack tapped the most experienced retail executive in the company. Bill Wade was pulled out of the Mr. Calculator stores he was managing in California and brought to Pennsylvania to set up a manufacturer's representatives organization. Wade was a large-framed, Oklahoma-born executive with the tact and personality of a dull ax. One Commodore executive described him as "the rudest man in the company."

Many people found Bill tough to deal with because he was all business and could be blunt to the point of rudeness. But he had one sterling quality: his ethics. He was the cleanest-fighting corporate warrior I ever dealt with.

In terms of personality and maybe philosophy, Bill and I were almost total opposites, but we recognized this and worked around it. We worked so hard, in fact, that if someone attacked Bill in a meeting I tended to jump in and defend him. Also, a few times when Jack attacked me in a meeting, Bill jumped in and took some angry and unnecessary flack just to take the pressure off me. That was the kind of soldier he was.

He was the only man I ever met that I could stand toe to toe with and have a knockdown, drag-out fight complete with personal insults, then walk out of the office, turn around and come right back and discuss a different topic—and Bill would deal with me as if the last confrontation never happened. In some ways he was like a cowboy of the Old West. He wouldn't shoot you in the back, but when he faced you in a shoot-out he used a double-barreled shotgun, which meant you couldn't beat him just by drawing fast.

More than anyone else, he was responsible for setting up Commodore to take the VIC-20 into mass-market retailing, although he received little or no credit for his accomplishments. Maybe this can be attributed to his abrasive style, which hadn't won him many friends in the company.

In his careful, plodding way, he set about the task of dividing the United States into manufacturer's rep territories, relying on his knowledge of which major retailers controlled which market areas, his own extensive experience in the retail industry, and statistical demographics. For many days, he hunched over photocopied maps of the U.S., painstakingly drawing and redrawing territories in different colored markers. He looked at consumer markets by state, region, and city. He listed and prioritized all the mass merchants, retail distributors, and manufacturer's reps in the country. It was one of the few times at Commodore that I saw anyone plan a strategy so meticulously.

Then he began interviewing and assigning reps to help sell the VIC. Manufacturer's representatives are very useful in helping to introduce a new product. If you sell your product through a rep organization, you don't have to set up a large company sales force until after the reps have established your product in the marketplace. It doesn't seem fair, but often after the reps establish a product, the manufacturer cuts them out and sets up its own sales group. Commodore did this.

In addition to the reps, Wade presented VIC sales demonstrations to major retailers like Montgomery Ward, accompanied by the best product demonstrators in the company. Neil Harris was a favorite because in addition to being knowledgeable, he always came across as sincere.

Bill was also responsible for putting together the first in-store display fixtures, which we patterned after an Atari display we saw in a department store, with modifications.

The rep organization quickly began to take shape, but the mass merchants were still gun-shy of the VIC. They were still having tremendous success with videogame machines like the Atari 2600 and Mattel Intellivision, but they weren't sure it was time for a $300 color computer. To speed the expansion of our retail organization, Jack split the sales organization into two divisions: the computer systems division and the consumer division. It was like dividing his army in two to attack two objectives.

He recruited Leon Harris, a 22-year veteran of Olivetti Corporation, as president of the systems division. Previously, as vice president, sales and marketing, dealer group, he had been responsible for setting up Olivetti's dealer organization. He assumed command of the computer dealer-sales organization as well as Paul Goheen's software group (Dieter Ammon had left the company to start his own business), and such activities as the user hotline which was staffed by college interns.

Alan Fink, formerly vice president of a cosmetics firm, was hired as president of the consumer division. Commodore was still selling watches, calculators, and electronic thermostats, but sales were dwindling to a trickle. It was the consumer division's new charter to move the VIC product line into the mass market.

For added support at the top, Jack brought in the heavy artillery in the guise of David Harris, an Englishman, to handle sales to mass merchants. A former associate of Jack, David was recalled after a long absence from the company. Everyone had great confidence in David, but Alan Fink was an unknown quantity.

Fink was a soft-spoken executive with steel black hair and drowsy eyes that always seemed to be bloodshot. Commuting back and forth to New York didn't help much, and four hours on the road every day had to be a drain, although except for his eyes, he didn't show it. He struck me as pleasant and capable but slightly standoffish. One of his first moves was to ask for Neil Harris to join the consumer division, and Neil and I agreed he'd be more useful in the consumer group, which needed all the experienced help it could get.

Fink's appointment did not make Bill Wade happy, especially when Fink passed over Wade to bring in Ron Glatz, with whom he'd worked before, as vice president. Wade was bitterly disappointed. After working so hard to set up the retail business for Commodore, the area was virtually taken away and given to someone else with scant knowledge or experience in the industry, and he wasn't even offered the number two spot.

Observers in the company had mixed emotions. Some thought Fink was aptly named, while others thought Wade was his own worst enemy.

This kind of thing happened a lot at Commodore. It seemed that no one was allowed to achieve too much success. As soon as you got something going and prepared to move on to the next plateau, Jack would take it away from you. I don't think he did it intentionally, but it happened so often that many people started to believe that too much success was almost as dangerous as not enough.

Alan Fink was a capable senior executive with many good ideas, but with little knowledge of the computer industry. Shortly after he arrived, Jack asked him to make a sales forecast and place orders for new products he thought he could sell.

About this time, Kit Spencer, Greg Pratt, and I painstakingly compiled a VIC sales forecast based on our own experience, dealer reports, and statistical information like actual sales ratios of peripherals to computers. We gave it to Fink thinking we were giving him a running headstart, but he chose to ignore it and submitted his own forecast.

It differed from ours. For example, Fink didn't think many people would buy disk drives for the VIC, so he reduced our forecast from 15 percent of VIC owners to 1.5 percent, with the result that throughout 1982 we had a serious shortage of disk drives. On the other hand, we needed more VIC software titles, so he pressured us to release some extremely marginal games which we knew wouldn't sell very well, and they didn't. He left the company in the summer of 1982.

David Harris was more successful. He was easily the most cosmopolitan executive in the company and a world-class salesman. Charm was his specialty, and he was adept at closing deals with retail buyers, although he was occasionally accused of giving away the farm.

While Bill Wade set up the reps and targeted the big accounts, David Harris closed the sales. In the ensuing years he was variously credited for landing between 30 and 60 percent of Commodore's U.S. computer business, depending on who you believe. There were always a few curmudgeons in the company who secretly envied his roguish attitude and tried to subdue or curtail him, but David's results spoke for themselves.

David's first and biggest retail client was a surprise to both the retail and computer industries. It was K mart, the discount store chain. Who would have imagined that a discount chain would be the first mass merchant to sell computers in America?

I sat in on a meeting in 1981 attended by Jack and Fred Shimp, K mart's powerful computer buyer. Shimp gets the credit for putting K mart into computers. At the meeting, Jack told him Commodore would always remember that K mart was "our first wife" in mass marketing. Shimp said something to the effect that some men go on to have other wives. "We won't forget you were first," Jack promised. "Our first wife will always be special."

A lot of people thought we were crazy. They said conventional department stores wouldn't touch a product marketed by K mart because customers would only come in to find out about the VIC, then go buy it cheaper at K mart. As it turned out, K mart was only the first in a long line of mass merchants who started selling the VIC, including Montgomery Ward, Toys'R'Us, Bamberger's, Service Merchandise, Kiddie City, Musicland, Target, and later Sears and J. C. Penney.

The computer store dealers were upset by this development. Before long, some dealers complained that they could buy VICs cheaper at K mart than from Commodore. Others charged that K mart sold VICs below cost. In any event, K mart soon became the world's largest retailer of home computers, an honor they earned, and deserved, as the first mass merchant to recognize the potential of the VIC. They believed as we did that home computers were ready to be sold like any other appliance or impulse item.

Christmas 1981 was a shining season for the VIC. Our William Shatner ads were on television; K mart and a few other mass merchants were beginning to carry our products; the press was raving about the VIC; and we knew we were selling more computers than our competitors, although market researchers and even prestigious publications like *Business Week* claimed we had a minority share of the market. Future Computing, the best computer industry research house, put us neck and neck with Texas Instruments, giving us 26 percent of the U.S. market in 1982. But our actual sales suggested we had a much larger market share each, and we felt we had a shot at becoming the first company to sell a million computers in one year. Kit Spencer went out on a limb and predicted, as did Jack, that Commodore would sell more computers in 1982 than the *entire industry* sold in 1981.

In January 1982, we announced two new computers, the Commodore 64 and Ultimax, and showed prototypes at the CES Show in Las Vegas. The decisive battle for the home computer market was shaping up fast, but to us in the Commodore booth it was clear we had crossed the Delaware. We were going to win the war.

We fielded our best and most extravagant CES booth ever, and our exuberance was clear to all who attended. David Thornburg, reviewing the convention for *COMPUTE!*, later wrote: "For sheer impact, Commodore stole the show with the announcement of two new color computers!" He couldn't help commenting that the Commodore booth "sported ear-to-ear grins."

Why not? We had the VIC. We had the Commodore 64. And we had the Ultimax—well, almost. The Ultimax was one of those products we showed more to gauge public reaction than to take orders, like when we brought the prototype VICs to the CES in June 1980.

One of my jobs was to get the Ultimax product line ready. Jack kept telling me we were going ahead with it, but I kept telling him, "Don't do it unless you add more memory!" He insisted it would sell, but this time I couldn't agree. Jack was wrong.

To me it was obvious. To begin with, the Max had a horrible flat plastic keyboard with little bubble-dome keys that I knew would get sticky and malfunction when the weather was hot. One of the lessons of the VIC was, you can't sell a computer with a substandard keyboard. We had set the standard with our own VIC: From now on, home computer keyboards had to have full-sized typewriter keys.

Also, the VIC had only 5K of memory but it was expandable, which the Max was not. We learned that being able to increase the VIC's memory to 32K was a major selling feature, but the Max had only 2K and wasn't expandable. What's more, the BASIC cartridge was extra, and when you plugged it in the Max, memory was cut to half a kilobyte. Finally, the target price of $149 was too high. By the time the Max hit the market, the VIC would be the same price.

On the plus side, the Max had a 40-column by 25-line screen display which was better than the VIC, and contained a special music synthesizer chip invented by Bob Yannes called the Sound Interface Device (SID).

Gamely, I wrote a Max user manual, and Kit Spencer worked with Ally & Gargano, our New York ad agency, to develop a launch campaign. He changed the name from Ultimax to Max Machine, and at the June 1982 CES we published a large full-color brochure with this on the cover: "Commodore announces the third-generation game machine: a true computer and music synthesizer that will out-zonk, out-zap, out-sing, out-think, out-program, out-teach, and out-sell the competition."

Jack said the Max would be even closer competition for videogame machines than the VIC. He saw it as a new category—a game computer. He was trying to achieve a starter computer priced like a game machine which could take advantage of the arcade games we had licensed from Bally-Midway. The press, and Commodore, were still talking about the Max in November 1982, and by that time the VIC was selling for as low as $179.

Finally they handed the Max project over to Bill Wade and he persuaded Jack to abandon it. A fairly large quantity had been manufactured, however, and were sold in Japan. As I had expected from the start, there were serious keyboard reliability problems.

Luckily for us, the Commodore 64 was a completely different story. While the VIC was opening the door to mass-market computer sales and the Max was in the process of being stillborn, the Commodore 64 was quietly being developed in tight secrecy by an engineering and chip design team headed by Charlie Winterble, Al Charpentier, and Bob Yannes. They worked throughout 1981 and into 1982 to come up with several new chips which gave us a 40-column color computer we could use to compete with Apple, at half the price.

The features of the Commodore 64 were extraordinary for a home computer:
• 16 colors (twice as many as VIC)
• 40-column screen display (against 22 columns on VIC)

- A built-in music synthesizer (the SID chip)
- Sprite graphics (easy high-resolution graphics)
- 64K RAM memory (compared to 5K on the VIC)
- A typewriter-style keyboard (of course)
- Two joysticks (the VIC had one joystick)
- Compatibility with VIC peripherals (disk drive, printer, modem)

The computer was shown at both the January and the June CES Show in 1982. It received rave reviews and went on sale strictly to computer-store dealers in September at a price of $595. The Commodore 64 wasn't given to mass merchants until 1983. Then the retail price promptly fell below $400. Computer dealers, who felt they got burned when the VIC went to K mart, now felt they were getting burned again with the Commodore 64.

Jack had a different point of view. He thought he was helping the computer-store dealers. Instead of going directly to mass merchants like K mart, he knew it would take several months to gear up to build the Commodore 64 in large quantities. He allocated his first six months' worth of production to computer stores so they could at least have a piece of the pie before the Commodore 64 fell into mass distribution. Nobody understood what he was doing, nobody reported it in the press, and even if they had I suppose the computer dealers wouldn't have believed it.

In the spring of 1982, Commodore moved to a sprawling one-story office building located in Wayne, Pennsylvania. By this time, the VIC commandos were getting a little cramped, so we moved them to the new building about a month before the rest of the organization relocated. They set up their desks and equipment in the large empty building, which still didn't have any walls or partitions (we were going with Herman Miller furniture again). More and more, the group was being called the games group, and we got ready to start writing our own original games. Everyone was excited about this, because until now we had largely just been converting games we licensed from outside, like Bally games. But converting a game can sometimes be as hard as writing an original game. We began having brainstorming sessions.

If we were to do original games, I felt the group needed some special compensation. I'd already gotten Jack to authorize stock options for the three senior members of the VIC group, but we needed some sort of a royalty structure as well to compensate them. You can't ask a programmer to create software that makes millions of dollars for the company and just pay him a salary. That's why programming groups kept leaving companies like Atari and Mattel, because they could make more money on the outside working for themselves. The most famous example is the half-dozen programmers who left Atari to form Activision.

I did a lot of detailed homework on special compensation plans and even presented my ideas to Greg Pratt, who chipped in some ideas of his own and approved my plan before I took it over to tell Jack.

It was late morning. A nice sunny day. I was happy as a clam. Jack had already approved the concept of giving the programmers royalties and I told them we would finalize the details this week. I went into Jack's office, bubbling over with enthusiasm and happy for the VIC group.

Then it happened.

I lost the VIC group!

Jack walked in, sat down at his desk, and before I could start he said, "You know you have a problem with the VIC group. They don't want to work for you anymore, so I'm assigning them to Charlie Winterble in engineering."

"Huh?" I was dumbfounded.

How could that happen? I had hired the group from scratch. I knew they wouldn't mutiny without telling me. Something was fishy, but I was so shocked and furious— furious isn't a strong enough word for my feelings—that I just sat their clenching my whole body, my lips pressed so tight I couldn't even speak without growling.

Kit Spencer came in to soften the blow, and he kept staring at me wide-eyed, afraid I was going to quit on the spot. He could hardly say a word to me because he was just as surprised as I was. But Jack had made up his mind.

It was another case of an executive getting ready to move to a higher plateau, and being knocked down by an improbable twist in politics. In this case, it was part politics, part misunderstanding, and part treachery.

Two members of the VIC group—one junior member who wanted to be a programmer but wasn't ready, and one dissatisfied senior member—got together with a disgruntled programmer in Canada and went to Charlie Winterble at MOS to suggest that they work for him. They said they wanted to sit at home and work on their own games. It was every programmer's dream, I guess, to sit home and make games.

Anyway, Winterble thought it was a good chance to expand his responsibility and get involved with software, so he convinced Jack to let the programmers come over, arguing that the Commodore 64 was such a "complicated machine" that the programmers would have to work closely with the engineers, anyway. What even Winterble didn't reckon on was that the programmer, the assistant, and the Canadian were making it seem that the entire group wanted to defect, which wasn't true.

That afternoon, I started getting frantic calls from VIC commandos, asking what the hell was going on. I told them I thought they knew, but they obviously didn't. A few days later, a half-dozen members of the group approached me and asked if they could stay with me. I told them, "Don't ask me, ask Jack. He's the one who thinks you don't want to work for me." I figured if they didn't feel strongly enough to complain to Jack, then let the die be cast. Besides, I knew it wouldn't work. But maybe it would convince Jack once and for all to stop tampering with successful operations. There were enough things wrong with the company that needed fixing, without trying to improve something that was already working quite well.

What happened next to the VIC group was a travesty. To begin with, they didn't get their royalties, although they were promised, and promised, and promised. Jack got so mad at their constant royalty demands that he told them if they wanted to get royalties so badly, he'd arrange for those who wanted it to step outside the company, pay them a minimum living wage instead of a salary (as an advance against royalties), and see what they came up with. Of course, no one was ready to give up his job security to gamble 100 percent on future royalties.

Joe McEnerny, an experienced but uncreative senior programmer, was hired to run the group. They were sent back to the old Moore Road offices, which we still leased, and took up residence alongside a new engineering organization called the production engineering group.

During the next six months, everyone in the group worked on games, but not one commercial product was produced by the entire group. The assistant who wanted to be a programmer was fired from the group a month or so after they moved. The disgruntled programmer from Canada sat home and worked on some software, in Canada.

A few months later, Jack dropped in on the production engineering group to see how they were doing—and promptly fired them. The group had been set up to get new products manufactured faster. They were supposed to pick up where research left off, and handle the more mundane task of getting products ready for manufacturing so the research engineers could move on to the next new development. It didn't work. The product cycle was moving just as slowly as ever, and in some cases even slower. Meanwhile, the group had ballooned to 35 people—designers, engineers, and technicians. Jack closed down the whole organization, practically overnight. Only a few Japanese engineers who had been with the company before were retained. It was a famous story around the company. Everyone was going around saying, "Did Jack really fire 35 people?" The final number wasn't that high, but he did close down the group, and for good reason. It was costing a small fortune to maintain, and it wasn't working.

As a result of all this, the Moore Road facility was closed and, in an almost poetic irony, the games group was sent back to where it got its original start—the same building where Jack sent me after my Jack Attack. The computer systems region was still there, and the games group established itself in a large, poorly ventilated room with no windows anywhere.

Joe McEnerny left the company, and the games group was given to Bill Wade, who had always wanted to be involved with videogames. It was surprising how many people who used to criticize the games group as a bunch of laggards and arcade addicts secretly wanted to take over the group.

For one month, even Steven Greenberg got into the act. A sharp critic of Commodore's game software, and a game enthusiast himself, Steven kept pressing Jack, and finally Jack told him to put his money where his mouth was. Jack agreed to let Steven take over the games group, with Wade remaining in charge in Pennsylvania and Steven giving directions from New York. About a month later, Jack canceled the arrangement. The reason given was that Steven didn't have time to run his own company in New York and also give the games group the attention it needed.

In all this time, *not one original commercial product was produced by this group.*

A year later, in 1983 on a car ride to New York, I told Jack I thought what he had done with the VIC group was the stupidest thing I ever saw him do. The only thing it did was ruin a great product group and destroy our chances to cash in on videogames. After listening patiently to my half-hour tirade, he just turned to me and said, "Everything you said is right."

In any case, right after I lost the VIC group, as if to rub salt into my wounds, I was taken out of product development altogether and assigned to public relations. I was always good at public relations and had done it before, professionally, but just because I was good at it didn't mean I wanted to do it, or that I couldn't do other things better. I told everyone—Jack, Kit, and everyone else—that if I wanted to do public relations I would have stayed in Beverly Hills and set up my own PR firm. I got into the computer business to market computers.

Jack said he understood, but told me, "If you want to get back into product management, you'll have to wait a few months." He didn't tell me what it was, but knowing he had something planned for me made it reasonably bearable. Still, watching the VIC group being tossed around, misused and not producing anything worth selling, was painful for me.

To make matters worse, the politics turned sour and the entire family of Commodorians came under heavy attack, from within. Jim Finke resigned in June 1982 after 18 months in office. He was candid in describing his days at Commodore, and his departure, to the press. He told the *Philadephia Inquirer:* "He [Jack] comes in like a lighted flare in a darkened room. He illuminates the scene with such brilliance that you're almost blinded. But his vapor trails take a lot of the oxygen out of the air. And when he leaves the room there's no more light."

Jack was quoted in the same article as saying, "Finke is a professor. He spent the first six months planning to do things and the next six months planning to leave."

But if Finke had the personality of a monarch, our next president was a dictator by comparison, and not necessarily a benevolent one. Robert H. Lane was appointed president of North American operations in November 1982. He came to Commodore from ITT Grinnell, and had been working in Saudi Arabia. Before ITT, he'd been a president and vice president with Northern Telecom in the U.S. and Europe. A Canadian by birth, he had some experience in marketing and product management and seemed especially proud of his achievements as product manager for Good Humor Ice Cream in Canada.

Lane was in his fifties, tall and athletic-looking, although his 1950s-style crewcut seemed out of place in 1982. We were all a little surprised when he was hired, and there was speculation Irving Gould was behind it.

Jack went out of his way to announce Bob's appointment to most of the Commodorians. He picked out those of us in the "in group" he thought Lane should get to know and asked us to attend Lane's first official meeting. We all assembled in a large conference room—Kit, Greg Pratt, myself, and several others. Lane came in, sat down, looked at me and asked very insultingly, "What are *you* doing here?"

"Jack asked me to be here," I replied.

I guess to Lane, not being a vice president meant I wasn't supposed to be there. Then Jack came in, introduced us to Lane, and left. Lane gave us a quick rundown of his credentials, asked us to introduce ourselves, then adjourned the meeting.

Unlike Jim Finke, who stayed above the organization, Lane plunged in with a vengeance. But instead of waiting to absorb the business, he started shooting from the hip. It seemed to me and to several other Commodorians that he was criticizing a lot of us behind our backs and making snide remarks.

At this time I was up to my neck in public relations. My job was to explain to the press what Commodore was doing. We wanted everyone to know that we had won this war by design, not by accident. In the six months I handled PR, we had virtually no unfavorable stories written about Commodore. The one glaring exception was a dagger-thrust attack in *Forbes* with the laughable title of "Albatross," which took the ludicrous approach of criticizing Jack's competence in the middle of our most successful year as a company.

What hurt us personally was that Jack and I had co-operated fully with the reporter doing the story. It was one of the very rare times Jack went out of his way for the press.

About two weeks after Bob Lane was hired, I had lunch with Jack because we were working on a speech together. He asked me what my first impressions were of Lane, and I said, "He seems qualified for the job, but he's done two things that might make it hard for him to succeed. First, he shoots from the hip. As a new president, it seems like he should spend a little time finding out the organization before jumping in and making hasty decisions.

"Second—and I don't know if he can recover from this one—he's attacked virtually every Commodorian in the company, mostly behind their backs. Jack, even enemies go tell each other if someone takes an unfair shot at them. I think most of us have had the experience of hearing that Bob Lane criticized us, usually to someone else in a private

244

meeting. He's even mentioned that he's going to get rid of certain people, and those people know it. This is not the way for a new president to win friends and influence people."

That afternoon, I was called into Lane's conference room, and in the presence of Bill Wade and Jim Dionne, Lane asked me what the hell I was doing going to Jack's office this week, and attacked me for daring to go see him. He didn't believe I was writing a speech.

"We know you go tell Jack every little thing," he charged, trying to pretend Dionne and Wade shared his view. He went on for five minutes attacking me personally, his voice rising to a high-pitched squeak as it always did when he got angry. I refused to take the abuse and responded "Bullshit!" or "That's ridiculous" to his comments, and finally I just left. It was a ridiculous scene, but I left the meeting worrying that Commodore was in the hands of a man who seemed trigger happy, and who was attacking his own generals and colonels.

Immediately after that meeting, a funny thing happened. Bill Wade—who tended to have frequent disputes with me—came down to my office and apologized for Lane's behavior.

"Michael, I was embarrassed to have to sit there and listen to that," he admitted. Wade's business ethics were always impressive.

In the following months, Jack went to Asia to rest and in his absence the Commodorians came under heavy fire. Lane seemed determined to get rid of Kit Spencer and me.

Bill Wade warned me to stay away from Jack because Lane represented the future of the company. Wade himself tried hard to be loyal to Lane, until he heard that Lane had told someone that he was planning to get rid of Wade. After that, Wade's loyalty evaporated and he started doing hilarious impressions of Lane.

When I mentioned Leon Harris's name one day, Lane responded, "There can only be one president" and hinted that he was going to demote Harris, or get rid of him. But Leon got disgusted before that happened. He quit the company after a bizarre incident in which Lane approved raises for Leon's staff and told him he could tell them, then withdrew his approval and canceled the raises after the people had been told.

Lane went after Kit Spencer, too, virtually ignoring him or hardly paying attention when Kit tried to brief him on the various projects he was involved in. Jim Dionne was next. Jack brought Jim down from Canada to run the systems division after Leon left, but Jim got frustrated and wound up going back to Canada. There were even rumors of racial slurs against Greg Pratt.

It was no wonder that everyone, even the lower-level employees, started saying that Bob Lane was going after everyone who had Jack's home phone number in their Rolodex.

By the first week in December, I was fed up with this nonsense. I told Kit I was thinking of quitting. It was bad enough I had to sit on my hands and watch the VIC group going down the tubes. Now all the Commodorians were being attacked, by our own president. Commodore 64 software was months behind, and no one seemed to listen when I complained that we had better get moving. What's more, I had to put on a happy face and play the merry PR role.

I began to lose my composure. I told Kit I had had it. How could they keep one of their best proven marketing managers out of product marketing, while letting the products get all fouled up? I was practically pulling my hair out.

One day, in the middle of the afternoon, Kit said, "Come on. You need a beer." We went to a bar and he listened very patiently while I poured out out all my frustrations. He reassured me and urged me not to leave the company.

"I don't know," I said. "I just don't know."

Then I realized why all the other Commodorians had left. Working your heart out to get something going and then being knocked down after you succeed is a quite a slap in the face. It smarts. It feels like being punished for doing well. It hurts inside and leaves you with twinges of bitterness and humiliation. It was a tough, character-building experience. I suppose I lost a bit of my idealism and became more pragmatic, but I also learned not to be smug about

246

success because anyone on top can get knocked down at any time.

During the few weeks I was having my crisis, I stayed in the company only because of Kit Spencer. He helped me considerably. I steadfastly refused to call Jack. This was something I had to work through myself. Later, it turned out I was the only one who didn't call Jack. Virtually every Commodorian was under attack.

Then, miraculously, everyone began to be saved, each in a different way. At the time I used the word *sheltered*. We all found our own way of dealing with Bob Lane, but the company would never be the same.

Kit Spencer had come under attack as soon as Lane joined the company. Lane hired Myr Jones as vice president of sales and marketing, and effectively gave him Kit's marketing responsibilities. Now it was Kit's turn to be furious. Exactly one month after I had gone through my crisis, he had one, too. This time, *he* needed a beer. I told him he was going through the same thing I had, but I had gotten over it and so would he. But Kit was perilously close to leaving the company.

I was beginning to think it was a law of physics that all Commodorians must climb a mountain, get thrown back down the mountainside to a narrow ledge, then have to leave in search of another mountain. The only problem was that there were an awful lot of us starting to pile up on ledges.

Kit's mountain was advertising. He had just engineered a brilliant Christmas ad campaign launching the Commodore 64 and pushing the VIC, which was the most expensive campaign (over $12 million) in the company's history.

With everyone in the company trying to kibitz and play Monday night quarterback on the advertising themes and content, Kit had to deal with tremendous pressures, not to mention the constant pressure of Jack questioning every detail of that huge advertising budget. But Kit pulled it off. He juggled the politics, finances, and creativity. The result was an award-winning series of ads by Ally & Gargano, featuring the voice of Henry Morgan (best known to TV viewers as the glib panelist on "I've Got A Secret" hosted by Garry Moore in the 1950s and 1960s).

To try to get even more mileage out of the ad campaign, Kit and the agency created a dozen humorous ten-second spots. One went: "Become great at a game machine—maybe you can score 16 million on *Space Invaders*. Become great at the Commodore VIC—maybe you can score 1600 on the college boards." Another spot showed a chubby actor sitting in front of a fishbowl with a joystick, thinking he was playing a videogame. Again, Henry suggested this might not happen if he had a VIC instead of a game machine.

The Commodore 64 ads were creative, too. One TV ad showed a college freshman going off to school on the train and coming right back again, suggesting he should have had a Commodore computer. Some teachers in California didn't like the ad. There were a lot of teachers who felt there was too much emphasis on computers. Many anti-computer teachers were against the machines simply because it meant they had to learn about computers themselves.

The Commodore 64 print materials used a fabulous endorsement from Shearson American Express that read: "The Commodore 64 could be the microcomputer industry's outstanding new product introduction since the birth of this industry." That line appealed to everyone—investors, dealers, and customers.

Kit had done a splendid job of scaling the advertising mountain, but for Kit and the other Commodorians, the mountain was becoming very slippery. Kit talked to Jack, and they came up with a solution that sounds like a fantasy. Kit would move to the Bahamas! We needed someone there anyway because we were officially headquartered there, and Kit could edit an international company magazine and still help troubleshoot international marketing, advertising, and public relations activities. It was ideal and Kit accepted. He departed in January, right after the CES Show.

In Japan, Tony Tokai had a similar conflict, and his solution was almost as creative as Kit's. He began taking Fridays off to play golf, and no one could dispute that after over a decade without proper vacations, he deserved the time off.

Another young executive in an international job actually had a nervous breakdown and physically attacked Jack, John Calton, and some other people. He subsequently recovered and retired to a more pastoral existence.

It seemed to be the season for crises, but gradually, slowly, we all began to find shelter. When Ed Kellow, the long-time president of 'Commodore Canada, announced his retirement, Jim Dionne asked Bob Lane if he would consider Jim for the job. As I heard it, the conversation went something like this:

"Nope. I need someone with a manufacturing background," Lane said, "and you don't have it."

"Well, then, may I assume whoever you hire will have experience in manufacturing?"

"No. You can't assume that at all."

Jim was furious. He called Jack, and Jack told Jim and Lane that Jim would hire his own boss. It was the kind of thing that could only happen at Commodore. Apparently, Jack felt Jim wasn't quite ready for the top job, but he trusted him enough to go find a candidate to take the job. In this way, Jim was sheltered.

Bill Wade was next. He decided to retire, although not for six months. Somehow, his retirement leaked out and people started talking about it, so those of us who knew about it started pretending it really wasn't going to happen, and the rumors dried up. But Wade was now sheltered.

Around this time, Greg Pratt was looking awfully sullen. Then he talked to Jack one night and the next day he was back to normal. After that, Jack started calling him the "orchestra leader." Apparently he had been given some kind of assurances which gave him a shelter.

When Kit left in January, I was assigned to Myrddin Jones, whom Lane had brought in as vice president–sales and marketing. Myr was a Welshman with a great sense of humor and a caring attitude. I recognized him immediately as a senior marketing generalist. His previous experience at

Magnavox, where he had been in charge of marketing Odyssey game machines, meant he knew something about our industry and could really help. I looked forward to the prospect of working for him. We talked about where I would fit into the new marketing organization, and he said he wanted to make me director of strategic planning.

That sounded perfect. Finally, I was going to sink my teeth back into product development and marketing. Wrong again.

Myr said all he had to do was get clearance from Bob Lane and he didn't think there'd be any problem. That afternoon he had a meeting with Lane, and after the meeting he sat down with me and tried to explain that they had decided that my title should be manager, special projects.

"Come on," I said. "Let's face it. Lane told you he wants me fired and refused to let you make me director of planning." Myr didn't deny it. "Look, Myr, how can I work for you and respect you as a boss when you don't even have the authority to give a job title to the people who work for you? I'll tell you what. I appreciate the fact that you like me, and I think we'd make a terrific team, but given the politics around here, I think I'll find my own job. Don't worry about me. Give me a few days and I'll tell you what I'll be doing."

It was beginning to look like I'd have to call Jack, after all. Maybe I would play my Jack card. It was said that all Commodorians had a Jack card which they could play by asking Jack for some special favor. In my case, I figured I'd ask him to set me up in a small games group and I'd develop some software and other products for him, working outside the company in a separate location, like a research cell.

I never got the chance to call Jack, because that same afternoon I got a call from Sigmund Hartmann. Sig and I had been chatting on the phone for several months. Jack said he was trying to get something going with Sig—maybe an outside software group—and asked me to help him if I could.

The afternoon Sig called, he had just been offered the job of president of the new software division, which he would organize and develop. Sig told me he was inclined to take the job, but he wanted to be sure he had some trusted people to work for him when he came. He said he had already asked Jack if I could work for him. Jack said it was okay, but only if I agreed to it.

"Of course," I said.

"You can name your own title," Sig offered.

"Don't worry about titles," I told him. "I'm just glad I can help."

Sig called me back later to tell me he'd accepted the job, and the next morning I strode into Myr's office wearing a broad grin and announced, "You can stop worrying about me. I've got a new job." Now I had my shelter, too.

Jack hadn't forgotten me. He took note of all the good public relations we were getting (*Forbes* excepted), saw the VIC reach a million units, and he was grateful.

December was bonus time at Commodore, but in my dismal mood I really wasn't expecting anything. Last year at bonus time, Jack had held a mysterious meeting with me, Kit, and Greg Pratt. He said, "Michael, I want to explain with Kit and Greg here why you're not receiving a bonus this year." Apparently Kit and Greg had gone to Jack and were lobbying for a bonus for me.

I shook my head and said, "Why should I get a bonus? I just got a raise and stock options. Besides, the VIC hasn't started making money yet. I'll tell you what, if the VIC does well you can give me a bonus next year." Jack smiled at Kit and Greg and said, "See?"

One day just before Christmas, Jack invited me to his office. As I walked in, Bernhard Witter, our vice president–finance, patted me on the shoulder and said, "Good job." Puzzled, I went in and took a chair across the desk from Jack.

He smiled at me and said, "Michael, you've done a good job and you're now on the executive bonus plan. That means from now on your annual bonus is 100 percent." I started to express my appreciation but he just waved me away and said, "You deserve it." Then the meeting was over. Just like that. Not bad.

As Commodore's financial reports reveal, 10 percent of the company's net income was reserved each year for cash bonuses. As my own example bears out, Jack believed in giving his best performers large incentives because he demanded a lot and rewarded us well for our contributions and sacrifices. Such rewards weren't limited to managers.

Employees of MOS Technology who joined before November 1980 had a special bonus plan geared to the price of Commodore stock. A block of imaginary shares was set aside, and the bonus amount to be split was calculated on its market value. One year, eligible MOS employees received a bonus equal to half their annual salary. Programmers, engineers, and others who made important contributions were also eligible for bonuses most years.

At the end of 1982, Jack asked all managers to submit names of people who deserved bonuses, and the recommended amounts. All the managers nominated virtually *everyone* on their staff for bonuses. Jack said everyone can't have a bonus, and if the managers can't be more selective there would be *no bonuses*. U.S. management interpreted this to mean no bonuses for anyone, although what Jack actually meant—he said so many times—was to pick fewer, truly outstanding candidates. As a result, few people outside the executive bonus plan got bonuses that season.

"I like to give a lot or nothing," he said philosophically. "If I give just a little [to him a little was a few thousand dollars] I might as well give a handshake." So that's what he gave as a bonus—100 percent (or at least a hefty amount), a handshake, or nothing.

Things were beginning to look up again. I'd come a long way from being broke with six dollars in my pocket.

NINE

The Jack-fighters zoomed in out of nowhere, sending the whole industry scurrying for cover.

"Battle stations!" someone yelled.

"Zap! Pow! Blam!" The lasers ripped through the industry.

"Look out! It's Jack Tramiel!"

"...and the Commodorians!"

"...and the VIC commandos!"

"The Assassin craned his neck and whined, "VIC commandos? I thought we got rid of them!"

"Kablam!" He tumbled off the catwalk and floated into space.

The Old Atarian twiddled his ears and poked his head out of the game arcade and muttered, "I remember Space Invaders—"

The minicomputer gang heard the explosions and said, "Hey, what's going on around here?"

We grinned and flipped our coins in the air. The Force was with us. We could feel it in our veins. No one had to tell us. It was like an earthquake, rumbling under our feet.

The men in the Battlestar snickered and readied their big guns, but they couldn't maneuver fast enough.

"Take that, Atari! Take that, TI! Bite the dust, Radio Shack!"

"Zap! Pow! Blam!"

"Benutzefreundlichkeit!"

Winning the War
& The Last Days of Pompeii

In June 1982, Clive Smith, an analyst with the Yankee Group, said, "Clearly this is the year of the home computer. The speed with which it has happened has surprised almost everyone." Everyone except Commodore, that is.

Despite all the crazy behind-the-scenes politics, Commodore was winning the Home Computer Wars. We were winning on cost, price, and technology. By January 1983, the VIC was still going strong and we were getting ready to move the Commodore 64 from computer stores into mass-merchandising chains, which would lead to considerably greater sales volume. We were manufacturing more than 200,000 computers a month.

The January CES was a gleeful event. I felt so good that Kim and I learned to play craps. Although we didn't win anything, we couldn't lose our $500 pot no matter how hard we tried. Kim always came to the January CES in Las Vegas, as much to share the success and good feeling as to gamble and have fun.

This time, we showed several new products and accessories including a portable version of the Commodore 64 called the SX-64. SX stood for sex, of course. Jack was always saying "Business is like sex. You have to be involved." Once he said that on the MacNeil-Lehrer report and the camera showed him making a slight squeezing motion with both hands. About twenty people watched the show with him in his office, and when that quote came up, everyone roared with laughter, except Jack. It was the only time I ever saw him blush.

The SX-64 was the first portable color computer. It had one built-in disk drive although there was space for two. Unfortunately, bulk shipments of the SX-64 would be limited to a few thousand units, and we had to back off from promoting it until we got larger quantities. Incidentally, we were going to call our portable the Executive 64, but Adam Osborne named his new portable the Executive before we could legally register the name, so we went with SX-64.

Our CES exhibit also included a new color TV monitor priced under $300, a color printer/plotter, and two music products which we never marketed—a keyboard music synthesizer and an electronic drum, both for the Commodore 64.

But the most exciting new product was the *Magic Voice* speech synthesizer cartridge developed by Dr. Rich Wiggins and his group in our speech technology division in Dallas, Texas. The speech module had a built-in female voice but could be programmed to speak in other voices, too. The module had over 200 words, letters, and numbers built into its existing vocabulary and could work with larger vocabularies, on disk. There was a slot on the top of the module for inserting a game cartridge, and talking Bally games like *Gorf* and *Wizard of Wor* were programmed to talk if used with the *Magic Voice*.

At CES I represented Commodore on a panel where keynoter John J. MacDonald of Casio recalled that only three or four years ago, a similar panel was debating whether there would be a home market for computers, and whether "home computers" was a proper name for the category. I made the point that just in the past year computers had graduated from being sold like videogame machines to being sold like stereo component systems.

I also gave several interviews and noted we sold over 65,000 Commodore 64s between September 1 and December 1, and predicted we would move from 10,000 dealers carrying our products in 1982 to over 20,000 dealers in 1983.

The *CES Show Daily* quoted me as saying, "Anyone who would bring out a games machine to sell for $200 has to be crazy. . . . The computer market will totally engulf the games field." Unfortunately, there were quite a few crazy companies out there, and companies like Atari, Coleco, Mattel, and others insisted on bringing out new machines that did nothing more than play games, that were priced higher than real computers that featured better videogames than these dedicated game machines.

One of the few annoying things at the January CES was Texas Instruments' gigantic booth, which was across the aisle from ours and literally towered over us. Ordinarily we would have felt blighted by TI's looming presence, but this time it didn't bother us because we knew we were beating them.

The press kept reporting that Commodore and TI were "neck and neck" in the home computer market. It was also reported that TI was asking its dealers to sell the TI-99/4A below their cost, and make up the money on software. But this simply wasn't sound business. Although half of TI's software was excellent, the other half was junk; and consumers had no way of knowing which half they were buying.

We also knew we beat them on features. For example, if you wanted to connect a disk drive to a VIC or Commodore 64, you just plugged it in. But connecting a disk drive to a TI-99/4A required an expansion box and a disk controller in addition to the disk drive, costing extra hundreds of dollars. We also had a better keyboard (theirs was cramped). Our computers ran faster too. But the key factor was our manufacturing cost, which in the end determined whether we would make money or not.

The cost of making a VIC was estimated by the press at less than $60, while the Commodore 64 was thought to be slightly more expensive. One reporter estimated that Commodore could sell the Commodore 64—introduced at $595—for as low as $99 and still make a profit.

By contrast, it was estimated that TI's computer cost over $100 to manufacture—including overhead costs like a large U.S. dealer and customer training staff, which Commodore didn't have. A former TI executive told me it was almost suicidal the way they were pricing against Commodore, while all the time they knew that Commodore's costs were much lower and Commodore could beat them in a price-cutting war.

There was a powerful underlying principle that helped Commodore win the cost war. In addition to being vertically integrated, Commodore continued to re-engineer and cost-reduce existing products by combining and reducing the number of chips and other components that went into each computer. We also kept renegotiating lower parts costs with vendors.

These tactics helped us to keep lowering our costs, which allowed us to keep our profit margins steady even if competition forced us to lower our prices. Jack knew we had to keep cost-reducing our products, even popular products like the VIC, because no one knew when the competition would squeeze their prices down. Getting caught between costs that are too high and prices that are too low is called a cost-price squeeze—something Commodore scrupulously and deftly avoided.

The competition had less success. But who was the competition? In our industry, competitors weren't so much enemies as fellow warriors in a way. We were all fighting the same battle, to put out better, friendlier, less expensive home computers. Many people at different companies talked to each other on a regular basis, especially programmers and engineers, and it was always easy to get information about other companies just by calling an acquaintance at that company.

In a nutshell, Commodore's U.S. competitors included the majors like Apple, Atari, Coleco, IBM, Mattel, Osborne, Tandy (Radio Shack), Texas Instruments, Timex (Sinclair); and the minors like APF, Magnavox (Odyssey), and Bally (they had a low-quality game machine for a while).

Apple had chosen not to enter the low-priced computer market, wisely deciding to stay up-scale and make more money per unit. Apple sold fewer physical units than Commodore, but for several years had higher dollar sales. Still, Commodore passed them in 1983 and became the first computer company to report a billion dollar sales year.

Atari started out with a simple arcade and home version game called *Pong*, and then went on to greater success with their Model 2600 videogame machine. They created the videogame market. But their Atari 400 computer was overpriced and had too few features, and the Atari 800 never truly caught fire in the marketplace because Atari's computers were always at least $50 higher than their competition. All this ended up costing Atari and its parent company, Warner Communications, over a billion dollars in losses.

Coleco fielded an excellent game machine against Atari and later broke new ground with a $600 computer system called Adam, which was packaged to include a computer, disk drive, printer, and simple built-in word processing software. The first units were notoriously unreliable, and there were various peculiarities (the on/off switch for the computer was inexplicably located on the *printer*). The Adam was later passed by Cabbage Patch dolls as Coleco's principal revenue producer, and in 1984 Coleco wound up giving away $500 college scholarships to sell its $600 computer system.

IBM made a huge dent in the personal computer market and gave Apple a real run for its money when it burst on the scene in 1982 and sold 200,000 the first year. IBM was like a huge, lumbering dinosaur, gaining a large share of the market mostly on the basis of inertial forces: its bulk and reputation. The IBM PC was well-received. The PCjr went sour when introduced because of its inflated price and a nonstandard, Chiclet-type keyboard (named after the shape of Chiclets gum.)

For more than two years Mattel had been announcing that their Intellivision game machine would be expandable into a computer in the future. It wasn't. They gave Atari some strong competition with good graphics and creative two-player sports and adventure games, though. In mid-1983 they introduced the $200 Aquarius home computer, with poor results. Mattel became the first major victim of the videogame and home computer shakeout, and by the end of 1983 at least two brokers were attempting to act as middlemen to help Mattel dispose of its electronic products inventory, which was rumored to exceed $150 million. In the first half of 1983, Mattel posted a loss of over $100 million.

Osborne Computer Company had a terrific gimmick: They traded stock in Osborne in return for software from various software companies. Then they included several of these sophisticated programs free with the computer. Unfortunately, after the Osborne I was introduced, Adam Osborne couldn't follow his opening act fast enough with next-generation products, and his company went under due to a combination of industry attrition, financial problems, and competition from more sophisticated portables like the IBM-compatible Compaq, which appealed to the same market as the Osborne. As fortunes tumbled, the company went from 1000 employees to 80 employees in five months and filed Chapter 11 bankruptcy in September 1983.

Tandy Corporation was a global electronics manufacturer and retailer with over 7000 Radio Shack stores worldwide. At first, it seemed that Tandy computers would catch on big, and for a while Tandy sold more units than any other company. The deficiencies of their up-scale computers ranged from confusing product names (was the TRS-80 Model III better than the TRS-80 Model II?) to peripherals that gobbled up memory and didn't leave much for the user to work with. The Color Computer was overpriced at $400 when it came out, and never really got low enough in price to compete with Commodore. In the end, Tandy's network of electronics store franchises, which we all envied them in the early days, turned out to be a limitation. They became captives of their own distribution system and were unable to break out into mass distribution beyond their own stores.

Texas Instruments had driven quite a few companies out of the business during the Calculator Wars in the 1970s. Now, less than ten years later, Jack had turned the tables and was using TI's own techniques to defeat them—vertical integration, aggressive cost-reductions, matching price cuts and more. TI insisted on cutting prices although they knew Commodore could match or beat them on cost. They remained optimistic and smug, until Jack administered the *coup de grâce* in June 1983.

Timex, the watch company, bought the rights to the Sinclair ZX-81, a $99 black-and-white starter computer with a flat membrane keyboard. The ZX-81, which was designed by inventor Clive Sinclair in the United Kingdom, sold in large quantities but generated proportionately small sales and profit margins. Several hundred thousand units were sold, but I estimated that most of the buyers outgrew the ZX-81 within 30 days and went out and bought a color home computer like ours. The Timex/Sinclair actually helped sell more Commodore computers. Later, Sinclair went on to introduce a color computer called the Spectrum, which was a hit in the U.K. But by the middle of 1983, a lot of us at Commodore had discovered that the flat, sloping case of the ZX-81 made it ideal for another practical use—as a doorstop. The ZX-81 worked better than a rubber door-step, and aesthetically, it looked great on the floor.

This, then, was our competition, and it was becoming clear that we were beating them in the marketplace on all fronts except one: software.

Jack's idea of forming a software division was excellent, and Sig Hartmann was the right man to head the division. Sig was like a giant panda bear, with a thick shock of long silvery hair that he kept tossing back with his hand when it got disheveled during a rousing speech. He gave many rousing speeches, and he knew the Commodore philosophy because he had once worked for Jack and subsequently be-came a personal friend.

Born in Germany and educated in Belgium and the United States, he spent 18 years at TRW, where his assign-ments varied from serving as an engineering manager on NASA space projects to running a division which included several hundred engineers and programmers. He had once interrupted his career at TRW to work briefly as a general manager at Commodore, and went back to TRW when it didn't work out. "This time, they won't take me back," he joked.

Sig sometimes apologized for his German accent by spelling out a word he was using, like ROM. "That's rom, R-O-M," he would say, "not ram, R-A-M." He used his accent to advantage and constantly mispronounced words and even people's names. He loved tossing out humorous malapropisms and puns, and you could see in his eyes that he enjoyed it when people chuckled. But behind those laughing eyes and panda bear exterior was a shrewd and calculating warrior who always knew exactly what he was saying and doing.

Sig was recognized by everyone, including Jack, as the best negotiator in the company. He had a complete arsenal of innocent-looking tactics that allowed him to make deals that sometimes seemed astonishingly one-sided. He would spend hours casually chatting with software authors and presidents of software companies.

"So if we give you a fifty cents royalty—"

"Wait a minute. I said eight dollars, not fifty cents."

"Right. So if we give you fifty cents—"

"You mean eight dollars—"

"Look, we want to make money and so do you, or else you wouldn't be sitting here. So if we give you a fifty cents royalty and guarantee—"

And that's the way it went, until the negotiations either ended or Sig called in our legal counsel, Nick Lefevre, to do a quick contract or letter of agreement. Often Nick participated in the negotiations. Nick was rare among attorneys— a lawyer who knew the computer and videogame industries inside out. He was personally interested in computers, an avid hobbyist. After he was hired by Lee Schreiber in 1982, everyone said that if he hadn't been a lawyer he would have been a programmer or marketing executive because he loved all aspects of the home computer business and was always a good, creative sounding board as well as an excellent attorney.

Effective sounding boards, and all the other troops and ammunition we could muster, were going to be needed if Sig were to fulfill his charter: to establish a software division and possibly turn it into a full-fledged software company, and more immediately, to provide a full line of software for the Commodore 64 before the June CES Show.

At this time, Commodore had two separate software groups, the computer systems group headed by Paul Goheen and the games group under Bill Wade. The first time Sig flew in, Bill Wade took Sig aside and said he didn't want me in the software organization.

"Of course he doesn't want me in the division," I told Sig. "They haven't produced one product in six months, and I've been their harshest critic."

That first morning, a software manager who worked for Wade and didn't even know me, threatened to quit if I joined the group. Sig told him to quit if he wanted, because I was joining the group, and in an important capacity. That day I took the manager to lunch and told him a little about myself. When we came back to the office he went straight to Sig, told him he was wrong about me, and withdrew his objections.

Paul Goheen, who was running the systems software group, also drew some criticism. Some people said he should be fired, but Paul presented himself so well in our first meetings that Sig began to suspect that the managers who were badmouthing Paul and me were themselves the ones who should be watched closely. For my part, I refused to badmouth anyone and quickly won a position as a trusted advisor and *consiglière* to Sig.

Within two weeks, most of the political fears evaporated. I think even Bill Wade was surprised at how few were the confrontations between us, given our stormy history. It turned out to be fun working together. Wade was a good warrior to have on your side. We all enjoyed watching him in action. His management style was colorful, unique, and fascinating.

For example, in meetings he had a way of leaning forward and physically stopping a conversation with his hands. He had large hands, and if he disagreed with something you said, he would lean forward and push those hands toward you with his fingers spread wide, say "Ex*cuse* me," and then tell you why he thought you were wrong. He had a whole repertoire of gestures that were guaranteed to interrupt any conversation. Sometimes he would stop you with his hands and say, "I love you—but you're *wrong*," and then go on to tell you quite bluntly why he thought you were being stupid or out of line.

But everyone's favorite Wadeism went something like this: "Excuse me. Either you're not paying attention or you didn't understand." Once, Myr Jones was meeting with Wade, and Wade complimented him on something he said. Myr replied, with a perfectly straight face, "Well, I must be learning then, because in all our other meetings either I wasn't paying attention or I didn't understand!" Then he turned and winked at me.

One thing Wade and I agreed on was the need for better quarters for the programmers. About this time, Commodore provided the solution by acquiring a 575,000 square-foot facility in West Chester, Pennsylvania, and announcing that all computer operations would be housed there. It was *huge*.

One floor was as big as several department stores. There was an area in the front for corporate offices including legal counsel and finance; a closed-off area for the technology and research group headed by Lloyd Taylor; and an enormous open area for sales and administration. The software division was located on the other side of a wall from sales and administration.

The sales, administration, and accounting sections were all thrown together in a huge, open area without any walls, low partitions, or cubicles. The employees used their file cabinets to try to create walls and were forced to work in the open among clattering computers, calculators, and people constantly on the phone. At the same time, Bob Lane, his three or four vice presidents, and the legal staff occupied sumptuous paneled "fishbowl" offices with completely glass fronts. These glass offices were strung out around the entire perimeter of the area, as if to remind the employees how enormous the gap was between them and the top managers.

To make matters worse, they purchased a limousine and left the price tag on the windshield for a whole day, and everyone knew it cost over $30,000. A lot of people complained that the brass was buying limousines and they couldn't even get office partitions. In the software division, we joked that it was the "let them eat cake" philosophy of management.

264

The software area was Herman Millered, with the kind of partitions and cubicles we'd gotten used to over the years, and everyone had their own semiprivate area. Sig insisted that his office be smaller than Lane's because he wanted Jack to see he wasn't going overboard on luxuries for himself. He really understood Jack's philosophy.

Extending down the wall from Sig's office was a string of four small glass-fronted offices which someone dubbed "the glass menagerie," but Sig turned it into a pun and called it "the glass mahogany." It was typical for someone to say, "Give this memo to the glass menagerie, or get the glass menagerie in here for a meeting."

The menagerie consisted of Bill Wade, me, Paul Goheen, and John Mathias. Wade handled operations, I handled marketing and documentation, Paul handled applications and productivity software such as word processors and financial tools, and John Mathias handled games. Assisting Mathias was John Campbell, a young engineer I'd hired straight out of college the year before as a marketing assistant and who had also worked for Bill Wade. Campbell was a tireless worker with the efficiency and tact of Radar O'Reilly from "M*A*S*H."

Larry Ercolino, who originally managed telecommunications, became a sort of administrative and operations troubleshooter and later inherited responsibility for software manufacturing, which was directly supervised by Steve Peaurt and Steve Wickham.

By this time, Andy Finkel—an original VIC commando—had become the software group's best technical brain. He was made technical manager and worked with Lloyd Taylor's engineering group on both hardware and software problems, and eventually became the product manager for Commodore's next generation of home computers, the 264 series. Later, Dr. Dan Kunz came over from the educational sales division and headed up our educational software program. In addition to the games and documentation groups, the division also had a testing and quality control section.

Rich Wiggins's speech group in Dallas was put into the software division, and John Feagans in Santa Clara joined the group and built up a small staff of programmers who became known as the *Magic Desk* group. Feagans, one of the inventors of the original Commodore PET, was working on a picture-driven program called the *Magic Desk*, which used picture commands instead of words. This allowed users to point at something on the screen by using a joystick to move a pointing finger, instead of having to type all the commands on the keyboard.

For example, if you wanted to use the Magic Desk Typewriter, you would just the joystick to move the finger on the screen to the picture of the typewriter, press the joystick button, and an animated typewriter would appear. To save or retrieve what was typed on a floppy disk, the user didn't have to use technical-looking disk commands. Instead, he or she simply pointed at the picture of the file cabinet on the opening screen, opened the file drawer, and scrolled through the files. The operations of the disk drive were totally transparent to the user.

John Feagans's picture-driven software was designed as a cartridge for the Commodore 64, and in many respects was similar to Apple's Lisa, a $10,000 computer system which included a very sophisticated picture-driven software system designed by Apple founder Steve Jobs and his programming team. Apple was excited about Lisa and about a future product called Macintosh.

John asked me to come out to California for a few days and help design the first *Magic Desk* software. He wanted to do some brainstorming and work on the graphics. I took Jeff Bruette, our best graphics programmer, with me, and by the time we landed at San Jose we had the opening screen-shot drawn in PET graphics on a sheet of graph paper.

We had to get the *Magic Desk* done by the June 1983 CES because Sig had promised Jack he'd have a ton of software. There were major complaints from dealers and customers alike about the lack of good software for the Commodore 64. We didn't even have a word processor or spreadsheet.

Sig and the rest of us tore into what Jack called the software menu for the Commodore 64, and our new division erupted with new software. Gail Wellington, an American settled in the United Kingdom, was in charge of software in the U.K. She and her staff contributed several key programs to the menu, including *EasyScript*, a word processor for the Commodore 64 which was so sophisticated that at least two people I know were able to write book manuscripts with it.

A complete small business accounting series was licensed from Dick Stahl, the president of Infodesigns in Detroit. It was to be sold at the unheard-of price of $99 per package. At Neil Harris's suggestion, we also licensed a series of Infocom adventure games on diskette, which were the hottest-selling games in the home computer industry.

The menu began to take shape.

Against this frenetic scenario, price skirmishes escalated into price wars between Commodore and Texas Instruments.

To understand price wars properly, it is important to realize that there are four numbers involved: (1) the *cost* of the product, which is what the manufacturer pays to have it made; (2) the *dealer price* of the product, which is what the dealer pays to buy it from the manufacturer; (3) the manufacturer's *suggested retail*, which is the price the manufacturer suggests should be charged to individual customers by the dealer; and (4) the *actual retail price*, which is the price dealers really charge customers.

Parry, thrust, parry. It was like a sword fight. We were all wildly slashing prices. *Home Furnishings Daily* ran a caricature of Jack Tramiel on the cover of their Computerware insert, depicting Jack in an admiral's costume, holding a saber aloft.

I guess we started the price wars when we introduced the VIC for under $300 when everyone else was selling computers for $600. The war really began to heat up in August 1982: TI issued a $100 rebate on its 99/4A, which brought the retail price down to $200. Commodore responded by dropping its VIC dealer price by $40, and letting the retail price float. For a short time we even stopped publishing suggested retail prices to let the market determine the retail price—it was capitalism in its purest form. In September 1982, Commodore began selling the Commodore 64 through computer stores, at a suggested retail price of $595.

Atari followed Texas Instruments's lead in December with a $55 rebate on the Atari 400 which brought the price under $200, and the dealer price of the Atari 800 was dropped from over $600 to under $500—still too high to compete.

TI responded by extending its rebate, which expired in December, to April 1983; and began giving away voice synthesizers to people who bought minimum quantities of software.

In January 1983, Commodore started selling the Commodore 64 to mass merchants, including K mart, and the actual retail price dropped to $400. The dealer price of the VIC was dropped to around $130 and mass merchants started selling the VIC at or below dealer cost to customers who also bought Datassettes, modems, software, or other accessories.

In February, TI cut another $48 off the dealer price of the 99/4A, dropping the retail under $150.

Then, TI uncovered a major technical problem: There was a potential hazard with their power pack (transformer). They had to stop cold in the middle of the war, fix old units, and substitute new transformers in units already in stores and in inventory. An article in the February 23 issue of *Home Furnishings Daily* carried the headline "TI Asks Dealers to Stop Selling 99/4A Until Hazard Is Corrected." For one month, it was as if TI's whole army had stopped cold.

We weren't elated. We were more sympathetic than anything, saying, "There but for the grace of God—" But our sympathy didn't keep us from proceeding with the war.

In April, Commodore hit hard. Dealer prices were reduced on peripherals and some software. Dealers applied these savings to the price of the VIC and dropped the price below $100—making the VIC the first color computer being sold under $100. TI announced they would match the VIC's $100 price point, but not until June.

Then Myr Jones came up with a brilliant rebate campaign. In mid-April, we told the public, "Send us any old computer or videogame, even if it doesn't work, and we'll give you a $100 rebate on a Commodore 64." Within weeks, there was a ceiling-high pile of rebate computers in our warehouse, everything from old VICs to Intellivisions, Ataris, and Timex/Sinclairs. A lot of people went out and bought Timex computers for $50 and sent them in to get the $100 rebate, netting them $50. I told Jack I was glad I wasn't Timex/Sinclair's product manager. How could you calculate software or accessory sales when you couldn't tell which computers were being bought for home use, and which were being sent in to Commodore? The rebate brought the price of the Commodore 64 under $300.

Atari suddenly had trouble selling its newly introduced 1200XL computer, even with a $100 rebate. In early May, Timex dropped the suggested retail price to $49. Atari offered a $100 rebate on the Atari 800, bringing the actual price below $400—still too high. By the end of May, TI could no longer wait for their announced June price cut, and started giving away $300 expansion modules.

Coleco unveiled the Adam computer system with great fanfare. The Adam bundled a computer, disk drive, printer, and built-in word processor in the same box for $600. Most dealers I spoke with said they saw it as a clever marketing scheme to persuade people to accept a new, untested computer, and pointed out that a Commodore 64 with the same peripherals would probably cost the same price by the time Adam was introduced.

Then, the *coup de grâce*. At the June Consumer Electronics Show in Chicago, Commodore cut the dealer price of the Commodore 64 to $200, causing the actual retail to fall between $200 and $230. The killing blow was administered by software, however. Not only did we announce 70 new software programs for the Commodore 64, but we also announced that we were cutting prices in half on all of our home computer software.

When the word was out that we cut our software prices in half, Bill Turner, the president of TI's consumer product group, came stalking over to our booth and asked why in the world we would possibly consider dropping software prices when that's where all the margins were.

The answer was simple. Thanks to Jack Tramiel's business religion, Commodore's costs were so low that we were making money on *both* our computers and our software. TI's prices were so high that they were taking a loss on their computer and trying to make it up in software profits. But we'd cut the profits out of their software and there was nothing they could do, and nowhere to hide.

Turner took the TI management team and whisked them back to Dallas. After putting their pencils to their pads, they formally and unexpectedly predicted they would lose $100 million in the second quarter that year. This was partly from lower sales in the first quarter (which we at Commodore had already suspected, but nobody else believed) and partly from increased reserves for rebates and price-protection payments to retailers caught with swollen inventories.

The story appeared in the June 13 *Wall Street Journal*: "Texas Instruments's tailspin could be an early sign that home computer makers have begun to glut the lower end of the market and that price-cutting has begun to take its toll."

It was true that price-cutting was taking its toll, but Commodore 64 sales remained strong, giving the lie to rumors of a glut. To think that TI had been defeated by some sort of a massive maturing of the home computer industry was merely wishful thinking.

The news report also said, "But so far, the other market leader among the three biggest companies, Commodore International, has shown immunity to any slowdown, reporting recently that profit for its third quarter, ended March 31, surged 124% to $25 million."

A few weeks later, Bill Turner resigned from Texas Instruments, and after that Texas Instruments made its fateful announcement that it was bowing out of the home computer business.

There were other dramas unfolding behind the scenes. TI wasn't the only company to lose a president at the CES Show. It was the last day of the show and we were gathered on our 300-foot boat. All in all, it had been a very good week for us. The whole convention was buzzing about Commodore's 300-foot boat exhibit. The boat was huge, white and stately, anchored alongside a pier a few miles from McCormick Place where the CES show was held. A special banner we had designed hung suspended over the gangplank, announcing "A Boatload of Software." In fact, we were announcing over 70 new software programs for the Commodore 64 and VIC. It was the largest number of products ever introduced at one time at the CES show.

Much of the new software was being demonstrated by software personnel in two dozen exhibits on the first deck of the boat, while upstairs on the second deck, visitors were invited to watch a very slick and emotionally stirring multimedia slide show which told "the Commodore story" with impressive graphics and music. It seemed somehow significant that the dominant background color in the slide show was a deep, blood red.

At one end of the main deck, there was a sizable dining area where they served breakfast, lunch, dinner, and nonstop appetizers. At the opposite end of the deck was a series of staterooms which we used as temporary offices and meeting rooms.

Sig and I and the other software directors held meetings and negotiations with journalists, software authors, mass merchants, and others. Meeting in the shipboard restaurant, in a stateroom, or while strolling outside on the deck was a nice way to do business.

In keeping with the nautical theme, Lane and a few people he called his trusted lieutenants wore special baseball caps he had made, with gold braid on the visors like navy officers' caps. Several lively meetings were hosted by the U.S. and Canadian sales groups for their visiting distributors and dealers, but Sig complained he hadn't been invited to some of the most important meetings. In typical Sig Hartmann style, he crashed the meetings and put himself on the agenda as a speaker.

In every speech, he predicted we were going to sell a

jillion software products. A jillion sounded like a lot of software and, for all anyone knew, it was.

The high point of the week was a shipboard press party held one evening with speeches by Irving, Jack, Sig Hartmann, and our Canadian managers. It went very well. But when the party broke up around 10:00 p.m., most of the press went outside and piled into our fleet of rented limousines, and didn't go anywhere.

Like many companies at the CES show, we had a handful of limousines for ferrying Commodore people and dealers between the boat, CES exhibits, and our hotels. The limousines were waiting when the press party broke up and the journalists poured into the cars, but instead of going back to their hotels the limousines drove them a hundred yards down the pier and left them there practically in the middle of nowhere to find their own transportation back.

Those limousines caused other problems, too. I spent most of the convention week accompanying Sig to various meetings around Chicago. Sig had been periodically borrowing a limousine to get him back and forth to his hotel meetings, but the limousine schedules kept getting rearranged. One time Sig and I were standing in the lobby of the Conrad Hilton Hotel, getting ready to go to a meeting, when Bob Lane stalked up to Sig with a walkie-talkie in his hand and demanded that Sig give him back the limousine he'd just been given for the day. Sig, who almost never lost his temper, exchanged harsh words with Lane and sent him away, but we took a taxi instead of the limousine, which caused him to be late for his next two meetings.

"I'm a president, too," Sig declared hotly. Sometimes, people tended to forget it because Sig bent over backwards to keep from flaunting his rank and tried to accommodate rather than dictate.

When Irving Gould arrived, Don Richard asked me if I could get someone reliable to take Irving's and Lee Schreiber's suitcases over to their hotel and check them in. I went over myself and took care of it. This sort of thing was one of the extra duties performed by all Commodorians—and, I guess, general's aides. Irving often flew in from New

York or Toronto to visit a convention, but he seldom stayed the whole week. Typically, he dropped in for a day or two, toured the Commodore booth, walked around the show, had a meeting or two and then departed.

This time, however, he lingered around the boat for the entire week, observing every little event. From the expression on his face, it was apparent he wasn't pleased. He was still very gracious, asked a lot of questions, and was more curious than usual about the software we were showing; but as he observed the goings-on at the boat, his expression grew steely.

On the last day of the show, Bob Lane left the company. I was one of the few people who knew about it the night before it happened. Anticipating events before they happened was a habit I picked up when I was a journalist; it was part of what Jack, and now Sig, called my nose.

I was there when Jack came to see Lane. He arrived in one of the rented limousines, walked Lane to the front of the boat, spent no more than five minutes talking to him, then walked back. Then he walked outside, said good-bye to his son Sam, me, and a few other people who were there, and left.

Whether Lane walked the plank or simply resigned, I don't really know. There was considerable conjecture in the press. In the June 27 issue of *Computer Retail News*, reporter John Russell wrote about Lane's departure and quoted "a former Commodore executive" as saying: "They bring in a man who came from a very structured environment and placed him in an environment of street fighters. Most people that work there [at Commodore] are from the streets and are successful because working at Commodore is conducive to being a survivor."

The source went on to say, "A president at Commodore has to come in and sit down with all the old people and marshal them as a cohesive unit. He [Lane] was given a honeymoon and grace period, but never accomplished that objective."

Although Lane did not survive as a president of Commodore, this doesn't mean his management style wasn't suited to other organizations. Obviously he did well before coming to Commodore, and by most reports he was successful after leaving.

In trying to explain Lane's departure, and the departure of other top managers at Commodore, many observers mistakenly concluded that Jack Tramiel held Commodore in an iron fist and would not share the power. But this was both inaccurate and simplistic.

The anecdotes associated with Bob Lane, and even my personal reactions as a Commodorian, reveal very graphically how difficult it was for any president to come into a tightly knit company with a predefined company philosophy. It was extraordinarily difficult for presidents like Jim Finke, Alan Fink, Leon Harris, and Bob Lane to walk in cold to a company like Commodore and begin dealing with an infrastructure which described itself with such smug and self-important words as "Commodorian," "family," and "disciples."

Myr Jones, who was always an extremely perceptive observer of the company, called it an infrastructure, and referred to the "hidden organizaton." One Christmas, Myr gave an unusual and symbolic present to his friends at Commodore: a copy of a military handbook entitled *The Rules of War*, by Lao-tzu, the sixth century B.C. Chinese philosopher and founder of Taoism.

A book that I found much more useful as a Commodore manager was given to me by Kit Spencer: *Management & Machiavelli*, by Antony Jay. In his second chapter, entitled "The State, The Corporation and the Devil," Jay writes:

> The first transference you have to make when studying political history in management terms is to read 'economic conflict' for 'military conflict.' Corporations compete just as keenly as states, and are impelled by exactly the same human emotions of greed and fear and pride, or self-interest and opportunism and a desire for security, or whatever else you believe to be the root of man's competitiveness with man. . . . Corporations, like states, can exhaust themselves by too much warfare, just as they can become fat and lazy

from insufficient exercise. But this transference only points up the comparison: a sales director planning an assault on a rival's market needs exactly the same qualities as a general planning an invasion: not just courage and a steady nerve, but, more precisely, knowledge of the enemy's strength and weakness and how strong his reserves are and how fast he can mobilise them . . . what the strength of his own force is and its endurance, how far he can push them, what ground they fight best on . . . where the likely counter-attack will come . . . and how to meet it—these sorts of comparisons can go on almost endlessly, since the essentials are identical and only the superficialities are different. The difference between killing and selling may, objectively, be rather more than superficial, but not the qualities they demand of those planning and executing the campaign.

After we returned from the June CES Show, it was back to the war, but now the war took on the trappings of a revolution. It had all the elements: purges, struggles, internal combat, and even a troika. And in the end, this revolution, like most revolutions, would result in one of the founders of the company assassinating his long-time closest comrade.

Meanwhile, a Commodorian was finally appointed to the position of president. Jack tapped his executive assistant, Don Richard, for the job. He was an excellent choice. Don had been Jack's assistant once before, left the company and returned, and he had a realistic perspective of the politics at the top.

Don's background included both engineering and top management, and allowed him to stand toe-to-toe with any engineering person in the company. He was also an insatiable reader. In casual conversation he loved to talk about great writers, and it was not unusual to sit and discuss, for example, the writings of Dostoevsky.

Don had what might be the best view of how Jack interacted with the Commodorians. Shortly after a trip to Japan, he described a visit to the ancient palace of the Shogun. The Shogun's sleeping quarters, he said, were surrounded by a "singing floor" cleverly made of nails that vibrated and sounded like birds singing when anyone approached. This was more of a warning than an aesthetic feature, for the Shogun was always subject to assassination.

Don said the Shogun sat on a raised platform, surrounded by a group of adolescent princes. The older feudal lords and military leaders sat at a lower level. Behind the Shogun's platform was a door. If a young prince attacked him, the Shogun was strong enough to ward him off. If one of his lords attacked him, the young princes would jump in and sacrifice themselves if necessary to give the Shogun time to escape out the back door. Don said this was how he saw the Commodorians. Jack was the Shogun and we were the young princes who sat between him and the other older leaders.

Like all Commodore presidents, Don was given a honeymoon, too. Publicly, his appointment was described as temporary, but he was widely respected inside the company and most people were pulling for his appointment to become permanent.

For a short time, the Commodore sales organization was run by a troika consisting of Sig Hartmann, Greg Pratt, and Jim Dionne, but this didn't work out very well because the troika never became a real management team. Each member of the troika had his own responsibilities— Hartmann, software; Pratt, operations; and Dionne, sales and marketing. The troika wasn't a bad idea, but each man had divisional responsibilities that required so much attention it was difficult for the three of them to step back and take a broad view of the whole organization.

Before he was named to the troika, Dionne had been working for Myr Jones. Now the roles were reversed and Jones wound up working for Dionne. A gossip column in *Computer & Software News* suggested, correctly, that Jones was interviewing for a position elsewhere.

The first thing the sales organization did was to disband the sales organization. It sounded preposterous, but all the regions were closed down and the people summarily fired. The regions had already been scaled back to skeleton sales/support teams when Commodore switched focus from business systems to home computers, but these organizations, as small and widely scattered as they were, held some of the most experienced and talented Commodore specialists in the company.

To the outside world, the firings looked like a major flip-flop. Those who were terminated included twenty district salespeople who had come on board only a few months before in April. District managers were asked to stay on as district representatives. A few experienced people tried it, but there were problems with compensation; and when major technical problems created an almost total shortage of disk drives in the fall, most of the independent representatives quit.

Commodore then began weeding out small distributors and dealers, and wound up with a list of about 65 major distributors who were authorized to carry the Commodore line. It was felt that dealing with major distributors only placed the burden of dealer support on the shoulders of the distributors, cut down the size and cost of Commodore's sales/support organization, and allowed Commodore to deal only with winners. This would force dealers who had previously dealt directly with Commodore to go through distributors to get their products.

The major exceptions were national accounts, some of which dealt direct with Commodore. However, even the national accounts began to work through distributors because of the special support they received, and a new phrase— rack jobbers—was introduced into computer sales jargon.

A few months after it was formed, the troika quietly dissolved. In October, Irving Gould brought in a friend and neighbor from the Bahamas, Sol Davidson. Sol became general manager of Commodore in the U.S., which was a position equivalent to a presidency, although there was some reluctance to appoint another president.

Davidson was a former art history professor who inherited a high fashion business from his father and, surprising even himself, became highly successful at it. Some people called him a "rag merchant," but it was only in jest. Sol, who was in his early sixties, was a shrewd and erudite manager with business instincts forged in the New York fashion arena.

During this time, I don't think anyone really knew that we were in the midst of a revolution. There was a feeling of uneasiness lingering in the air, but it was impossible to define. It was almost like a fog. You couldn't touch it or brush it out of the way, but it made it hard to see the organization clearly. For the first time since joining Commodore, I had trouble sensing what would happen next; the future was unclear.

I continued to handle a variety of software marketing activities and also pushed to expand Commodore's commercial book business. In June, I was asked to prepare the 1984 annual report and, working closely with Don Richard and Julie Bauer who was in charge of packaging and media, I tore into the project, mostly doing the writing with Don and working with Julie on layout and design.

Don pointed out that 1983 was Commodore's twenty-fifth year in business, so we decided to do a silver annual report cover. I had an artist do a colorful and vibrant red, white, and blue drawing that showed a computer chip blurring into a computer. The drawing was placed at the top of the cover as a small horizontal strip. Everyone liked the cover, except Jack.

"It's too Picasso," he complained. "No one will know what it is."

"You're wrong." I told him.

"I'm not wrong," he said.

"Yes you are."

He picked up the large board that held the drawing and walked out into the sales and administration area. I started to follow him, but he turned and held up his hand. "Tut-tut-tut—you stay here." He said if I came along the people would know what I wanted them to say, just from looking at my face. I guess he was right.

Then, to quite a few people's surprise, he walked up and down aisles, stopping at nearly every desk, asking them what they thought the drawing symbolized. After several minutes he walked back, handed me the drawing, and said, "You're right and I'm wrong." We used the picture on the cover and it turned out to be our classiest-looking report. We also broke a record and came in on time. Jack told us it was the first time an annual report had been completed on schedule.

Our fiscal 1983 sales hit $681 million, up 124 percent from the previous year. Our net income of $88 million and earnings per share of $2.86 were both up 117 percent, and shareholders' equity increased 80 percent. We were clearly on our way to the billion dollar sales level.

Meanwhile, the software division started feuding with the sales division. Sig and Sol conducted a friendly ongoing dispute. Sig said the sales division wasn't ordering or selling enough software; Sol pointed out that a huge unmanageable backlog of VIC games had been allowed to build up—stretching back to 1982—and this was good reason to be cautious in ordering Commodore 64 software.

Both men were right. But the situation was complicated because the sales organization, having just terminated most of the hands-on salespeople who understood the software market, was short on people who could properly evaluate, and sell, software. Also, the sales group was more oriented toward hardware, and in the national accounts area, which was still headed by David Harris, most software sales took third billing after computers and peripherals.

To further compound the problem, the price wars we had waged in the spring and summer began to catch up with us. It seems no one took into account the impact of price protection. Price protection means a manufacturer guarantees to certain large dealers that if the company drops the price of a product, the company will cover the difference, either financially or—more commonly—by giving the dealer more products with a total value equivalent to the price difference.

But the problem was bigger than we thought because many of our dealers had built up huge inventories of VIC games in their warehouses and the price cuts caught them with large quantities of software they had purchased at the old, higher dealer prices. This turned out to be a good lesson because we started requiring our mass merchants and distributors to give us periodic inventory reports. Nevertheless, the short-term bottom line was that we had to give away a lot of the Commodore 64 game cartridges and other software instead of selling it. As a result, the sales organization didn't gear up to sell software as they otherwise would have had to do if the Commodore 64 wasn't given away under the price-protection program.

Another problem we faced involved software manufacturing. At the June CES, Sig promised to deliver all 70 software programs by August 31. Unfortunately, much of the software couldn't be manufactured that quickly. As a result we drew some criticism both internally and from outside although most of the programs were available by Christmas.

Since our formation, the software division published very thick monthly and quarterly divisional reports which it was my responsibility to prepare. At first I wrote nearly the whole report under Sig's direction. Later as everyone got more comfortable, we split up the chores among the various software directors.

I moved into Bill Wade's office, next to Sig's office, when Wade retired at the end of May 1983. I have to admit a lot of us missed his colorful presence and occasionally wished we had him with us to help win some battle which was suited to his special hard-nosed skills.

In November, Sig, I, Paul Goheen, and Bob Russell from engineering attended the first official international software conference, which later led to an international software coordinating committee. The three-day conference was hosted by Gail Wellington in London and included representatives from more than a dozen countries. On the last day, Rich Wiggins flew in and demonstrated a German language tutorial which featured authentic pronunciation and worked with the Commodore 64 and *Magic Voice* speech module. We Americans gave presentations as well, and Gail and I teamed up to chair some strategic planning sessions.

Afterwards, I was joined by Kim, and we took a working vacation to visit several Commodore friends in Europe, including Eli Kenan, our Commodore distributor in Paris, and Jim Bachmann, our general manager in Italy. We missed seeing Harald Speyer in Germany, but by this time he was busy anyway in his new role as head of European operations.

Commodore Italy was an especially lively place in 1983. They were going through a renaissance and their staff of aggressive young managers like Vico Angeli and Rinaldo Farina reminded me of the original VIC commandos. It was not surprising to discover that their renaissance had been inspired by Jack. A few months before, he had visited Italy, had seen that their VIC sales were slow, and had told them to cut the price in half. Jim Bachmann admits he was a trifle chagrined by the idea, but they did as Jack suggested. Before long the VIC was the best-selling computer in Italy, and the Italians had enough money to start advertising on television, which gave them even better sales. They went so far as to predict they might match the sales of long-entrenched Commodore strongholds like the U.K. and Germany, which was practically heresy in Europe.

While in Italy, Kim and I spent a few days in Florence. In addition to seeing the works of Michelangelo and da Vinci, we learned something about Machiavelli as well. One of our guidebooks said Machiavelli "wrote as a politician deeply troubled by the sight of his beloved state falling to pieces." His best work, *The Prince*, deals with the absolute authority of a strong political leader who commands total obedience, and engenders a form of civic humanism expressing confidence in the power of men to control events.

Contrary to popular belief, Machiavelli was not himself the prince or the benevolent dictator he espoused. He was merely the commentator and chronicler of that style of politics. I couldn't help noting that he was in the military for a while as an officer, and for some reason it seemed significant that he wrote *The Prince* while in self-imposed exile.

Apart from its Machiavellian insights, our European tour was a tremendously uplifting experience, because it got me involved again with the international management set, which I missed since Kit Spencer had left and my job had changed from product marketing manager to software marketing director. I found that I really enjoyed the international arena and missed the challenges of multinational marketing.

Back in the States, we were working on our next home computer, which was nicknamed the 264 Series. There were two models, the Commodore 16 and Commodore PLUS/4. Sig and the rest of us in the software group felt we could and should field a computer with built-in software. We said it could be done, and quickly. The engineers working on the project said it couldn't be done, at least not in time to launch the project.

Jack said, "Do it."

The built-in software project became a pet cause of Rich Wiggins and Tom Brightman in the speech technology and robotics groups in Dallas. (We had robotics, but the group never fielded a product.) After they showed the engineering group that it could be done, and quickly, the engineers started working on it, with support from Andy Finkel, who was named product manager.

As a result of everyone's almost superhuman development effort, Commodore went to the January CES Show in 1984 with several models of the PLUS/4 which featured built-in software. The plan was to introduce several models, including machines with built-in word processing, an electronic spreadsheet, and Logo, a popular computing language used to teach children how to program.

The sales division was scared to death of the project. They didn't think they could sell several different models and kept lobbying against building in software. At the very least, they said, we should market only one model. Jack was insistent that we should have several models, "just like General Motors."

His theory was that we could segment the market according to interest groups, and he was planning to do the same thing with professional computers. A licensing agreement with Zilog gave us the 16-bit Z-8000 microprocessor chip, and a Z-8000 computer was being developed to help get us back into the business market. Another computer called the Hyperion was licensed, to give us IBM-compatible technology. Within a year, Jack predicted, home computers would have the power of small business computers like IBM and Apple—but would be priced like home computers, perhaps as low as under $500.

We went to the CES Show with a giant gray and blue carpeted exhibit that included all sorts of interesting displays. There was a column of television screens which ran nonstop videotapes of our television commercials. In the middle of the booth, we had a small stage where Canadian Commodore guru Jim Butterfield described and demonstrated the new 264 Series. His sample programs were displayed on an oversize screen above the stage. Butterfield is universally recognized as the foremost authority on Commodore computers. One row of displays near the stage was devoted to Rich Wiggins's speech technology products.

An open corridor contained about a dozen Commodore PLUS/4 displays (we were still calling it the 264 Series at the time), but this aisle got so crowded on the first day that we had to cut down on the number of displays just so more people could fit into the space. More than two dozen practical software programs were shown for both the PLUS/4 and Commodore 64, including an improved version of *Magic Desk*, *EasyCalc 64/264*, a graphics package called *B/Graph*, and much more.

The built-in software program—called 3-Plus-1 (a take-off on *Lotus 1-2-3)* was the first integrated software package to be built into a personal computer. In this case, integrated software meant the program included a word processor, file manager, financial spreadsheet, and business graphics. Using the PLUS/4's windowing capabilities, 3-Plus-1 provided a word processor and spreadsheet which could be viewed simultaneously on the screen, and the data was interchangeable between the programs.

Our booth had other attractions, too. A darkened, partially closed room was outfitted like a giant video arcade and was used to display more than 30 new software programs, mostly for the Commodore 64. For the first time, large backlit signs were used to describe each program, in addition to the program itself. As you went into the arcade room, you passed two pedestals containing the "Two Millionth VIC" and the "One Millionth Commodore 64."

Upstairs, over the arcade, was a large meeting area with sofas all around, a small room for private conferences, and a large, plushly decorated office for Jack. There were constant meetings in that office. Tony Tokai was here, along with Sam Tramiel, Kit Spencer, Ira Velinsky (our industrial designer who was working in Japan), and several other Commodorians.

I took a few snapshots during these meetings. Ironically, the only snapshots I ever took at Commodore meetings were at the first meeting in Europe in 1980 and at this one. Little would anyone suspect that this would be the last meeting Jack would hold with his disciples.

Our press conference was impressive, with Irving and Jack announcing that, during 1983, Commodore had become the first personal computer company to hit one billion dollars in sales. We also announced that we had sold over three million computers and 600,000 computer books in 1983. Sig and Sol introduced our new products. The dinner party that followed was understated and worthy of the world's leading home computer company.

Then, before the week ended, Jack resigned from the company.

We knew something was fishy when he abruptly left the convention after a three-hour meeting on Tuesday (January 10) and drove home in the new car his family had given him for his birthday two days before. A few people who didn't know for sure actually said they thought he might be leaving. It was uncanny how much ESP there was in this company.

But why would Jack resign?

It wasn't widely known at the time, but Jack was planning to bring his sons into the company. It was rumored that Sam was being proposed as president. Gary would work in finance. And Leonard, who had just got his doctorate from Columbia University, would assume a software role.

Irving Gould apparently objected. Gould wanted to bring in his own president—Marshall Smith, a 54-year-old manufacturing and finance specialist with extensive experience in the rough-and-tough steel industry. It was reported that Smith refused to join the company with Jack Tramiel there.

On January 13—Friday the thirteenth—Jack resigned from the company at a board of directors meeting in New York. He walked out in the middle of the meeting and was on a plane back to California before the meeting was over. I heard about the resignation while the board meeting was still in progress.

At Commodore, everyone was stunned. All we knew was that Jack and Irving had a falling out and Jack resigned. In the coming days and weeks, rumors flew around the halls as we all tried to guess what had happened.

Irving said Jack brought the company to the billion dollar level, but now it was time for professional management to come in and take the company to the ten billion dollar level. Besides, he said, he was worried about Jack's health and wanted to see him enjoy his success rather than die at his desk.

"Yes," Jack said sarcastically, "let's see how the 'professional' managers do with the company."

Another theory was that Jack wanted to keep Commodore going and bring his sons in to make sure it happened, and Irving, the company's largest shareholder, wanted to set up the company to be sold. After all, Smith had engineered the sale of Irving's shipping container company, Interpool, and maybe Commodore was next on the list. Whatever the reason, it was the end of an era. It was the end of the revolution.

The Home Computer Revolution was over. The Home Computer Wars had been fought and won. We found ourselves in the Post-Revolutionary Period, where politicians were more important than warriors. We were like rangers, trained to kill, coming home from World War II, or Green Berets coming back from Vietnam. Warriors without a war.

With the wars mostly over, at least for the time being, the home computer industry was settling into a rare period of stability and orderliness. It was a time for politicians, not warriors, or so the politicians thought.

There was ample historical precedent. Revolutionaries and zealots who begin an insurrection and go on to win the war are rarely allowed by history—or their associates—to remain in power after the revolution succeeds. The most aggressive or radical leaders are always the first to go and are imprisoned, exiled, or assassinated. They are quickly replaced by politicians, administrators, and bureaucrats. This is the lesson of history, and it's a bitter one.

After Jack's resignation, Commodore changed dramatically. It appeared the same on the surface and in its day-to-day operations. But it changed in the sense that the earthquake had stopped. When Jack was there the ground was always moving and shifting, and we had gotten used to the tremors and the sounds of stress. Some people who had always said they hated Jack's methods, suddenly felt an eerie stillness. They were abruptly afloat in a frightening silence. It was as if the wind had stopped and all the background noise had suddenly dropped away.

The pace of work began to slow down too. Smith joined the company February 21, and from the very beginning he didn't share his views or plans much with anyone except presidents and general managers. The rest of us had no way of knowing where he was going or what he was planning to do with the company, and it seemed that he didn't especially care if we knew or not.

In the army, I learned an important lesson about sharing information. You can get a whole battalion to charge up a hill, knowing half of them will be killed in the attack, but you have to tell them *why*. Not knowing where we were going, or why, gave us a hollow feeling and robbed those of us who were used to aiming at high purposes of the conviction we needed to keep going.

The first four executives to resign after Jack's resignation were Don Richard, acting president of the U.S. company; Myrrdin Jones, vice president of marketing; Bill Miller, systems engineering director; and Roy Thomas, who oversaw chip-making and computer assembly operations.

Smith picked up the reins of the company very slowly. He had managed a billion dollar company before and prudently studied the company before making changes. Before joining Commodore, he was president and chief executive of Thyssen-Bornemisza Inc. (formerly Indian Head Inc.), the U.S. holding company of the Dutch firm which had the same name.

In the coming months, he was described in the press as low-key and affable, but one reporter called him crusty. A top manager who Smith later fired called him a jock, and another disgruntled manager said, "He thinks he's Lee Iacocca." Irving Gould told me he had tremendous confidence in Smith and said he was not the kind of president to encourage or get bogged down in company politics.

Smith was over six feet tall, had heavy Scandinavian features, and a pink complexion that contrasted with his long, snowy white hair. He seemed to favor cronies his own age. In meetings, he kept a serious poker face and absorbed what he was told without committing himself until he had all the facts. My personal experience was that he was extremely receptive and enthusiastic about young managers' suggestions, and if he heard something he liked he would smile and say, "Amen!" A few senior managers who saw him socially described him as fun-loving and noted that he liked to carouse a bit.

I continued working in software marketing with Sig and the glass menagerie, but my heart wasn't in it. Things that hadn't seemed important before now became important. Sig had been promising to make me the first vice president in the software division since last October. He even told my wife and announced it to the glass menagerie. But he had not come through on his promise because, he kept saying, "The politics aren't right." That didn't make sense. If someone's ready to be a vice president and he's doing a vice president's job, he gets the title. Mentally, I gave him six months to make good on his promise.

It turned out that almost everyone had decided to wait six months before deciding what to do. By May, all our silent alarm clocks started going off and, one by one, we decided to resign.

About this time, Kim and I spent an evening with Jack, his son Leonard, and their wives in New York. This was shortly after Leonard got his doctorate from Columbia University, and he had also gotten married recently, so there were good things to celebrate.

During dinner I had occasion to tell Jack I was seriously thinking of resigning, but I still wasn't sure if and when. We discussed it for a while and then Jack advised, "Stay as long as you're happy. If you're not happy, don't stay." He added that another way to measure it would be whether the company is practicing at least 70 percent of The Religion. He also reminded me that I'd been threatening to write the Commodore story ever since I joined the company. "You must have at least three books in you," he said. But he advised me to make it *my* story and base it on my experiences, instead of just a history of Commodore or Jack Tramiel. I asked him if he'd help; he said no, I'd have to do it on my own. I think he wanted to make sure I wrote the book independently, without anyone looking over my shoulder, or prejudicing the contents.

After dinner we saw a hilarious Broadway comedy which Leonard recommended, *Little Shop of Horrors.* After the show Jack suggested, "Why don't you buy the rights and make a videogame?" He was always on the lookout for business opportunities.

During one fateful week in the middle of May, nearly a dozen top managers resigned. Some people thought there was a conspiracy. They thought Jack wiggled his finger and everyone resigned, but I know from talking to the people that most of them resigned for personal reasons because they didn't like the new management style of the company.

It started in the middle of May when Sam Tramiel resigned, followed by Tony Tokai. Sam had stayed with the company for a few months to help keep manufacturing going, but now it was time for him to leave. Tony had stayed out of loyalty to his employees, to insure a smooth transition.

Next came Shiras Shivji, one of Commodore's best research engineering managers, along with three members of the engineering staff: Arthur Morgan, John Hoenig, and Douglass Renn.

The exodus turned into a stampede. Other departures included Lloyd Taylor, president of technology; Bernie Witter, vice president of finance; Sam Chin, who ran the financial organization in the Far East; Joe Spiteri, who ran manufacturing; his assistant David Carlone; PET pioneer John Feagans; and operations vice president Greg Pratt.

To minimize the impact, Commodore gave a vague statement to the press that hinted Smith was conducting some sort of purge of the Tramielites. Actually, the Tramielites were abandoning ship.

A few Commodorians stayed with the company, like Sig Hartmann and Kit Spencer. Bob Gleadow stayed in Hong Kong, where he had been supervising manufacturing operations; and Elton Southard stayed in charge of the semiconductor group. The European general managers stayed on, as well.

On May 15, Ira Velinsky dropped in, unexpectedly. He was over from Japan to talk about some new product designs. He walked into my office and we started talking about the people who were leaving. I was surprised when I heard myself telling him I was leaving the company, too. The words sounded strange on my lips, but also good.

"Nobody cares if we stay or leave," I told Ira, "and I like to work where I'm wanted, not where I'm taken for granted."

That day I called my wife and told her I was resigning. She agreed it was time to move on. Then I called Jack, Kit Spencer, and Robert Lock. I told Sig I was leaving and we discussed the arrangements.

Later that day, Sig told me Irving seemed disappointed by my resignation. That was the only moment I felt sorry I was leaving. The next day I called Irving and thanked him for all his kindness over the years, and said I was leaving because "there's just no place for me here." As always, he was very gracious. When *The Wall Street Journal* reported my resignation, instead of listing my title they described me as "a long-time favorite of Jack Tramiel." It was a wonderful epitaph.

Of course, leaving Commodore was a big decision. The company still hadn't settled down yet and would probably do well in the future. Also, by leaving I gave up two years' worth of stock options worth up to $200,000. And, of course, my steady salary.

Some people thought it was a gamble. I leapt off with no guarantees, no assurances. But warriors know when the war is over. And Commodorians can usually find some way to prosper. My friends throughout the industry implored me to go home and write the story of Commodore. I had become Machiavelli. Here I was in voluntary exile, in the country, writing the story of the Home Computer Wars.

TEN

"Is this the end?" I asked.

"No, that's just a feeling, not the truth," said the Jack.

The Dormouse closed the door and said, "This is what you get for living in the future."

"But was it real?"

"Yes and no. It was a door to another door to another door. It was a war, and like any war, just because it's over doesn't mean there won't be other wars."

"So who are we?" I asked.

"We are all the Jack," said the Dormouse. "All rogues and thieves and geniuses, all playing cards and poker chips. Some get shuffled, some dealt, some cut, and some get tossed on the table and win the jackpot."

The Jack smiled and said, "Don't worry. In the end we are all the Dormouse."

The New Atarians

When the Commodorians disbanded, it looked for a time like we would all be thrown to the winds. Then the unexpected happened. The Commodorians came back, but not as Commodorians. This time they were wearing the uniforms of Atari. They had become the New Atarians.

Some said it was a reincarnation of Commodore, but it wasn't a reincarnation. It was a metamorphosis. Jack Tramiel, called the "heart and soul of Commodore" by *The Wall Street Journal,* had become the "conscience of Atari." But how?

When I talked to Jack shortly after he resigned, he said he had no plans to get busy again. First he and Helen were going around the world. And they did. Then one day I called him at home in California and he said he was making a sandwich. "I have to learn to make lunch now that I'm unemployed," he joked.

He told me he didn't plan to get back in the industry unless he felt he was really needed, for example, unless he thought the Japanese were coming into the market in a big way and Commodore couldn't beat them. I interpreted this to mean he wasn't getting back into the business, but I should have caught the cryptic message, because the Japanese *were* planning to invade the U.S., with a secret weapon called MSX.

Several Japanese companies had pooled their resources and planned to introduce computers that used the same MSX operating system developed by Microsoft, Inc. Presumably as many as a dozen companies were preparing to descend on the U.S. with software-compatible computers priced under $200. Even if MSX was a dud, it was clear that twelve companies could wield a lot of advertising muscle. I began to wonder if Jack was going to do something about it.

Then the news started leaking out. Jack had founded a new company called Tramel Technology Limited—TTL. A friend of mine told me the proper pronunciation of Tramiel was TramEL, not TramEEL, so when they formed the new company, they called it TramEL Technology Limited.

This was all fine, but I was just getting used to TramEEL. Some people called Jack's disciples Tramielites, which I always thought sounded like a bunch of junior Jack Tramiels running around like rug-rats on the floor of the computer industry. I preferred Tramieleons (rhymes with chameleons). But maybe Tramelions (rhymes with hellions) was appropriate, too.

Then the rumors started flying. One disciple after another—some who had already left, and some like David Harris and Mel Stevens who hadn't—were going to California to join Jack: John Feagans, Greg Pratt, Joe Spiteri, Tony Tokai, Shiras and his engineers, Ira Velinsky, and more.

A lot of people thought I would go, too, but I didn't. I had my three books to write.

"Finish the book!" Jack declared.

Then the story broke in the press. Jack had bought Atari.

It was incredible, but completely in character for Jack. He wanted to bring together his sons and his former Commodore family, and Atari was a perfect vehicle. The company was even close to everyone's homes in and around Silicon Valley.

The prospect of buying Atari had come up in May, after Jack told me he was "learning to make sandwiches." Jack met with the top executives of Warner Communications, Inc., Atari's parent, but the negotiations didn't click. It was reported that Jack thought the deal was dead. Then Warner reopened the discussions and in an all-night weekend meeting with Stephen J. Ross, Warner's chairman and chief executive officer, Jack and two of his sons worked out the purchase arrangement. The deal was concluded in the wee hours of Monday, July 2, after a long Sunday night. When it was over, Warner and TTL were shareholders in each other's companies—partners, really—and TTL owned Atari.

Jack wasted no time. As soon as the terms were finalized, he hopped on a plane and flew back to Atari's headquarters in Sunnyvale, California. Thanks to the three-hour difference in time zones, he was able to walk in the door Monday morning at 9:30 a.m. It was clear he didn't want to waste a second.

But Atari was called a billion dollar headache for Warner. After hitting $2 billion in 1982, its sales fell to $1.1 billion last year, and instead of making money, the company lost hundreds of millions of dollars—a total of $538.6 million in 1983.

Under the agreement, Warner sold most of Atari's assets to Tramel Technology Limited in exchange for $240 million in notes, reported to be at below-market interest rates, with interest to be paid starting in 1985.

Securities analysts tried to evaluate the impact of the deal on Warner Communications stock. Financially, the deal was described as Warner selling Atari to Jack, and then loaning him the money to buy it. As a result, Warner indicated it would incur a quarterly loss of over $400 million, partly from operations and partly because of the terms associated with the Atari sale.

Tramel Technology Ltd. acquired Atari's assets and also received warrants for one million shares of Warner common stock. The notes were five-year warrants and exercisable at $22 per share, the market price of Warner's stock when the deal was cut. Presumably, Jack felt that without Atari, Warner's stock should start going back up.

For Warner's part of the bargain, Warner received warrants for 14.3 million shares of TTL common stock, representing over 30 percent of the company. Warner also agreed to assume obligations for certain debts and contracts.

But the big question remained. Could Jack's business religion resurrect the company he helped defeat? Could Patton implement the Marshall Plan? Could the warrior become a military governor?

There were several clues that hinted he could do it, almost from the beginning. Jack wasted no time conforming the company to his philosophy. That first morning he walked in the company and immediately took over from Atari chairman James J. Morgan, who had managed Atari for less than ten months. Jack's three sons were installed in top management positions. Sam became president, Gary was given the responsibility to collect Atari's $300 million worth of receivables, and Leonard was put in charge of software. Jack said "He's in training."

A shell-shocked Atari employee told me that on one of those first days in the company, Jack was being shown some new products, and to show what he thought of them he dumped them on the floor.

"Every single area of the company will need trimming," Jack said.

Three days after acquiring the company, he started slashing personnel the way he slashed prices during the Home Computer Wars. Atari had grown fat, attesting to Jack's belief that any company will hire too many people if left to itself.

Atari's marketing department of 300 people was more than ten times the size of Commodore's 25-person marketing staff. "The product managers don't even know how much the products cost," one of the New Atarians complained. In less than a month, the world-wide Atari staff was reduced from over 5000 employees to under 1500.

I called Jack after a long day of staff cuts, and he said, "I suppose you want me to put down my machine gun and talk to you?"

It was rumored that the Atarians who were dismissed received a healthy severance check from Warner, amounting to up to five months' salary for some. Hearing that rumor, one New Atarian said, "Warner likes to do things right. Jack likes to do things that work."

Someone else told a reporter, "Tramiel is a boss, not a manager."

Atari was bloated with physical facilities as well as people. On the day Jack and his team started, Atari occupied over 40 separate buildings, most of them leased. By the end of the first week the total was down to 7 buildings. The closings left a warehouse full of used office furniture, much of it more plush than Jack and his group were used to at Commodore.

Most of all, Atari needed an injection of new product technology. The software and engineering groups immediately started working on a new computer, scheduled for introduction at the January 1985 CES Show.

Shiras Shivji and three engineers who had come with him joined Atari to form the nucleus of the technology team, but in mid-July before they could physically move, Commodore filed a lawsuit charging they had taken confidential research information and prototypes with them, relating to Commodore's Z-8000 machine.

"This complaint is just a lot of bull," Lee Schreiber, formerly Commodore's lawyer and now Atari's, was quoted as saying. "There was nothing to steal, and nothing was stolen. These are honest people of integrity."

The suit was filed while the engineers' household possessions were still en route from Pennsylvania. Commodore sent a contingent of a dozen people, including a security guard, to wait for the moving vans to arrive. Atari's legal counsel Lee Schreiber watched with the engineers as their belongings were pawed over by the Commodore search team. The engineers cooperated in the search, but they were nonetheless chagrined to have strangers going through all their belongings.

Meanwhile, in late July former Atari officials trying to return to the United States were denied exit visas pending payment of tax liabilities accrued while Atari was still part of Warner. It was one of many nuisances TTL had to deal with as it streamlined the company along the lines of The Religion.

By this time, many investors believed all the management defections and TTL's purchase of Atari might damage Commodore. Commodore's stock dropped below $20, but then climbed back above $30 after Commodore purchased Amiga Computer in August—in an all-night meeting similar to Jack's meeting with Warner. Marshall Smith and Nick Lefevre did the negotiating.

Atari immediately fired a shot across Commodore's bow, in the form of a $100 million lawsuit. It seemed Atari had bankrolled Amiga before Jack came on the scene, to the tune of $500,000. It was reported that Amiga gave the money back to Atari and turned around and sold their developments to Commodore for over $20 million. The developments included new semiconductor chips and a computer thought to be a next-generation computer similar to Apple's Macintosh.

The press conjectured the suit was intended to slow down Commodore, but it was based on the terms of a deal which occurred between Atari and Amiga before TTL took over Atari.

Chuck Peddle was quoted as saying, "It's a great harassment lawsuit." Another observer suggested they were canceling out each other's lawsuits so they'd have bargaining positions when they get to court, even though neither one would ever admit it.

Commodore's purchase of Amiga signaled a major shift in philosophy which was already occurring while I was still there. Instead of designing new technologies in-house, top management felt new technology could be purchased from outside the company. As a result, some research activities were cut back or eliminated altogether. It seemed to me that Commodore was taking a risk putting its technological destiny in the hands of other companies, but on the other hand, the period after any revolution is traditionally a time when treaties and alliances are formed.

To streamline the balance sheet, Gould and Smith started eliminating some research programs and consolidated Commodore's physical facilities. Commodore shut down its Santa Clara facility, where I was first hired at Commodore; and in June a 65,000 square foot facility in Dallas was sold for $3.5 million.

The Dallas-based speech technology division under Dr. Rich Wiggins was closed and Wiggins, one of the foremost computer speech experts in the world, immediately started his own think tank at a Texas university, where he expected to continue his research on artificial intelligence as well as on speech technology. Rich felt computers could have natural sounding speech and sentence patterns within five years, given sufficient research. He was one of the inventors of Texas Instruments' Speak and Spell product line.

When the Dallas plant was closed, Commodore also canceled its robotics program under Tom Brightman. The company had been working on a consumer robotics product for more than a year.

But these actions had no effect on TTL and Atari. Jack was dealing with an entirely different set of problems. For example, Atari had a full warehouse of computers—including over 100,000 Atari 800XL computers which TTL bought for $80 each, according to Mark Halper of *Electronic News*. With the Commodore 64 selling for $199, it was expected that the TTL team would reduce the retail price of the Atari 800 to under $160. They would also have to reduce costs, estimated at over $130 for the Atari 800XL. But these New Atarians were well versed in that aspect of the business.

Getting vertically integrated would be a major problem, though. Semiconductor facilities no longer came cheap like they did in 1976. Another problem they had to tackle was erratic production and a sloppy manufacturing setup in the Far East. The experience of Sam Tramiel and Tony Tokai would pay off here. Collecting almost $300 million in outstanding debts owed Atari by its dealers and distributors was another challenge.

These are only a few of the walls the New Atarians had to climb or break down. They had a small but experienced army—all veterans—and a military handbook written by Jack which they carried around in their souls. It was going to be a tough campaign, and it would be some time before the New Atarians would be strong enough to sally forth again to do battle.

The groundwork was being laid for the next phase of the Home Computer Wars. Unlike the first phase, it wouldn't be fundamentally revolutionary. It would be fought with a strange mixture of unconventional products and conventional business weapons.

The Commodorians have become the New Atarians. What remains of Commodore is poised in midair, ready to fall into another company's lap—and may well be sold to AT&T or another multinational company.

Meanwhile, back at the ranch, Jack Tramiel and the "family" have become Tramel Technology Limited. TTL is poised in midair, too. But TTL, alias Atari, is in partnership with Warner and has already entered the next phase of the Home Computer Wars. This new phase will involve solid alliances, individual skirmishes, and strong lines of defense, instead of all-out war.

Jack Tramiel continues to shape our technological future. It seems likely that his philosophy—which he was kind enough to share with his disciples and teach by hard example to his enemies—will be quoted widely in management books. The principles he developed and practiced and communicated so colorfully already echo in our lives:

"We make computers for the masses, not the classes."

"Business is like sex. You have to be involved."

"Business is like war. You have to be in it to win."

"The Japanese are coming, so we will become the Japanese."

The Japanese are still coming, and perhaps one day they'll arrive. In addition to MSX, they're working on something called the Fifth Generation computer involving artificial intelligence. That may prove to be a significant new technology. And the Europeans are still taking a cautious approach.

For all of us who were involved, the lessons of the Home Computer Wars have become an indelible part of our lives. For me it meant joining a war and being on the winning team. It meant going from six dollars in my pocket to a house in the country. It meant learning the technology which will, more than anything else, shape our future. It meant absorbing a new, effective business religion.

In the footnotes of history, this era, these well-fought wars, will be nothing more than a brief notation. And I hope the future of computers arrives soon, because computers have to get larger and more powerful, and less expensive. In any area of technology, we have to keep dwarfing the past. We have to turn whole chapters of science and industry into small notations. That's progress.

Within a few years, we'll all be able to afford to have computers in our homes which are just as powerful as the biggest scientific computers now being used by governments and universities. Uses for these computers will be so numerous and pervasive that not even science fiction can predict them.

Right now, all that prevents computers from talking in normal sentences, and understanding what we say, is *memory* and *speed*. It will take a lot of memory for computers to store enough words, idioms, and grammar rules so they can communicate out loud with us in normal, spoken English. It will require much larger memories to store and recognize enough voice patterns so the computer "knows" what we say. And, of course, the computer will have to run fast—much faster than today—in order to interpret and respond to all the permutations that our brain performs every second. The result will be artificial intelligence. And that will lead to robotics. What that leads to is anybody's guess.